Conversations with Daddy

The Understanding of Identity and Relationship

By:
God, Jesus, Holy Spirit
&
Mary Jo Mayes

WESTBOW PRESS®
A DIVISION OF THOMAS NELSON & ZONDERVAN

WestBow Press books may be ordered through booksellers or by contacting:

WestBow Press
A Division of Thomas Nelson & Zondervan
1663 Liberty Drive
Bloomington, IN 47403
www.westbowpress.com
1 (866) 928-1240

ISBN: 978-1-4908-9039-5 (sc)
ISBN: 978-1-4908-9040-1 (hc)
ISBN: 978-1-4908-9038-8 (e)

Library of Congress Control Number: 2015910859

Print information available on the last page.

WestBow Press rev. date: 08/19/2015

DEDICATION AND ACKNOWLEDGEMENTS

This book is dedicated to my family, beginning with my AWESOME DADDY, BEST BIG BROTHER EVER, and the ONE who comforts and guides me. There are no words to describe the level of love and gratitude I have for the three of you, especially for your level of patience with me!!

To my earthly family—
Thank you, Wendell, for encouraging me in my communions and trusting that I was hearing from God.

I want to thank my kids, Miracle, Brianna, Joshua, and Gabrielle for believing that Daddy God can speak to or reveal Himself to you at any age, that there is NO Jr. Holy Spirit, and that you can do ALL things through Jesus Christ. Thank you all for supporting me during my times of communion, while putting this all together, and allowing my transparency to be your transparency.

I'd also like to thank my mom and sister for being such big cheerleaders even before I knew my communions were for the public!

Ivana and Jennice—I love you. You two played huge parts in my past few years. Thank you for everything.

Gateway:61—Thank you for being a church house that loves to host the presence of God as well as ALL of his children! John and Diane, I love how passionate you are about everyone experiencing the love and freedom that Daddy God gives.

Lastly, I'd like to thank Dr. Chauncey Crandall for putting his story into print. I'm not much of a reader, but in 2011 I borrowed your book from my mom, and that was the first book since high school that I read cover to cover! While I grew up believing in miracles and the supernatural, your book showed me that it wasn't just for pastors and evangelists; God wants to use us all.

AUTHOR'S NOTE TO THE READER

I hope this book ministers to you. I hope that my obedience to print this book, with its grammatical errors and all, is beneficial to you. When Daddy said to leave it as close to how it was written, I cringed as I thought about my mother who cannot stand grammatical errors, and just said, "Yes, God." I fully believe that Daddy speaks to us in our own 'language' and style. He meets us right where we are. I understand that when you hear Daddy God speak to you, it most likely will not sound the same as my conversations with him. I simply celebrate you as you seek to hear your Daddy's voice. I want nothing more than to encourage you on your journey of communions.

Please note that although some had to be edited for personal reasons, I tried to leave the people and conversations the same, not for entertainment purposes, but for transparency purposes. This is who I am. This is who I am with my Daddy, the one who created me. This is not my journal. This is not a record of all our faults, things we do well, prophetic words, or ministry we did inside or outside of the home. This is just a compilation of conversations with Daddy.

Key:
Jo=Regular font
God= Bold
Jesus= Italics
Holy Spirit= Bold Italics

INTRODUCTION

July 22, 2014

Good morning. I think yesterday went kind of well. I worked on everything on my list at least! That's a good day to me! How about you? Was it good for you?

You mean did you please me? Yes, you pleased me. Remember, I delight in you. Everything about you. You're my daughter, how I could I not be pleased with you? DON'T START QUESTIONING WHETHER OR NOT EVERYTHING YOU HEAR IS BIBLICALLY SOUND!!! Just LISTEN to me. You know me. So stop doubting and thinking about the lies being spoken to you. Listen to my voice. Hmph. It's the same thing you tell your kids really, "When you hear my voice, stop and listen. It doesn't matter who else is talking around you. Listen to MY VOICE!"

Ha. If only we, your children, did that, huh? I know that would make you happy!

Yes, it would. There are so many who I want to speak to like this. You need to help them. Jo, you've been right, this isn't just for you. Haha. Again, just like you say to other people—though normally when they're going through hard times—"It's not just about or for you, it's for the one coming behind you." THIS is for the one coming behind

you. Yes, put this out. Yes, people will read it. And it doesn't matter how many and it's not for a profit—it's to help the one behind you.

I'm telling you stuff you know. This is your heart. I know it's not about money. At first it is because of the investment on your end, but I'll take care of that. Watch me. Whether it be your husband, whether it be a gift, whether your crafts sell, don't worry or think about the **HOW**. Just wait on me and watch. You'll see how I do it when I do it. Just get the book edited. Start combing back through it now.

What **YOU** think is personal and useless, to a book reader, might be exactly where they are. So don't go through it and start cutting stuff out. You don't know what the audience needs. If it's something that needs to come out, I'll let you know. And be sure to ask me while you proof, but don't just go crazy and start changing everything around. And even leave the punctuation. Again—this is how I speak to **YOU**. I don't talk the same to everyone. You know that, but someone else may not. Someone else may talk like you and need to know that I, God, their Father, wants to talk to them **AND** I don't speak in the "Thou's" and "Thy's" so they can understand me in their speech—that's going to be a big deal for someone. Put the book out there close to how it was written. I say close, because I know you have to change some names. But I really want you to put this out there the way it is. My voice to yours.

Is this going to be as hard as I'm starting to think it is?

Well, you're looking at the editing and someone else's opinion of the book as being hard. So that's your choice to allow that to seem hard to you. What I know is going to be hard for you is to put it out there the way it is. To bare all that we've talked about with the one to one hundred people who may read it. Comparing this journey to the copied journeys of others. So it's not deep, and you didn't ask me about the affairs of the world and parts of the Bible…that's not what EVERYONE is interested in.

You came to me like a daughter asking for guidance in your marriage, your parenting, your house, your ministry, your hobbies. How many other people do you think are out there who wonder about the same things? How many do you think know they can come to me and talk just like this?

Jo, this is the point I'm trying to make to you. This is what I want you to get across. This is your assignment right now. Work on the book; I'll show you when it's time and who to go with. Just do your work; do your part. Now go, the kids are calling you.

THE BEGINNING

January 19, 2013

God keeps telling me to write, plan, and be obedient. I keep telling him that I have no idea what to write or what to say or do, but he keeps telling me to just sit, write, and be obedient. I'm going to put myself in position to be obedient so that when he speaks and tells me what to write, I'm already ready.

January 19, 2013

Timing and season. I want you to pray. About your gifts and your calling.

What do you want me to pray about?

Empowerment. Practice your gifts. The time has come to move forward. Open your eyes to see my thoughts.

God?

Yes.

Don't stop talking.

Don't stop listening.

Is it possible to listen all the time?

The sheep know my voice.

What do you want me to write?

The plan.

What plan?

You have the plan right there.

This seems so hard.

It is, because you keep trying to do it all on your own.

January 21, 2013

What do you want me to do today?

Write. You did a good job last night hearing from me.

Thanks. So what do you want me to say today? I'm sorry. I'm a little troubled about the house.

Don't be troubled. Just focus on me.

Okay. So what do you want me to write today?

How great I am.

How great you are? Is that you? Did you say that?

Yes.

I think I said that.

Okay then.

[I heard it like, "You don't have to do what I said, but you asked, and I answered." Then I remembered the list of names that describe God and his attributes through the alphabet!].

January 26, 2013

Should we leave the house for sale?

Yes.

Do we stay with our current realtor?

Yes.

Should we build a house?

No.

So our house is already built?

Yes.

When are we going to move?

Soon.

What do you want to teach me?

Everything.

(Chuckling) Where do we start?

Here.

When?

Now. I want to show you things that you haven't seen. New things. Things that the people you look up to haven't seen.

Is that possible?

Yes.

There's so much I don't know.

I know.

What do I need to do?

Listen.

It's hard to hear here.

I know.

[I glanced and looked at the book, *Children and the Supernatural* (Toledo 2012).]

I have a book for you. In you.

It's so hard to hear here.

Focus on me.

So do I need to be like that guy who wakes up and asks what you want him to do every day?

Yes. You feel so uneducated, but I don't need an education. I need someone who'll listen.

Okay, so what do you want me to do today?

Pray.

Can we talk about the house more?

No.

What do you want me to pray about? (I keep getting "stuff," so I keep asking, waiting for a different –better—answer.)

My eyes.

Anything else?

My vision, my spirit, my love, my patience, my joy, my peace that sustains, my comfort, my joy, .my love.

That's it?

That's it.

January 29, 2013

I'm so excited to talk with you!

I am too.

So what do you want me to do today?

Pray.

That's what you said the other day.

I know.

I forgot what I was going to talk to you about. Is there anything you want to tell me?

Yes. Love me.

Anything else?

Yes. Serve me.

Is there some way I need to serve you more?

Yes. Joyfully.

Are you my best friend?

If you let me.

What do you want me to do about children's church?

Pray.

Is that not what we're doing now?

No.

Okay. So I have to stay there, right?

Yes.

I can't remember what I was going to ask you about. When are we going to move?

Soon.

Have we already seen the house?

No.

Do I still know your voice?

Yes.

How do you want me to seek your face?

Like this.

Do you have a word for Ivana? Can I ask for words for other people here?

Yes.

Do you want me to ask about Ivana?

You can.

Do you have something you want me to share with Ivana today?

No.

You're funny. I love you.

I love you more.

I miss my daddy.

I know.

Is he there?

He's here.

I want you to be pleased with me.

I am.

But I can do more?

Yes.

What do you want me to do?

Write.

What do you want me to write?

Everything.

That's a lot!

I know.

Like go back and write the stuff that I deleted even?

Yes.

That's hard.

You're going to have to write hard stuff.

Is there someone you want me to give a word to today?

Yes. Joseph. Tell him that I love him.

Is that it?

Yes.

Are there any books you want me to read?

Mine.

What part?

James.

If I ask you every day will you tell me what to read?

Yes.

Is my friend okay?

Yes. She's tired.

Do you have a word for her?

No.

Is there anything you want me to do today?

No.

Can I go listen to that guy [a prophet in town]?

Yes.

Do I have a mentor?

Yes.

Have I met them?

Not yet.

Anything else for today?

Just that I love you.

I love you more … (laughing) … Okay, I love you, too! God, I want to see.

I know. In time.

June 4, 2013

It's been a long time.

I know.

What do you want to say to me today?

That I love you.

I love you, too. I'm concerned about GFC (Generation for Christ).

I know, but don't be.

Do I need a plan for the whole summer?

Yes, but I'm going to orchestrate it.

How will I know who to invite?

I'll tell you.

Do I need to submit this through church?

No. I've got you.

This is scary and a lot of weight.

I know, but you can handle it.

I want to call you "Daddy."

I know. You will. You'll get the fullness of it later.

God.

Yes.

I call your name a lot. I'm like my kids, and I say that they're bugging me!

I know. But you're not bugging me.

I'm sorry.

For what?

For not being the parent that you are.

I forgive you.

Teach me how to be like you.

I will. Where do you want to start?

You're asking me? Where I want to start??

Yes.

Oh wow. I don't know! I don't know. With joy? That's all I can think of. And you probably put that there, huh? Because I can't think of any other word! Where's my husband?

He's coming.

It's going to be crazy!

It is.

I'm excited for it.

You're going to have to hold on [Like hold on to the ride once Wendell gets it. Like holding on a roller coaster is what I was seeing.].

Is there anything more you want to tell me today?

That I love you.

I mean. Like, any great or revolutionary word?!

My love is greater.

Than anything?

Than anything.

I want to ask about moving and my husband's job so badly.

I know. But just follow me.

Okay. What do you want me to teach the kids [who come over for GFC]?

Who they are in me.

What else?

What they can do with me. What they have power over. That they have no limits.

Teach me to see.

I will.

Are we supposed to be at this new church?

Yes. This [church] is your hub, but your ministry is here.

Here where? Our house or Illinois?

(Chuckling.) Just follow me!

July 9, 2013,

So what do you want me to do?

Wait for me.

What? I just went! I thought you told me to go [referencing the email sent about GFC yesterday]?

I did.

Okay....so....

Now wait.

On what?

Me.

What do you want me to do while I wait?

Stay with me. In My presence.

Okay.

I want to breathe on you. Fill you. With my spirit. A fresh wind.

Am I ready for this?

You will be. It's in my timing.

God. You just want me to stay right here?

Yes.

How will I know when to get up or move [like physically up from where I'm sitting]?

You won't leave my presence. It's not about where you sit. You will stay in my presence all the time.

Oh wow. Will I hear your voice?? All I hear is dog and refrigerator!

Focus.

God, I just want an encounter with you so badly!

I know, it's coming.

[I keep feeling like I need to do something more, picture him, praise him, DO something more than what I'm doing (just sitting with laptop) and He's saying, "Just stay with me. Stay in my presence."] This is hard because I feel like I'm not doing anything.

This is waiting in my presence.

What am I waiting on?

Me.

This is hard for me.

[Chuckling.] Do you want me?

Yes.

Then this is the cost. You have to learn how to quiet your spirit and wait patiently on me.

Can I talk to you while I'm here?

You can. But I really just want you to listen.

Okay.

(Maybe one minute later) I love you. You're doing fine. Just go with me. Don't worry about others. I have you. I'm keeping you. You're my child. I'm proud of you. I'm pleased. I'll guide you. I'll show you. I'll teach you. I'll instruct you. My ways will be your ways because you will wait on me. You will let me guide you. You won't step out without me. You'll be in my will. At all times. This ministry will be run right, but this is the cost. Waiting on me in my presence. No matter how hard it is for you to sit and just listen. This is the cost. You will serve me and love me with all of your heart. I am your God. No one will come before me. [There was weight coming down onto my head.] You feel the weight of this mantle. It's heavy but I will carry you. I am with you. You're mine. I will not leave you. I will show you everything you need to know. Like this. You will not hurt these children because you will wait on me. These are my words. Arise.

July 10, 2013

So what do you want to talk about today?

You.

What about me?

Who you are.

Who am I?

My child. My creation. My love. I made you for a purpose and you're about to walk it out. I love you. I accept you. I made you. You're mine. You can't undo that. You can't mess that up and change any of that. You're mine. I've chosen you. You were made for my glory. You were made for my people. My children. My loves. I love the church, but she is hurting. I want to help her, but they won't let me. I'm calling you to step out into something that may hurt. Friendships. Relationships. Things you haven't thought of yet

Is this you?

Yes. I'm calling you to a people who are not accepted as my own. As my soldiers. As part of the army, but they are. They're Mine. I created them.

Who are you talking about?

Children. Youth. The unloved. The un-churched. The forgotten. Those are my children. My creation and I love them. I want them back. Back in my church. The way I created and designed them to be. Not left outside because they're not of age or dirty on the street. They're mine. I've called them. They have purpose and destiny, and they can rise up and do far greater than the church because they

will have been touched by me. They know my power and my grace. The church is satisfied with routines and the four walls. But I'm calling you out. You have to go. At all cost and any cost. It's time to go.

So what do you want me to do today?

Write. Write my words. Stay like this. Before me. In my presence. I'll give you the words to say. I'll teach you. I'll train you. You will be ready for where I'm taking you. Keep staying with me. In my presence. Yes, your thoughts are mine. You hear me clearly. Stop doubting me. Doubting your ability to hear. These are my thoughts. These are my ways. You're a willing vessel, so I'm using you. I'll give you the abilities you need. Stop questioning everything. Just go with me. You place limits on yourself. Those are lies from the enemy. You think you can't do anything because you're little. I don't see you as little. I see you as great, because you're coming to me and seeking me. Your faith is strong. The healings will come. Just stay with me. Let me guide you.

Can I share this?

You can, but this is for you. This is your calling. Not your [extended] family. Your family is great. You have a great purpose. Keep doing what you're doing [music]. I've called your children to do great things. Stay focused on me. Don't worry about Miracle being a martyr. I've given her a heart for them so she can pray. She's a warrior. Don't worry about her. And Brianna is my child. She'll be fine. I've got her. It's in my timing. My love. My love is greater than anything you've ever known, and you don't know the fullness of it yet. I will show you things you can't explain, but you will believe me. You'll know it's me. People will

not believe you, but you will know it was my hand that did it. Don't doubt. Don't worry on it. It's me. I'm doing it. You stay with me. My hand. My ways. My doing. It will be all about me.

What's my husband's gifting?

He knows his gifting. Just like you ran from yours and what I called you to do, he's running from his.

Was that you?

Yes.

I have a hard time discerning when it's personal.

I know. If you can't hear my words as mine, then don't ask.

Sorry.

You don't need to be sorry. Just trust my voice. You know it.

Will I be able to hear you like this when it's not quiet and I'm not typing as you speak?

Yes.

I interrupted you. Was there more that you wanted to say?

There's always more…but I know your limitations! I want you to know that I care for you. You're special. You're my daughter. I love you. No one can stop that. Not even you. You'll finish strong. You won't be a quitter. I know you need that. You're not a quitter. You will finish well. But you do have a long journey ahead of you. I've got big plans for you. You're going to have to hold tight! These kids are just a tip of the ice. You've got a world before

you. You're mine. Don't put limits on me. I've got your calling. I've got your purpose. I am greater. My ways are higher. I've called you to nations. Don't be limited here. Don't settle here. Go. And be what I've called you to be.

Where does my family fit in this?

Your family is it. You're all called. You will see. Stay with me. Follow me. I've got your husband. He's cautious, but he's Mine. You stay with me. You're going together. His heart will change. He will see what I show him. He sees. He hears. He lacks confidence, but it's coming; I told you you'd have to hold on. You won't be able to go fast enough. He's quick. Elevated. On a fast track. His wisdom is from me. I gave it to him. He's mine. I've got him. He's good. I love him. I chose him. You two are a power couple. You'll work out your communication because you'll become more like me. I'll consume your thoughts, your actions, your behaviors. You're mine. I put you together. Great things are coming. In my timing. You'll move in my timing. No thoughts about the house. That's mine. I've got that. That's my doing. Just watch my hand. Keep going where you're going (the new church). Your purpose is there. Your destiny starts there. This is right. I've put you there. Follow them. Watch them. Get before me there. That is where you are to be. Leave now(the old church). Go. Follow me. I've called you there (the new church). It's time. Don't look back. Friendships (from the old church) are fine, but I've called you there (the new church). Go now. Don't look back. I'll tell you when to go back, but don't go any sooner. You ask me first. Wait for me and my timing. Not your desires (I was thinking about youth conferences!)]. Hear this.

Yes sir.

Relax. I just want to make sure you get it. I know you like to doubt sometimes!

You love me.

I do.

Thank you.

No problem. You're still doubting!

I'm sorry! You're just so real and yet so far away.

I know. But you know me. You know my voice. So stop doubting me. Stop doubting you.

So am I done for today then??

No. Read.

Read what?

Your new book. (Toledo 2012)

Okay.

She's got wisdom for you. And finish the other book. He's on point. (Schambach 1991)

Can I craft today?

Most definitely. I love when you create art!

Will you help me? Give me ideas or designs?

Yes.

Thanks Dad.

You're welcome. I love you.

I love you too.

July 11, 2013

God. What do you want to say today? Though I think I'm having a hard time hearing today. Open my ears to hear Your voice and Your Spirit.

I love you. You CAN do it. You are more than a conqueror. You have been chosen for this. You're not off track. Yesterday was not a failure. That was preparation. You will get it. You will get through this. My ways. My thoughts. I speak to you. You listen. We work together.

So what did I miss yesterday?

You missed me.

I don't understand. I asked you for help many times. You gave me things to pray about and I did. But nothing happened. Nothing broke.

Just because you can't see it doesn't mean that nothing is happening. There's just more there. There's more work to do. You are not finished.

So what do I need to do? We can't have deliverance sessions every day till it's gone…

No and it won't take all that. I'll show you.

When?

Now.

Okay…

You're impatient. Even the way you type to illustrate your thoughts. Like you're waiting on me impatiently. This all happens in MY time, not yours. Do not get impatient with me because you'll act out of yourself, your flesh. And

it won't be by me or my doing. THAT'S when mistakes happen. But they're caused by you. Not Satan. Do not act out of your flesh desires. Follow me and I will show you what to do and what to say. Don't touch unless I tell you to. Stand back and watch. You don't need to touch a spirit to address it and cast it out. You don't need physical control over the person's body. Not for tantrums. Other things require other things, but with what you're dealing with you just need words.

Your flesh tells you that you need control over their bodies. It's the parent-child tendency, but that's not what you need here. This is spiritual warfare. They're not respecting you as a parent. They're fighting with the Holy Spirit in you. Don't get down and play their games. They're teasing you. Making fun of you because if you can't get control over their bodies then you think you've lost. You can't control them, they won't listen to you as their parent and so you think you can't fight and win spiritually. They've got you off your game. Stay focused on what's at hand—and that's a spiritual battle. You get too distracted too easily. Good job with oil yesterday though!

So just speak to the spirit and not the child at all?

You can speak to the child, but know that you're not looking for them [the spirit/s] to submit to you as their parent. You address those spirits directly, by root name if you get it. Yes, write that--by name if you ask me for it. I'll give you the tools you need, but you HAVE to ask me. You can't be in it one minute with me and then try to go off and fight on your own. STAY WITH ME.

Okay.

My peace and love I give you to you. Stop stressing over stuff. Don't worry about failing in praying for your kids or school even. Just follow me. Let tomorrow take care of itself. Stay with me. My ways are most important. If you don't follow me, then you're off track anyway and nothing will work right by my design. It's simple. Stop thinking about school. Yes, your kids need an education, but they're put here for MY work, not yours. Don't box them in. They'll know their callings in the right time, and they will have learned what they need to have learned. Too much pressure on education and not on things of my kingdom. Can they read and write? Then they can read my word and write. Let the world take care of the world. Be about my Kingdom. That's your goal. Worldly successful kids don't matter—unless I put them there, but that's not your kids. Focus on me.

God. Is there anything else you want to say?

My peace I leave with you. Get it. Receive it. Walk in it. You're on track.

What about my kids? What should I be doing or praying?

That they'd know me. Follow my ways. Seeking my face.

Like that? That simple? Just a basic prayer? I'm asking if I need to be doing some big or deep warfare stuff?

You follow me. I told you I'd show you. Learn to talk and listen to me when you're out. When you're with your kids that you think are loud. Get used to hearing my voice over the noise. You want immediate, and that's not how I'm doing things because I'm trying to train you. You won't always have immediate deliverances, and you're going to

need to know how to hear me when it's loud outside so you'll hear me in the fire. It's training time, so practice.

So…what do you want me to do with these spirits in my house?

Cast them out. You know what you're dealing with right now, so deal with it. You have the power and authority over it. Will it be a big deliverance session? No. You just keep commanding those spirits to leave when you see them rise up. They can't stay there. Deal with them when they show their heads. My words. Use the word to chase them out too. They hate the word. Can't be returned void. Find the scriptures that deal with the spirits you're dealing with—rebellion and disobedience. They must subject to the authority you have. Not just as a parent, but I'm talking spiritually. Those spirits must submit. Now go and do something.

Like that?

Yes, have a good day. Make something.

Okay…

I've given you what you asked for. You can talk to your pastor if you want to, but I told you I'm training both you and your ears. I gave you homework with scriptures and training your ear. You don't need more, you need to follow what I've given you. Now have a good day [and He's talking while walking away from me]!

Okay.

July 15, 2013

Good morning.

It is.

[Lots of side small and some silly conversation. Half thoughts-not worth typing.] God I need you to teach me everything I need to know. My mind seems blank.

I will. I told you I would when I called you. I said I'd never leave you. You're doubting so much today. Why are you troubled?

I don't know. I feel far away, distant…like our lack of communions over the weekend would cause you to stop talking to me because you were upset with me.

I don't operate like that. We may not have sat down and had one on one together like this, but you talked to me all weekend. I don't hold grudges like that. I'm not man.

Okay, I'll try to shake it off.

Just do it. Be shaken!

You love me.

I do!

Thank you. So my kids are home today…what are we going to do?

Seek me. Come together as one and seek me as a group. Like you did last week. Keep doing that. They'll get it. Remember that you're in training mode. You do what I say and it's all going to work out in time. You just like to rush. You have to slow down and follow me. I'm not someone you can lead. It won't work and you'll fail. Wait on me and my direction.

Your peace you give.

Exactly. So do communion (conversation—not juice & crackers) with the kids and send them off to be obedient. It may stretch you too. Just go with it. My peace and my grace…

Okay….What do you want me to do [I thought about Wendell, but not like—what do you want me to do ABOUT him. Just thought of asking God about him.]?

He's good. He's on the right track. This move is good. You'll both see. He has my plans in mind and that's to follow me. My spirit will guide him. Don't worry; don't think about the house. I know you're getting tempted to do so, but I said to just follow me and I'd work all of that for you. I told you to watch my hand move, you just follow me.

Yes sir.

Not legalistic. That's not how this relationship works. You're my daughter and I love you. Don't make me your boss. Don't be afraid of our relationship when you think my tone changes. I'm talking to you. Don't shut down [like your daughter]. Take correction, take guidance, learn from it, and keep on. Don't wallow in what you think you heard or understood. There are no undertones. I know how to speak clearly. You will understand what I'm saying to you. Relax. Rest in me.

So—off topic. Can we write music together like this?? 'Cause that would be good, right?

Yes, but you'd have to listen. They may not be what you'd expect, and then you'll doubt the whole time. You may want to wait.

Okay. Is it okay to try?

Of course, but you've got to be willing to trust me, and you're still having a hard time doing that.

Do you expect me to be able to hear you over people? Over the noise and know and recognize that my thoughts are you speaking?

Yes, at some point. You will get there. You're going have to get there for what I'm calling you to. You know kids are loud, but it's beyond that. I'm calling you into the depths. You can't be timid and full of doubt of my voice. Yes, you need to practice talking to and hearing from me when you're listening and talking to other people. I WILL be giving you words for them—like you ask——but you ask and then walk away from me. You're not expecting me to answer because you haven't heard me before, and you credit that disconnect to me, and it's not. I always answer; you just fail to listen. When you ask me for a word and I tell you to say that I love them, but that sounds too cliché for you, and so you don't give the message—is that MY disconnect or yours?

Mine.

Okay. See that I hear you, and I answer you. Every time. But if you walk away or don't listen or don't have your ears trained to hear my answer and my voice, then you still have work to do. That's why we're here. To train you. Keep resting in me. Everyday. Yes, when you're at VOA you're going to have to get up early to do this with me. Am I requiring it of you while you're down there? No. But is it required of you? Yes. [I'm not going to make you do it—but this is all a pre-requisite to your calling and where you're going. Choice is always yours.]

Okay.

You can hear through noise. Trust ME.

Okay.

I know that you want to talk about other small things. Like church and houses and locations, but if you notice, I usually only want to talk about our relationship. Getting you where you need to be. I don't mind giving you a word for someone else and your family, but this time together is sweet, and it's about us growing together. I'll take care of that other stuff. Yes, you'll be released from church, and yes, you'll move on. Your husband's reputation is fine, do not cross over the line for selfish ambitions. Keep your mouth shut. Your lights will shine through me. I don't care what other people may say about you and your husband. I know what I say about you two. He's mine; I've got him. No one can touch him. He's covered. My vessel. My willing vessel. Continue to support him and pray for him. His time is coming and IT IS quick. There is no time to prepare. This is a now thing.

Yes, I heard you [thoughts of us "getting ready" for whatever God is going to do.]**! My time IS NOT your time. I know. But I don't need you cleaned up, fixed up, perfect in order to use you. I just need willing vessels and that's what you** [two] **are. You're choosing me. Above anything else. You're understanding service. You will be on one page, one accord, but he'll be higher than you. Almost pulling you along, but not like it was before when you got married. This is spiritually. This is different. This is not a bad thing. This is momentum. This is him being unstoppable. You want him to go, and he's about to go. I keep telling you you'll have to hold on. He's fierce. A warrior in my army. He's battle strong. He's heavy with my burdens. Things that vex my spirit. He hungers for**

truth. He wants what I want. My time is not your time. You don't have to see all this now, but these are my words. You can look them up if you want to, and that's fine. It's your lack of trust of what I'm giving to you, but you look them up for your own peace of mind. That's fine. You'll trust me.

Your husband is my servant. Don't worry about the job. He hears me, and he knows me, and I will prompt him. I will tell him and show him when to go. Yes, she's influential [the lady lawyer he met on the plane], but that's not his job [there]. Follow me. It's in St Louis, but you will be too. Yes, it's coming. Things are coming. My timing. My hand. You just get ready to move. You can't get ready for me spiritually like you think you have to, but you can get ready naturally for the move you'll be making. Clean up and out. THAT you CAN do. But that's about it. My wind is strong and fierce, and there's no way you'll be prepared for where I'm taking you. Both short term [St Louis] and long term [abroad—see like a globe here]. No, you're right. You won't be in the states forever. I'm not telling you where or how long, but yes, you will both travel. This is not just for you and Miracle. Your husband will go too, but of his own choosing. You won't have to suggest and pray about his mind to change. It will happen on his own. He'll be so wrapped up in ministry that he longs and is hungry for it.

Don't hold him back. Let him go everywhere I call him. Don't hold him back for selfish reasons and motivations. You prayed for him to catch it. I heard and I answered. He's about to walk into his destiny, and you're going to have to check your heart and motives. Stay with me because the enemy will try to use you to cause him to slow

down. I told you to hold on to him [roller coaster again]. That's your job. You hold on to him while you stay with me. I will continue to direct and lead you every day if you seek me.

Don't stop this, though, because the enemy is lying in wait to creep in your heart from jealously. Purge those things now. Idle time is not your friend. Games aside. No time wasted. Stay with me. At all times. Guard your heart, your eyes, your emotions. Be strong in me. I guide you. Bridle your tongue. It's fierce and will get you in trouble in this stage, in this hour. Learn to be quiet with your husband. My ways may not be yours. That is your flesh. Be quiet. Follow me. Seek me. Search me. I'll guide you. Watch and pray and listen. To ME.

Your husband leads from this point and this transition. You follow. You pray the mind of Christ on him. Don't worry. Not dominant and dominion over you, just healthy, where he should be. My ways will be his. Don't stop following him. Ask me about reminders. You will no longer be a nag. Mind of Christ for him. That's what you pray. My will be done. My kingdom. My will. My peace. My joy. My love. I give these things to you. Freely. Take them. They're yours. Walk in them. Day and night. Go to bed earlier. You need your rest. I'm requiring much of you, and you can't be tired.

Will he be healed?

Yes, he will. In My timing. I'm not revealing that to you.

Wait, of narcolepsy or feet?

Both. But IN MY TIME.

Okay.

My peace and joy I give to you. Take it. Walk in it abundantly. You have all rights to them.

Are you lifting already? Don't we need to talk about GFC? I need your help.

I know, When you're ready to talk about GFC, I'll be there. I always am. But you need to edit and digest what I just said to you. Go ahead. It's okay. Read it again.

But when you say we can't get ready for what you're about to do—what do you mean? You don't mean we can't read Bible or books, do you?

No, but I'm saying that no matter how much you think you're soaking up, and hopefully memorizing all you're reading, it's my spirit that is going to move and shake things. Not by your hand and your head knowledge, but by my spirit. That's how you'll be moving and travelling, really! By my spirit. HOLD ON! Because it's coming fast. It's coming strong. It's a rushing wind coming for the two of you. Just hold on. (I was seeing us in a cloud! Like we were both in/on a cloud and TRYING to hold on because it was moving so fast, but of course that's impossible because there's nothing to hold on to in a cloud!)

July 16, 2013

What do you want me to do today?

Seek me.

Today is Ivana's birthday. Do you have a word for her?

Go where I tell her to go.

That sounds like her red light green light!

Yes, she's following me well. I am pleased with her. She makes me smile. I want her to go deeper in me. To some it may not seem possible, but I have very deep depths for her. I'm taking her to new places. Follow me. I will comfort her in her hard times. She'll know me in a new way. Again, not possible for some to fathom, but she's my child, and I'm pleased with her, and I want to show her new things. She's a faithful servant. I love her. This is another year for new things. Her path is unknown to her, but I have it, and I see it. The time is near for her to be released. Released to do my kingdom work outside. She will understand. For you[her family], it's time to let her go. This is her time and season that I've brought her into. Don't worry about who's left. She's planted her seeds well. Even watered. But the harvest will come later. She's fruitful. Nothing will be forgotten. Her family will be okay.

Seek me. I am good. I'm all you need. My faith goes before you. Follow her. Lead my people. They are waiting, and they are hungry. It is a hungry land. Not like those who are here. These people are desperate for me. Follow me and feed them. Give them the depths that they desire and need. Their souls are hungry for truth. And you'll feed them. Like my sheep, but not in that pastoral role. Just that you're a willing vessel that sees a need and meets it. I'm pleased with your service. You please me. You make me joyful. I want to use you in a mighty way. You will bring up a nation. An army. In my time, but you will. You're obedient. Your brother will be okay. He's not going with you. I have a place for him. You just follow me. My timing. My peace. Follow me. I love you. You're my smile! Keep on doing what you do.

People are uncomfortable because they don't like me. They don't want my presence. It brings conviction because of their sin. They reject the truth you bring. And that's okay. Just keep following and serving me. It will all work out in the end. They, and you, will see. Their time is not yet. I will take the blinders off. I will be their leader, but in my timing. Those who reject truth reject me. I cannot help those who reject me. My heart aches for them, but they've shut me out. Do not fret over them. I will watch them. You just watch me. Follow me. I've got you. My peace I give to you. Follow me. I love you. Speak my words. Only. Follow my lead. I am coming. In fullness to you. Watch and wait. You're at the beginning, but its time to go deeper. Don't press it. Don't try to do it yourself. Just wait on me. I'm coming for you, and you will know.

My timing will bring peace and clarity, and you will know it's me because it will just fall into your hands. You will know. Just go with it and follow me. My ways are clear to you, so don't ask a lot of questions with your carnal mind. Just follow the way I put before you and the people. You will know who. Don't question your spirit because you already know it's coming. Just follow. They'll all be okay [those you're leaving "behind". I see you looking back at friends and family as you're walking away, but not in a Lot's wife kind of way, just a slow goodbye]. They, too, will encounter me in a new way and go deeper with me. The seeds you planted are deep. *They're safe from the elements. Know that they're already growing, you just can't see it. My peace. My timing. Is perfect.

Okay, let's talk about other stuff. What do you want me to do with Teen Bible Study?

Serve.

Okay. Anything else?

Serve me. With your whole heart. Follow me where I take and lead you. Yes, you're called to kids (youth). But I will show you what to do.

So am I SUPPOSED to be working with the group, or am I just praying?

You will serve there. To what capacity, I'm not revealing to you yet. You may run [thoughts of a leader OR cook go through my head]!

Well, thank you. I understand that and appreciate your withholding! Anything else?

Keep on until they move—in regards to your house. I'm proud of you all for opening your home. It's a great start. Great blessing for you all. There's more to come. But this time has almost ended, and you will fill this time with something else.

I don't understand. Will I be apart when they move?

Yes, but not on that night.

Okay.

You will see.

Okay. Am I supposed to work at Bible study during the day?

Yes. Yes, of course, I know what age [I was wondering about what age group I was supposed to work with]! I'm not revealing that to you either. Your leader knows.

Okay.

And don't worry about school. You will have a good year. You're following me, and I will bless your school year. You'll have your OWN testimony about it. It won't be like someone else's.

Okay. And GFC??

GFC is coming. You're doing fine. You're on track. Don't worry about those who don't respond. You just keep going with what I give you. Remember that this is still my timing and doing. If it's just one, then you do your kids and the one. Make it happen. It will grow. Small beginnings. But still my hand and my doing. Follow me.

I'm still waiting for you to give me a layout or something—the plans.

I gave them to you already. Look back through my notes. We may not have been talking this way, but I've already spoken to you.

What about the lessons I have to make up?

I will be there in your studies. But make sure you set the time to prepare. I will guide you once you get there. You just have to get there! Remember, no idle time. This is important. I may be guiding and teaching you, but you need to be a good student. A studier of the word. You can't just show up at class and get it all. You need to do your homework on your own.

I understand. But you'll keep telling me what to read, right?

Yes.

And will you help me to read more? Faster?

Yes, but your pace is fine. You just have to give yourself the time.

I'm so tired all of the time. And reading makes me sleepy. [Kids came down. Loudly. Feel off course now. Can't go back into that conversation.] God what am I doing with my kids?

Praying.

What or how do I need to pray?

Like I instruct you.

Seek you first?

Exactly. You HAVE to do this, Jo. I have all the tools and keys you need, but if you keep trying to do things on your own, it's not going to work and end up the way you want it to.

So what about all those people who teach that we shouldn't have to pray for every little thing? You want me to pray about everything, don't you?

Yes. If it's a decision, then you should seek me first.

And since life is all about choices then….

Exactly.

Okay, I get it. You're interested in us, but if we do it on our own, we shut you out a little, huh?

Sometimes a lot.

Right. I'll try to do better.

Yes.

So GFC. You'll give me the plan when I sit down and am ready to work, is that correct?

Yes.

Okay when do I need to start that?

Today.

Okay.

And tonight, after prayer, work on it some more.

Okay. What were my friend's intentions when she gave me that Bible study book?

She wants you to lead.

Hmmm. [Paused to email and ask her the same question!] So what do you want me to do?

Lead. Wherever you are and in whatever you do. You should always be a leader. Lead my people. I'm not saying always be the boss or the one in control or running the show. I'm talking about being a Christian example and leader wherever you go.

Got it. So you're still not talking to me about Bible study and Teen Bible Study right now, huh?

(Chuckle) No not yet.

Okay. I tried…

Yes, you did!

Well my kids are active now. Anything else you need to leave me with?

Keep trying. Keep trying to be consistent. You'll get it. It will come. Your kids will flourish, just give it time. You keep wanting immediate results. And that's not always how I work. Healing, deliverance, joy in your home are

coming. They're just in my time, and that's not immediate. You will see. Just hold on and wait. I'll give you patience; you just endure till the end. My peace I give to you! I love you my child. Have a blessed day.

July 17, 2013

I feel like I need to get in the zone today because I'm so tired

Yes, you had a late night last night. Not what you had planned.

Why does this seem so hard sometimes?

Because you doubt. Both me and yourself. You've got to stay in my presence during the day more. It is, and should be, normal to hear my voice throughout the day. Walk with me. I'll guide you.

Speaking of guiding me. I was reading that book last night and I feel like I am SOOO far over my head! How in the world am I supposed to teach people about hearing your voice and all the stuff and steps that she's talking about? [*Forever Ruined for the Ordinary* (Dawson 2001)]

Look at her audience compared to yours. Your audience won't be coming with so much baggage and so many stipulations. Most will be coming with a heart to believe and receive. It won't be so hard to break through or get through to them. Especially the younger they are. Just follow me.

Okay, I HEAR you, but….I didn't feel like you were guiding me last night.

That's because you weren't coming to me like this last night. You read some of the book and started typing. It's

great to have a general idea or an outline, but you didn't ask me what I wanted you to say. If you ask me, and you wait for me to answer, you'll have everything you need. Stop wasting time.

Are you angry?

No, you're just wasting your time. I told you that idle time is not your friend. And I saw that you stopped playing your game, but I'm talking beyond that. Wasting time doing things that don't need to be or shouldn't be done is a waste of your time and you have things you NEED to be doing.

Ooo. Like what?

Like GFC. Like cleaning your home and purging excess things. You have a future to prepare for and arguing over chores won't get it all done.

Ouch.

Yes, stop worrying about what they're doing and if they're getting what you call 'their work' done and you focus on what YOU are supposed to be doing. Let them be kids. It's okay to play all day. They're young. They don't have to work half of the day so they can "earn" half a day of free time. Let them be free today. No math, no history, unless THEY want to. If they want to do the fish, let them. [Clown fish art video.] Say yes. You say no too much. You are not nice to these kids. Follow my ways and examples. Speak to them kindly. Stop yelling. They can hear you. They choose to ignore you because of your attitude. THAT'S YOUR thorn. Fix your attitude. I'll help you. But it still comes back to you LISTENING for and

to my voice. Above the noise, Jo. You have to listen for me above the noise!!

Okay.

You get your work done today.

Well what's that? Are you going to tell me what to do? Write my to do list?

I can. But you're smart enough to figure out most of it on your own. I've given and we've talked about things that need to be done. You don't need me to give you a step-by-step plan in order to clean. Now when you sit for GFC, then I can talk to you there.

Okay.

Call the plumber though.

Okay. I'm concerned about the floor and walls and how bad it might be. I was always hoping we'd get out before anything major needed to be done.

Don't worry about that. It'll all work out.

Okay. Anything else for today? I'm excited about VOA.

Yes, there are great things in store for you all there. Don't worry about money [(in regards to my family meeting us there.]. Everyone will be taken care of.

Okay. Is it by us??

You'll see.

Okay.

Be generous though [down there]. That is when you will be face to face with your destiny. You're going to see

amazing things down there, but it's still only a glimpse of what I'm going to do with you. And your family. This is just the beginning.

Bible study …

(Sigh.) You've got to understand that you all are waiting on a man and men to step up. If they're not listening for and to my voice, then they're going to miss what I'm calling them to. I know that you're waiting on them. I am too! You all just keep doing what you're doing. The Bible study is a good idea. It's always a good idea to study my word! So do that, and then just wait patiently. Don't become anxious. I didn't tell you what you're doing because it may not be here [In Illinois]. And you know that from your natural mind. You're not going to be here forever, and you may not be able to give that two-year commitment they require. I know it's your future. Keep praying, keep studying, keep seeking me and listening to my voice. I'll tell you when to stay and when to go. Your family is moving. In more ways than one. Just be obedient and follow me. My ways are perfect. I'll show you.

Hey what about that guy and our money. Are we ever going to get that back?

In time. In my ways. Not in your ways.

Okay.....

You'll see.

Okay. Anything else for today?

That I love you. And my ways are perfect. Keep praying for people. Stop getting caught up in what you "don't

know." Just follow me. I'll take you. I'll guide you. I'll keep you.

You said there's a book in me?

Yes, there's a book. Not now though [like—we're not going to talk about that right now though].

Okay. So plumber, clean, GFC, take pictures to sell stuff….

Say yes to kids and love them.

Okay.

They're mine. They may frustrate you sometimes, but they're mine. Treat them as such. Even in how you spank them. Spank them as if they were not your own, but you were given permission to discipline in that way. How would you spank them then?

Okay.

They're gifts. Don't break them.

Yes sir.

Okay, that's it for today. I love you.

I love you too.

July 18, 2013

So how do you feel about communing like this? Am I missing my prayer time? Should I be going into deep prayer first and then coming to listen to you? I would think that because of who YOU are, it'd be better for me to come to your feet and listen before I start talking. Even if some of it is my praise to you. What do you think? What do you want?

I just want you to come to me.

Like this?

Yes, like this. I want you to sit at my feet and listen. That's how you hear me. You miss me if you're talking all the time. I want you to know MY voice. I know yours. I hear you when you speak—both good and bad. But you need to train your ear to hear MY voice whenever I speak, and the only way to do that is by sitting and listening to me.

Okay, but I need to have my prayer time too, right?

But you pray throughout the day. That's what I want. I want us to speak to each other all the time. Not just during certain hours. I want to become a part of your life all the time; where we are in constant communion and conversation. But when we come together in the morning and I express my heart to you, then I expect you to do what I've said. If I give you something to pray about, then that is your task for the day. Until I say something else, you keep praying for that thing. You can't just pray for your husband one or two times. You need to KEEP praying until it comes to pass or I say otherwise. Follow the instructions I give you. Am I forgiving when you mess up? Yes. But what you CAN do, I expect you to do. Do YOU understand?

Yes.

Okay. So let's get on with today then, because you have some trust issues going on. I saw your tantrum and meltdown last night. It was so bad that you were looking at garbage [some silly videos online that were making fun of people]. My creations being made fun of. It's not cool. I told you that idle time was NOT your friend. Don't waste

your time. Fill it with reading, praising, reading my word, worship, conversation with your husband…something beneficial to your body. Not mockery. Yes. Laughing at Joshua was mockery. You know better. Do not discredit my word when it is given. Even by a child who is upset.

Yes sir. I was just upset because I'm lazy and this is going to be a lot of work and I don't have that paper to copy [something related to GFC that I couldn't find].

I didn't create you lazy. I don't say that about you. You can overcome this tendency that you may have, but you are NOT lazy.

Yes sir. Okay. So you said that the paper is in my head?

Yes and I will give it to you the way I want you to present it. JUST FOLLOW ME. Do I not keep saying that EVERY day?

Yes.

Then just do it.

You sound frustrated today.

Well I'm not, but isn't this how you sound to your children? Isn't this the way that YOU parent? We can keep going this way until you decide what you think about it and if this is the way you want to be parented.

Okay… I don't like it.

There's more.

It's not as fun as our other conversations. It makes me feel like I just want you to get to the part where you help me with GFC and then we're done so I can go.

Exactly. That's exactly how your kids feel. So stop wondering why they disrespect you. You're not nice to them. Your speech. Your tone. Your frustration. You're unkind. You're unforgiving. You hold grudges against your CHILDREN. You're not loving. Does this sound familiar the way that I'm saying it to you?

Yes.

Good.

Sigh. So now what?

Repent!

Huh. Like right now? I remember in those Korean stories in *Baptized With Blazing Fire* (Kim 2009) that you were not pleased with someone's asking for forgiveness. Do you need me to fall out on the floor and be in tears or can I just talk to you?

I know your heart, dear. I can see what's real and what's not. Just like your kids, when they repent, you want them to mean it. I don't need a show if your heart is not broken from your sin. If you can't do it right now that's fine, but you have sin in your life that needs to be dealt with. You can't walk around hollering at them because "they don't want to be free" when you're carrying around your own sins that you don't want to look at. It's more than what I gave you [a previous prayer time when he revealed some "planks" in my eye.] This is a DAILY thing. You need to come to me to search your heart EVERY DAY so that we can deal with the things that creep in. Every day there is sin in your heart. Every day you should be broken and repenting for your sins. Every day. Not on Sundays before communion. This has to be a lifestyle, or the sin that goes

undealt with becomes a monster inside of you, and then you'll have to work to get it out.

Okay, I understand.

Do you?

Yes.

Then show me. That's one of your lines too. I don't think you like the way you talk and parent, do you?

No. (Tears now)

There you go. That's what I'm talking about. A repentant heart. I see your heart. I don't need a show. I see the aches in your heart from your sin, and THAT'S what needs to happen for you to come to me and repent and be forgiven.

(After crying and seeking forgiveness…) God I don't even think I can fathom being nice, kind, talking kindly to them. Like, it would take a miracle.

That's because this has been your habit for a long time. This is the way you were raised and the way your father parented you. I understand the reason behind WHY you are the way you are, but that's not how I created you to be and to act and to operate. This is not part of your destiny and called place. You can't continue to operate like this. Yeah, when it comes to kids and working with them, I'm proud of you for recognizing it's me calling you there, and you're walking in obedience to where your flesh doesn't want to be. But it's time to do more and go deeper and get rid of those attitudes, thoughts, perceptions, and behaviors that are not of me.

You cannot operate with these mindsets AND fulfill what I've called you to. You cannot. These things have to break

and change. Through my word and soaking. Not all of your own doing. You'll have to work at it. But this is also coming from a transformed mind that will start from the inside out, and the first place it starts is with a repentant heart. Seeing your ugly ways for what they are, seeking forgiveness, starting with a clean slate EVERY day, and then working on breaking those bad habits.

That's the way you'll overcome this. This won't be immediate. This will be a process. For both you and others following behind that you will lead through and instruct by your progress. This isn't just for you. This is to share. And back to the front [beginning of this conversation today], yes, it all starts with communion every day.

Okay. [long time of silence.] I'm very tired.

That's because you haven't been going to bed when I told you to so we can get up early and talk.

Do you want me to start GFC this Monday?

Yes.

Ugh. I think this is too much.

Stop doubting me. Just bring the kids who can come together. Open up with the goals of the group. Get to know each other—this is really what you already wrote out. Talk about what the group is for, and go from there.

Go from there where? I need specifics since I lost this paper.

STOP DOUBTING! My ways, Jo. My timing. It's perfect. JUST FOLLOW ME. Stop trying to do this all on your own, okay? Have the kids come over and just do this informal meet and greet. Yes, you can talk to them on

ways to hear my voice. But don't make it so deep. Ask them to talk about how they hear me or how they sense my presence already. Talk about the "something told me's". Explain that's the Holy Spirit. Explain why we have the Holy Spirit. He came when you accepted Christ. He leads and he guides you. He helps you. He speaks to us for you. He intercedes. That's enough for now.

Okay, so back to GFC! What else should we do?

Your first day is going to be informal. Talk to them about the importance of prayer and spending time with me every day. This will be good for your kids too! I'm going to show you scriptures to send them to each day so that they can be reading my word until you meet again.

I'm not sure my mind is clear to get scriptures from you right now.

I know. We'll do it later.

Okay.

So you'll talk about prayer for them to be doing privately at home, and then you'll talk about the prayer you're going to do when you all come together. Prayer is THE MOST IMPORTANT part of GFC because it's through prayer and communion with me that they'll draw in and closer to me. Then they'll be able to hear my voice when you get ready to do treasure hunts.

Okay.

So you can introduce them to popcorn prayer, but explain that the goal is for EVERYONE to pray. They don't need to worry about being impressive. We're learning new things, and it's time for them to stretch. Buy them

all a rubber band so that you can illustrate how big and powerful a rubber band can be when stretched. In its natural state, it is just flimsy looking and not very strong. But when it's stretched to new lengths, you can easily see how strong and powerful it is and how much it can hold. I'm going to give them a lot. Power, knowledge, understanding. This is for all, not for just a few select kids. This is for all who come. Keep the rubber bands around for the new kids who come. But not to be played with as toys by your kids. These are special rubber bands.

Okay cool!

So they're going to make room for me to stretch them.

This is cool! You really are giving this all to me!

I told you I would. You've got to work on your trust of me. This goes deeper and beyond you just trusting that this is my voice.

Okay. I'm sorry.

I know. I forgive you. Okay, first day: meet and greet, rubber band, prayer. How I speak—sometimes quietly, the still small voice, sometimes loud like a shout; sometimes they'll be able to smell me/my presence; sometimes I'll show them a picture or a movie; sometimes they'll have a dream. These are just SOME of the ways that I communicate with my children. With you I just talk in a normal father-daughter talking voice. So share that too.

Have the kids share what they THINK has been me speaking to them before or how I speak now. Tell Miracle to hold back only a little! Don't keep my truths away from people, but don't have her lead. Tell her to use discernment and for her to listen for me to guide and instruct her in

what to share, how, and when to share. This really should take you through your two hours, but since I know that you want more...

Give them an assignment this week to watch and listen for my voice. Also tell them to look to my creations for peace and thankfulness. Encourage them to start looking at things with a thankful heart. Tell them to make lists of what they're thankful for each day. Bring their lists or notebooks back with them. Give them a notebook for GFC so they can take notes while together, journal, write down what I've said to them or showed to them or their dreams. But give them a journal that is just for GFC type of stuff so all their things are together and they can bring them each week.

IF you have time left over, which you won't because you have your prayer time in there and YOU don't know how long that is going to go, then just hang out and have some fun while you wait for their parents. YES, write out the agenda/lesson plan because the parents ARE going to want to know what their kids did (and what you're teaching them).

This is REALLY good!

I know. I told you I'd help you. You've got to trust me, dear. And you're not doing that. If I say I'm going to give something to you and teach you and train you, and all you have to do is follow me.....THEN FOLLOW ME! No, I'm still not mad! But you have to get this. All those people you look up to-Ravi, Heidi Baker, Robby Dawkins, Todd White, Will Hart—they follow me. They know my voice and they FOLLOW ME. I'm the same to you that I am to them. These things I have for you, too. Just hear me and

follow! I'm going to let you go because your kids need you now. I see that and you know that. They need you. Love on them. Let them feel like the gifts that they truly are. Remember you gave them back to me. They're all mine. Please treat them as such. Treat them kindly.

Yes sir, I will. Thank you for today. All of it. Rebuke and all.

I didn't rebuke you. You'll know a rebuke! I just let you hear how YOU are.

Okay gotcha. Thanks God.

Really?

Thanks Dad.

July 19, 2013

Our time together is sweet. Are you ever going to stop being here? Like stop talking to me like this?

No, I'm always going to talk to you.

Isn't this for everyone? [Communion like this?]

Yes, it is. If they'll listen.

Well this is a great trial run with Joshua sitting next to me and talking to me the whole time. I think I'm going to have to go upstairs to focus though.

You don't have to. It's a choice. Just like you told him about fear—hearing my voice above the noise is a choice. You have to purposefully tune your ear to Mine. [I'm running through my mind wondering if that made sense.] Yes, it makes sense. You will hear what I hear.

[In my room now so that Josh doesn't have to TRY to be quiet…not because I was having a hard time hearing. I just felt bad for him sitting and doing nothing since he's up early.] So what are we talking about today?

You.

Man, what about me? I thought we talked about me a lot already lately. Have I done something else terribly wrong?

No.

Okay, so what are we talking about me? Or what are YOU about to say about me?

That I love you.

I know *that.*

You think you know it. You know it in theory, but I want you to know it in relationship and its magnitude. It will be very hard for you to do because you'll have to free your mind a lot more than what you are right now.

Okay, so how do I do that?

See how you want steps and instructions? It's not like that. You can't follow steps in order to feel my love for you. To KNOW my love and the depths of it. There are no plans to follow. It's just in your freedom in me that you will experience it. But you have to be free. Tonight will be a good class for you. For you all. You may even get to share. But be honest and tell the truth. This is not an arena to hold back or pretend to be humble. They are searching for truth like you and need freedom in all that I give them. So if you are asked a question, you answer it in truth. All of the question/s they may ask. You'll see. Just know that I've given you permission to speak tonight.

Okay. Anything about Teen Bible Study prayer today?

My peace and patience I give to you all. It will come in due season.

If we faint not?

Yes, keep doing what you're doing.

Should I tell people what you've said? Like, "Daddy said that he's giving his peace and patience and the Bible study is a good idea and that you heard him correctly?" Do people WANT to hear that? Will they receive it? Do you even want me to present that way?

I want you to be you and be free in that. Because I give your freedom. No one else. If you ask me, I'll tell you want to say. But if you don't ask then you're relying on the Holy Spirit to prompt you and guide you.

Wow. So like Wendell said last night...I really am coming and talking straight to you every day? I am not communicating with or through the Holy Spirit?

That is correct. He's here. And of course we all [the Trinity] hear everything that's being said so we all know and are accountable, but you are talking directly to me.

Oh wow. Should I have my shoes off every day then?

(Chuckle.) No you don't have to. I take you as you are! You're my daughter.

Okay! You're so kind. I wish I were like you. [Not as *God*, but as a parent.]

You will get there. It's a process.

[I'm imagining what He looks like.] Will I see you?

In time. One day.

When I'm in Heaven?

Yes.

Okay. Did we finish about people WANTING to hear what you say to me each day?

Your family will want to know. Always. They think it's neat. But it's not a super power, like some will look at it. So you have be careful and use discernment on who and what to tell. Some may be easy or beneficial to share, but some is just for the, "how cool is this?" factor. And that's what you have to watch out for. You don't want people to think that this is JUST for you or Ravi or "special people." This REALLY IS FOR ALL!! They just don't get it or see it right now. Keep telling them it is. Share what people ask to hear. [Don't bombard them like you do your husband!]

If people know that you talk to me every day, if they want to know something, then they'll ask you for it. Don't start taking requests for words, either. I'm not a Genie, and if people ask me what I want to say to them, they may not like what I say. Either people have a lot of sin that needs to be dealt with—that they don't WANT to talk about—or their future has a lot in store, and they'll get scared or try to make it happen on their own. Then it will be messed up and out of order. So don't take requests and try and do them there.

If someone asks you for a word, tell them that you "will ask Daddy about it next time we talk and he may or may not give you something for them." And you can explain to them what I just told you about hidden sins or doing things out of poor motives. Because with that, the Holy

Spirit in them can begin to work and convict them of areas of their lives that need to be dealt with. When you answer them, tell them I told you to release the power of the Holy Spirit in their lives to begin to work in their hearts, to find the hidden areas that no one sees, and to set them free from any bondage they may have. Ask for a fresh wind to blow in their lives, and when things start to change, know it was the work of the Father and the Holy Spirit that you called out to be released.

Don't let any credit come or fall on you. Give all glory back to me. You know that. That is NOT a place you want to be. That's where men fall, and I told you that you'd finish well. That's not going to be your story, but remember to verbalize that all glory and honor has to come back to me.

Okay.

This is fun isn't it?

Really? Is this fun for you, too?

Of course. I love being with you and my children. I just wish that more came to talk with me. They talk TO me a lot, but I want them to sit at my feet and listen like this too.

Well why don't you talk to some of them? Like when they're praying? Or when they ask you a question and then pause or wait even? How come you're not speaking to them so they can hear you?

Well, just like you had to work through your own doubt that you were actually hearing me, that this was really MY voice you were hearing, they have to do the same. They can't just ask me to answer, sit there and wait, and expect

me to shout. They have to learn to recognize my voice in whatever manner I come to speak to them. Some people are going to hear my audible voice, others pictures, and some will have to wait until they sleep to get dreams! But they have to listen in whatever manner I speak to them in. I told you, I'm NOT a Genie.

Okay so if I were trying to convince someone that you DO want to talk to them in this way, in communion, what would you want me to say?

That I love them. I've chosen them. I've created them to hear and to know my voice. I give my peace. So they should have a peace when I speak to them. I should be comforting to their soul. I don't bring confusion. They can rest in my words. I am here to bring life and not destruction. So if I speak to them and they experience peace and life and hope, then they've heard from me. Now take those same steps again to hear my voice again. If I've done it before, do you not think I can, or will, do it again? They need faith to believe that I DO hear and I WILL answer. If they don't believe, then they're shutting me out. I cannot work with a vessel that is unwilling.

They need to be open to receive what I have for them. And since I'm not that Genie, I can't live in the box they try to shove me in. I don't speak out of that box. Well, I don't speak FREELY out of that box. My box-lovers know me, they just don't KNOW me in my fullness and know who THEY ARE IN ME. I'm still their God. They just put so many limits on me and what I can do and what I get to do for them. When you take me out of the box, then I have full range of motion to do what I want where I want.

You take me out of the box and give me power over your tongue. Yes, you heard that correctly. Freedom in me is relinquishing yourself to me. You're free to trust that what I'm instructing you to do is good and right. It's still not a puppet or a slave mentality because this is by your free choice. But you're choosing to give me free access to every part of your being. Including your TONGUE! It will be mine. The words I speak will be the words you speak. You'll be my mouthpiece. You're going to shake nations. You're going to use my voice to be your voice, and we will change lives.

Don't worry about anything else. Give me control over you, again, not a slave or false mentality of how that sounds. You know what I mean. Dying to your flesh so that I can live in and through you. You have this. You have the concept. You just need to walk it out every day. Your home, your kids, your thoughts...my ways will be your ways because you'll follow me.

Yes, this would be good in book form. You can do that just for easy reading when you come back to it. Memorize what you need to memorize. Some of this you won't want to forget, but some of this will be brand new every day or every time your season changes or every time a habit is broken. These words will always change for you. When your vessel is clean, then this will just be instructions and commending every day. Like, "I'm proud of you. You're doing a good job." Those are the words I will speak to you. And not that I don't feel that way right now, I'm just talking about how right now we're trying to clean your vessel and train your ear. Seek me today at prayer with the girls [Teen Bible Study]. Seek me right in the middle

of prayer. I'll tell you what to pray. You follow me. Don't worry about who's there.

Okay.

Now go eat. You're going to be late if you don't go now. Read and edit this later. Yes, there are good things that you should highlight! You know that. But do it later today; you'll have time then. But right now you don't! I love you!

I love you too!

July 22, 2013

I am so mad tired and I never feel just right on Monday mornings. Almost like I need to do SOMETHING to get in to talk to Daddy because "I'm so far away" on Mondays. I guess if I would continue to go to bed early so I can get up early to talk to him on the weekends too, I wouldn't feel so far away.

Daddy?

Yes.

What are you doing?

Looking at you.

Okay. Want to talk this morning?

I always want to talk to you.

Alright. I'm feeling kind of distant, so I'm going to let you lead the talk today if that's okay. I can't think of anything to come right out and ask today.

I've forgiven you for that movie. You can stop thinking about it. That's the enemy messing with you. Let it go. Shake it off and keep moving forward [we had watched

some movie with too many bad words in it and it was really messing with me while we watched it and I finished watching it anyway].

I'm trying.

Try harder.

Okay. I really am starting to get the Daddy relationship thing.

I know. I'm glad. You're my baby.

Baby girl? Like the word I got before?

You are my baby girl, but you'll see how that [word] plays out. Not yet. Not time.

Okay.... So what are you doing today?

Waiting on my people. To rise up. Take ownership of what is rightfully theirs and seek my face for direction. I'm waiting for them to come to me with humbled hearts so I can move on their behalf. But my people won't repent for their sins. They keep on doing things their own way with their lustful desires. They won't find true relationship with me. I'm what they need and are longing for. Not drugs or sex or violence or women. Just me. I love them. I'm waiting on them. Just watching and waiting.

Dude, what is the deal with North Korea?

It's sad, isn't it?

To say the least.

I know [he just left this like this wasn't a conversation for us right now].

So what do you want to say to me today?

That I still love you. I know you sin, Jo. You're human. But the more time you spend with me and long for my presence in every area of your life, the more you'll become like me. Not like a god, but you'll take on my love and my character. You'll see things differently—through my eyes. That's what you've been praying for. I prompted you to that twelve years ago. Those were my words for you. You will see with my eyes, but you will be hurt by the things that hurt me. You have to be prepared for pains that you've never known before. The sins of this world are great, and they contain much weight. You will carry that weight in your heart because it will grieve you so.

But don't worry. Don't fear. Don't despair. I am greater. My love is greater. I'm still on the throne. I'll still get all the glory. You'll learn to separate ministry from personal life. I heard you talking this weekend to Miracle and Dell about the time when your dad's friend told you that[he said that I wouldn't be able to separate work life from home life and not to go into social work]. He didn't know my power and strength or how I was going to use you. I put those burdens to help me in you. I put that rescuing spirit in you. I know you want to help people. I put that there. Don't run or try to change from that. You will long for justice and freedom for my children. My people. That's all from me.

Yes, separate it from your family time. Don't bring and carry those burdens at home when you should be enjoying your children and the freedoms you have. But know that I put those things in your heart. It's part of who I created you to be to carry the load that I have for you. Yes, this is still scriptural. Yes, I know it says my burdens are light, and I told you you'd carry heavy loads, but I know what

you can handle. There won't be more than you can bear, and many have born them before you. Yes, it may have cost them their lives, but to die is gain, Jo!

Don't stress over how these words sound to your human, comfortable ears. I'm just saying that what I have for you will have a cost. To do the work I have for you, you will the feel pain that my children are going through and carrying. Their bondage. Their slavery to sin. You will understand how they feel. You'll be able to minister to them. Don't worry about any of this. Just follow and serve me. You will finish well.

Will I ever talk to Jesus and will he ask me a lot of questions?

You can. If you talk to him. He's always here. But you were right—it IS me who you're talking to, so it doesn't have the same characteristics of when your big brother talks to you.

That's cool. You think I should try to write those down when I talk to him?

You can.

I feel like I should try to talk to him during the day.

Whatever. Like I said. He's always here with us when we talk.

I think it'd be hard for us all to talk at one time because I would have a hard time typing it out so I knew who was who talking!

You're funny.

That's how you made me! You know GFC is on my mind today.

Yes I know. It's going to be good. No, you don't need the other mom to help you. You know that she's just interested

and hungry though. So I'm glad you typed your agenda out to make copies. And copying that paper is a good idea, too. Just hand it out. They can go over it themselves. It's self-explanatory.

Okay anything else for today. I still need scriptures or a memory verse, don't I?

Yes. Don't you think you can find one?

Yeah….but wouldn't I rather have it come from you? You gave me everything else!

Romans 12:1

Ooo. I think I'm going to have them learn Romans 12:1-2.

That's fine.

Okay cool. Thanks. So when are you going to speak to my husband?

I am.

So why isn't he hearing you?

He's cloudy [I see, like, big chunks of white wax; they look like corks in his ears].

Cloudy with what?

Judgment.

Yours?

No, his own. He's listened to other people talk about him in addition to the lies that the enemy has told him. Now it's hard for him to think clearly and understand My voice and that I AM talking to him. He can't hear me above the noise of the enemy.

Can't you talk louder? He wants to hear from you.

Then just like you need to stop thinking that I'm still thinking about that movie you watched, he needs to stop listening to the lies in his head telling him that he's not good enough, he's too far behind and can't catch up, and that he doesn't hear my voice. THOSE ARE ALL LIES!

So I'm to continue to pray for the mind of Christ on him is what I'm thinking here. Anything else?

No, just pray for him. You can ask him about judgment but I think you know now that he wants to hear things directly from me. He just needs to move those things out of the way [I see him having to move large file cabinets from in front of a door of a big open room. All that's in it are these black tall file cabinets.].

Okay. It's just hard to watch, you know. I hate to see him frustrated. And doubting himself and his abilities. You know for years I've watched the job and church just wear him down. I've always thought it boiled into, or down to, a poor self-esteem and lack of confidence.

Yes.

Was that the root of those judgments or is that something different? I mean, if I were going to pray against something, what should I be calling out specifically?

You can continue to just pray for the mind of Christ. He's judging himself based on his earthly performance, whether it be work, life, or church/ministry, but that's not how I'm looking at him. I don't see him like that because that's not how I created him; that's not how I see him now. He needs to forgive himself of those things that need to be forgiven so he can quickly forget them and

move on. It's just not the way I see him. He needs to let his past go and walk free and clear into the future that I have for him.

Hey. I'm glad that yesterday was our last day at the old church.

I am too. Not that it's bad there, but it's time for you all to get ready for your future, and that's why I've called you out to your new church. This is your birthing place. This is where it will all begin. Just wait for me. I will show up, and you will know without a shadow of a doubt what your next move in me will be. This is the birthing place for both of you. Together. Yes, together. You'll see. It's going to be great. You WILL make a good team.

Yes, you have issues to deal with, and you will [deal with them]. But this is where it all begins. Don't go back [to the old church] unless I tell you to. I will release you when the time is right. I know your kids won't understand. But stand your ground. They are children. They don't understand everything. But I see the big picture, and I reveal it to you. You carry it out. Yes, your husband will lead you. Follow him. But he will hear and recognize and follow my voice as well. One army. That's what's being birthed here. One army for the Lord. Don't get caught up in what people are doing [at the new church], just follow me. I will instruct you for everything.

Can I go hear Prophet Todd Hall this weekend?

Yes you may go. He has a word for you. It may just be in his message, but he has a word. Go and be filled.

So you don't have just one style, do you?

No, I'm everywhere, doing everything.

That's cool.

I know.

Well, kids are up. Anything else for today?

Just that my peace and love I give to you.

Oh hey, the big girls and I keep getting words about joy. What's that about? When is that? Will we know it? Notice it?

You'll see.

Okay.... I'm gonna go. Talk to you later.

Okay. Talk to your brother today too [Jesus].

Okay. I'll try that. It seems like it'd be funny though. Like awkward. Sorry. I don't know why. I think I'm used to your conversation, Daddy. Will talking to him bring confusion to me? Will I be able to differentiate the voices? Ahh...I don't know if I'm ready to go there and do that yet. Is that okay?

Yes, of course. And no, he's not mad. He understands!

Okay. Thanks.

July 23, 2013

God, I love You, and I need You. I can't do anything without you. It's hard to even wake up without you pulling on my heart to rise. I love you so much, and I know there's room to do deeper in you. There's still love that I haven't experienced yet. You're just waiting for the right time to pour out more of your love on me. Thank you Lord. I have this nagging feeling like someday you're going to lift and we won't be doing this anymore.

Why do you feel that way?

Because until I said that, you weren't saying anything, so I didn't think you were there.

I don't interrupt. You should try that skill…

Funny…

Hmm mmm.

Okay, so what did you think about GFC yesterday?

It was good.

That's it. You weren't pleased?

Oh yes, I was pleased. You had a good turn out. But you have to be careful to follow me only. No one else. No distracting diversions. Stand your guard. Follow what I give you. I'm your planner. No one else. I don't care if it is a good thing, if I didn't say do it, then don't [We were talking about giftings and using your gifts in ministry/God giving us things to do in visions, etc. Someone brought up the girl who painted Jesus who Burpo mentioned; we went online and looked up her art.]**.**

Yes sir.

I'm not mad at you.

I know. I'm just listening and saying yes sir so you know I get it. Should one of the girls bring her guitar?

She can bring it, but I haven't asked her to play. This isn't a show. This is teaching ground. You all can do praise and worship with music on your own. This isn't that time. Just teaching and training RIGHT NOW. It could change for you in the future.

Speaking of future…I sure don't want to do this!

I know.

I feel like how I felt in another children's ministry. That's not good, right? The responsibility of coming up with everything. Not just using a lesson already made right out of the box… ugh. It's so much work.

I told you I'd help you. Didn't I give you the entire lesson for yesterday?

Yes.

Then why are you worrying? FOLLOW ME!

Okay… I'm so tired today.

Another late night. You'll stop doing that. You'll start going to bed earlier. You'll see. You need to arrange and schedule those quiet talking times with Miracle and your husband during the day. Don't wait until after bedtime to have a deep conversation. It may seem weird at first, but just do it. Block off thirty minutes for you and Miracle to talk each day. It sounds like a lot. But you can do less. Just try it out and see how you like it. It will help you stay on task better.

Yeah, that reminds me of school. I think I'm overloaded right now, and I haven't factored in school. Should I drop something? GFC??

No. If you need to drop something, which I don't foresee, then I'll let you know what when you ask me. You CAN handle this school year though. Whatever it brings this year—you can handle it.

Okay.

Did we finish GFC? Was it good?

Yes it was good. You did a good job. We'll work on next week tomorrow.

Okay.

What's next?!

You want to work on music. Follow me. The lyrics will come. You're doing the right things with the melodies. Keep doing what you're doing. You may be getting parts right now, but it will come together. You'll see.

Well, I noticed they were all slow songs. Originally I was hoping the kids would get some music to minister to kids…

I told you that you may not like what I give you!

Yeah, you did. I actually do like what I've gotten. Just wish I could get a complete thing.

It will come.

Okay.

Hey. Will you give me an idea or ideas for making art type stuff? But wait, ideas I can actually do? I'm not that girl [the girl who painted Jesus]. I don't have the time, patience, or desire to go into the detail that she does.

Oh you don't want a masterpiece, you just want some random art? That may not mean a lot to anyone?

Well, I was thinking about putting scriptures on them…

Hmm mmm. We'll see where that goes and how it turns out for you.

So what should I do about my kids?

I told you what to do with them. You have to be consistent in bringing them to prayer. They need to talk to me and hear from me every day. You have to be consistent!

Ugh. Okay. This is all getting harder. The more we talk the more I'm responsible for.

Yes, exactly.

Not necessarily fun.

It will be. When you get over yourself and self-pity and your attitude of laziness. Just remember that I said you'd finish well. Changes are coming. You'll see. They'll be good. Just hold tight.

Okay. Are we going to write music today?

We can, but make sure you get your other work done.

Okay. I'm really tired, and this is hard for me today. I'm not giving you the attention you deserve. I'm going to just talk to you later. Is that okay?

Yes, I understand.

Thanks. Love you!

July 25, 2013

[Conversation about me feeling distant & not coming every day, my sin that separated me, and asking for forgiveness. Thinking about VOA, how I'm going to do communion there, how the rest of my family hasn't purchased their tickets yet.]

God, thank you for providing all of our needs and taking care of us.

You're welcome. But I'm taking care of them, too.

I know. It just looks different than ours.

Exactly.

So did you miss me yesterday?

Yes, of course. I love our time together. And I hate what being apart does to you mentally.

Yeah. You said hate.

I can do that. Because what upsets you and causes that feeling of separation is not just the enemy at work in your mind, but it comes from sin. You make bad choices, he pounces on the opportunity to get in your head and lie to you, and then you carry around guilt. It's all amounting to sin that separates us, and I hate sin. So yes, I said it!

Okay I get it. You know I want to talk about GFC.

Yes, it's weighing on you. Just like you trusted me last week, I need you trust me for every week to come. Stop stressing. I know it wasn't comfortable for you. I'm glad you got nervous so that you relied on me. Just remember to stay focused so you don't derail. I will still give you the plan. You're looking like you're not ready to receive though. Your mind still isn't clear. We can do it later when you're at rest in me and trust that I'm bigger than any of the sin in your life and that I can give you whatever I need to give you regardless of how you may feel. My will will still be done. Hey. Did you like that music time?

Yes, but I only got parts! I was hoping to get a whole song like I did when I woke in the middle of the night and wrote a complete rap song. Will you give me the rest of ALL those songs or do I finish them myself?

I can help you. Or you can work on them. I know you want a few fast songs, so I'll help you be creative if I don't give you the exact melody or words. But when you write the rest of the words, stay in the same flow that I was in, like that one where I'm talking throughout the song. Keep that flow the same way.

I'm guessing I could just keep that the length of the song in terms of words and just make it go on.

Yeah.

Okay, I'll go back to them later. Maybe tomorrow. I'm planning ahead to be tired today and go back to bed! Help me to do exactly what I need to do today [I'm thinking about going to the store and farmers market later though I'm tired and have to deliver food to a friend today].

I will.

Hey do you have a word for Doris?

Are you going to trust me with it and for it?

Yes…I can.

Okay, then do it. I don't mind you asking for words, but you have to say what I say or it won't work right. And yes, you can share it with whoever you ask for—and I give it to you—I'll let you know who I'm not going to give a word for. But if we talk about her and I give you "REST." Then you send her a message that only says, "REST." Do you understand?

Yes.

Being my messenger is a very important job. It's serious. I don't take it lightly. It can make or break someone's life. Do you think I can trust you with that?

Yes.

Okay then. Let's go.

Doris,

I love you very much. You have pleased me with your work; both in your life and with your children and family. I want you to find your rest in me. I'm all you need. My grace is sufficient. Follow me, and I'll give you peace. I am all that you need. Keep on my path. My ways will be your ways. You'll see the way I see. You have done well, but I'm taking you to new heights AND new depths. You will be pleased, and you'll bring your husband honor. You can finish the race before you with my strength. My timing is perfect. They will come home. I love you. I'm here with you and for you. There is no lack in me. My peace I give to you, and my grace is sufficient. My love will pour down and overflow from you. I have graced you for this season. Don't run from it. This is my doing. Just stay with me. You are my child. I have you. I love you. I hold you in my arms. You are my child and I'm pleased, just like your big brother. Just rest in me. I'll make all your paths straight. My love abounds. I'll lift you up. Follow me. Honor your husband. Respect his wishes for you. I'm leading you. I've got you. Stop worrying about things that don't matter in my kingdom. My grace and love abound. My ways are perfect. Just rest and go with me. In my timing, all things will be made clear to you. But now, just REST and follow me. I love you, Doris. You make me smile. I love to hear you sing to me. Teach your

children well. They will worship me. You have done well. I'm proud of you. I'm all you need. Come to me all who are weary and heavy-laden and I will give you rest. I leave this with you my child. Just rest in that.

-Daddy

Okay. I know you're tired. Don't think about the email. You know she's busy!

I know.

Get your rest right now. I'll show you what to do today. We'll meet again for GFC. I love you.

I love you too!

July 26, 2013

So GFC is definitely for you, because I don't think I want it anymore. I sure am glad you said I'm going to finish well, because I sure don't want to finish anything I start. And when you said that I wasn't thinking of GFC at all, I was just thinking about my life as a whole, in general.

That is correct.

Okay. So I'm not sure how to pinpoint the root reason of me feeling like GFC is too much for me, and I don't want to do it. All these kids looking at and to me to teach them something. Knowing that I'm not there to entertain, but feeling like I need to….I don't know how to describe my feelings.

You don't have to. I know your feelings and their root cause.

So you can reveal it to me then, right?

If I need to. If you don't figure it out. The Holy Spirit can and will help you. And your brother can help you get over it too when you cast out these imaginations and habits and you purposefully walk away from the thoughts that keep you bound. We're all here to help you, Jo. You're not on your own. We each have different parts in your life, roles to play. You just have to learn to utilize all three—even at one time! THAT'S when you get real power!

Ha…I'm not even thinking of obtaining power right now. Just want to get through these next two weeks of GFC without looking like a fool in front of these parents!

Well, you WILL need the power that comes with using all three of us at one time, so just remember that, and practice communicating and using us at different times. Not just one of us at a time. Angels can help, too. Call on them to war and to cover as well.

This is cool stuff. Thanks!

You're welcome. [I'm] here to teach and train you, remember?! There's way more to your life and training than just GFC!

Okay. I love you.

I love you more.

"I love you more!!" *(Jesus!)*

Oh man! Yes, You do. I know that you both do.

So today I want to lay out the plan for your next meeting. Maybe even the third one if time permits since Joshua is waiting on you [wink]. This week you're going to go over their findings. How I revealed myself to them.

Is this how we're starting?

Well, still pray and invite all three of us in, and then this will be your first bullet.

Okay.

So go over what they journaled. You need to read Joy Dawson's book (Dawson 2001) **today and tomorrow. Don't stress about how MUCH you read, just read both days. I've got you.**

Okay

Talk about their different stories and examples. You need to fast that day so you'll be in tune with the spirit to help you interpret what's presented.

Okay.

Try to have everyone share something. If they didn't notice me speaking to them, then they at least need to share some new things that they gave thanks for this week. And that will be your next go-round the circle. So after sharing what they got, you may have some pictures in there too, then you'll go around and share what everyone was thankful for this week. THEN you pray.

This should help to open kids up to want to hear more, see more, desire more and press in to get more from me and our relationship. Coupled with the time of shared thanksgiving—hopefully you'll get more prayer time out of them. Remember to be patient. These are kids. The long, quiet pauses are okay here because they're building up courage to bring our relationship to the public's eye. Let me encourage them to speak. You just wait and be patient. No, you don't need to look at your watch and tell

them you'll wait three minutes at the most. You wait on me. ASK ME. I'll tell you when prayer is over. Just ask me!

Okay.

Alright, so after prayer time, you're going to go into teaching.

Teaching what?

Please don't interrupt. You're waiting on me. Wait on me to give it to you.

Yes sir.

The different ways that I speak. I know that you handed out that paper last week, but you're going to need to go over some things. When you go through sharing time you may have some kids who didn't experience me this week. First of all, that's okay. But second, remind them of the ways that I speak. Ways that I may appear to them. I know you went over this last week, so it won't be so in depth.

I also want you to talk to them about making sure that their hearts are ready to receive me. Use the sections in Joy's book (Dawson 2001) **as headers/reasons. Bullet each one of them and give brief descriptions. Tell them that in order for their vessel to be used, it has to be a clean, clear, usable vessel. Take her sections and make them for kids. Be mindful of the ages and maturity of your kids. Don't worry about boring the older ones. They understand you have a wide group. Make sure the 'littles' understand. If Joy** (Dawson 2001) **has scripture in each section, make sure you use those on your paper that you give to them.**

Okay.

This week's assignment will be working on your vessels so that I can use you all.

Okay.

You need to talk about honesty this week. The importance of it in your personal lives as well as in this group. You can look up scripture on that on your own. Make it relatable, and use it for the kids. No, don't lead with it. Put it on the paper so it's already there. You're going to be talking to kids who may have flubbed in the beginning. Let the Holy Spirit bring conviction to those who may have stretched the truth at the beginning. Let him deal with them all week in this area. They must be honest before me and before you all. Lying to themselves only holds them back. If they want to move forward in life, or in ministry, they will have to be honest vessels, or I can't use them to their fullest potential.

Is this going to fill two hours?

It can. I really want this group to do a lot of interactive stuff. I want them to talk and share more. This is how you're all going to grow in your faith.

Okay.

If you still have time, you can start with your next lesson. Introduce words of knowledge to them. Just do a brief overview of all of the steps for the prayer model, because that's the goal of what you're doing—that's the next step to prepare for prayer. This is actually going to be how you close out your meeting. You're going to go over these steps, then find some videos of Todd White or others of street ministry and how they're using the model to pray

for healing. But first you need to introduce/briefly go over words of knowledge.

This week, focus on them asking me for a word for someone and seeing what they get. How they got things this past week should prepare them for how they get things now—words in their head, words above someone or something, pictures, movies, speaking. Do the notecards. They may be nervous or feel like they're not ready. Tell them it's okay. Just write down whatever comes to them. Pray first to help them clear their mind and be in tune with what I'm revealing to them. They'll be okay! This is just practice. If they make mistakes, that's fine. Yes, the parents can participate. This is training ground. This is where our ears get tuned. If they get nothing, that's fine.

Sounds like a fun week.

It will be. Now go and get some fun videos to get them all fired up!

Yes, I will. Thank you.

You're welcome.

I'm going to read today.

GOOD! You need to be reading every day! You need to work on your schedule; you know that. It's coming though. Don't keep beating yourself up. You'll get ready for school and your new schedule. You'll figure out what time you need to go to bed. It will all fit. The things that NEED to fit and get done, WILL FIT. If it doesn't fit in your schedule, then look at it again to see if it really needed to be there. You'll have more time if you schedule your day. Make time for your kids too. They need to play every day. Not just at nighttime.

Okay.

Okay. Go get some work done now!

August 5, 2013

It's been a long time.

I know.

Wow, you're still there?

I'm always here.

You're awesome.

I know.

So what would you like to talk about today? [My mind's racing with all the things he could want to talk about since I've been "gone" so long.]

Stop talking.

Yes sir.

Just wait and listen. Yes, I'm still going to talk to you the same. Yes, you're still going to know my voice. I don't change, Jo. And I always want to have these sweet times with you. Whether it's been a month or a year. I don't need religion. I want relationship.

Okay.

Okay. Now, let's talk about your habits.

[I'm surprised about the topic, but not sure what he's referencing.] Okay…is there too much narration?

A little bit! Let's focus here; you can add that in later.

Okay!

So what about my habits?

They need to change.

Which ones?

All of them.

Ugh. Huh?

Your habits need to change. They need to be more like mine.

Do you have habits?

Yes.

Okay I don't know what they are then. At least not that I can think of.

Then that's your first problem. You don't know me.

Oh.

I know if you sat and thought about it, you'd be able to think of my characteristics, so use those as a guide to my habits.

You're not just going to tell me what your habits are that I need to follow?

No, because that would be easy. And YOU—need to work!

Okay…

Good. Next thing. GFC.

What about it?

You have a meeting today. Are you ready?

No.

Why not?

'Cause I didn't work on it.

I know. Jo, you're going to have to do work. Not just for the kids but for yourself. In whatever area you work, it's going to be work!!! You can't think that just because we talk that elevates you and that I'm going to give you all the answers all the time. I give the plans; then you have to fill in all the blanks by doing your homework. You have to study. You have to commune. You have to pray. This communion together does not count for everything. YOU HAVE TO DO YOUR WORK! Your side of the bargain. You're not going to receive everything you want and desire JUST through THIS. Do you understand that?

Yes.

I'm not mad, but you have to know and understand this. Communion is NOT a substitute for food and nourishment. That's what you get from studying and praying—and you NEED those things—especially for the day-to-day things of life. You need scriptures in your heart and a desire to pray for people. This is when you listen to me. That is when I listen to you. Are you taking that the right way?

Yes.

You know I listen to you all the time, and I hope that you will begin to listen to ME all the time. But for natural purposes here—you do the most talking in prayer, and I do the most talking in communion, understand?

Yes.

Okay. On to the next thing. Your fear. It needs to be dealt with. Yes, you pushed it to the side to move forward. But yes, just like you said to your husband last night, it needs to go out of your life. YES, you CAN have a life WITHOUT FEAR! Trust me. It's possible!

Okay. I want that then!

It's going to take work. And you don't like work. So we'll see how bad you want it.

Are you going to tell me how to get rid of it?

You know how to get rid of it.

Hmmm.

See? It's going to be work. You've been listening today, right? Perhaps you'll see what I've said when you go back and edit all this. YOU HAVE TO CHANGE YOUR HABITS! Stop being lazy, Jo. You can't move forward AND be lazy. Your callings are going to require a lot of work. And I can't even reveal them to you if your work ethic is so bad that you run because you know the work involved. You've got to learn to press! Get dirty and work hard.

Ugh…

I'm not going to tell you anything about GFC. Just be ready. To fly or to flop. It'll be on you.

Okay…...I'm so tired.

Then rest. But look at me; I worked hard and THEN rested. Go learn ME. You'll be okay. You're on a good

track for this week. Keep it up. You're doing good. I love you.

I love you too [but feeling overwhelmed and tired].

I know!

August 24, 2013

Good morning, Daddy.

Good morning.

Talk about distant. I feel so far today.

You're not.

Okay. What do you want to talk about today? I'm really tired.

I know. We should talk about you.

Ugh…should we?

Yes.

What about? Bad stuff, huh? I was hoping that this wouldn't be all a rebuke.

I didn't say it was going to be a rebuke; I just want to talk about you.

Okay. Shoot.

So I've noticed that you aren't spending time with me like you should.

Uh huh.

And your face seems sadder than it should. You don't look happy or joyful. Any of the time. Even at that conference with all of those believers, you still didn't look happy.

Okay.

Okay. What do you think?

What do I think? Wait, who am I talking to?

Your Dad, but I'm asking you a question. What do you think about what I said?

Well, I knew I wasn't spending enough time with you. That's why I wrote out that new schedule…

Which I saw you haven't put anything dealing with me in the evening during all of those free hours you have.

Right. I'm still waiting to see what Wendell is going to want planned for the evening before I put in "book time."

Okay…

Do YOU want to plan those free hours??

I could, but I'll wait to see what you put there first. Just know I'm watching!

Right! Okay my face. I don't know what to say about it. I'm tired a lot.

Yes, but this goes beyond being tired. This is your attitude and your perception of life. There's a disconnect there. You should be joyful all of the time. I'm not asking you to look like your friend. I'm asking you to be joyful about who I am and who I am in you and your family. I AM going to use you, Jo. But don't wait until I do to try to change how you look and appear to others.

Like the song, "don't wait….shout now?"

Right. Start changing these ugly habits now. It will make it easier for me to move in other areas of your life if you deal with these now.

Wow. You called my face an ugly habit…what do you thinking about bad habits that are actually considered "bad" down here???

I know what you mean, but remember that it's all bad to me. Sin is sin. It's all equal. Please always remember that when ministering to others so that you don't judge them. You keep looking for the big things to convict people with, but that's not how I see things. What you consider small is big enough to separate man from me. So it's big enough to convict, make people cry from remorse, and to flood an altar. Don't discredit "small sin" for there is no such thing.

Okay. Today. I really don't want to go. I'm tired, and I think I'm tired of not seeing anything. I'm trying to keep my faith up, but I feel like it's getting weary.

Don't grow weary in well doing. You know that, Jo. Don't despise small beginnings. I've purposed you for this. I'll give you words; you'll see my hand. Don't quit on this—on ME. Just wait; you'll see. Keep doing what you're doing. And DON'T discourage my children from praying for people, because you may not have the faith to believe that my miracles have no limits. I'm not bound by peoples' handicaps. You pray for every person you feel led to pray for or every person your kids feel led to pray for. DO NOT DISCOURAGE KIDS BECAUSE OF YOUR LACK OF BELIEF.

Yes, you <u>do</u> keep hearing the Holy Spirit say, "Thrill of Victory, Agony of Defeat" (Clark 2014). **Listen to it.**

But also remember that most of the people you listen to say that they prayed for people for months with nothing (seemingly) happening, and then one day… But what if they had gotten discouraged and stopped praying because they looked at their track record? You wouldn't know of Heidi Baker and Will Hart. YOU just keep believing. Yes, be happy just planting the seed. You will never know the impact of all of your prayers, even when you can't SEE something happening. But I know. And I'm pleased with that. Your job is NOT to please people; it's to please ME. Be obedient to my voice and what I tell you to do.

August 27, 2013

Good morning Lord. I'm starting to feel overwhelmed today about the fall schedule.

I know.

Is there anything that I need to take out of the schedule? Though I really don't see anything that's removable; it's more that I have to manage it well. Is that the case?

Yes.

Then I REALLY need your help.

I know.

Are you going to show me something? Or make my schedule for me?

No.

Uhh…well why not?

I'm going to grace you for it. You are preparing for a new season and a new day. This year, the rest of this year

is going to seem very stressful for you. Overwhelming. Too much for you to carry. But you will—because I'll be helping you. I'm allowing you to go through this to train you, to equip you, to strengthen you. You're going to need to know how to manage and balance and carry the weight of this season. You CAN be a minister of my gospel and homeschool and be a good mom and wife. You will find the balance because I will grace you for this. This is training ground.

Uhh…is there a prerequisite for your grace? Like, can I get out of line and you'll lift that grace that I'll need?

No. You WILL make mistakes, but I'll help you to see them clearly so you can recognize them and learn from them right away. Your eyes will be clear to see what I have before you. Your vision of my path and my plan will become more clear for you to see. You will learn to make sound choices more regularly because you'll recognize me and my presence and my words when it's time to make decisions. You will not question if it's your flesh or the enemy. You will know it is me speaking to you. YOU HAVE TO HEAR MY VOICE WHEN YOU ARE MINISTERING!

Stop trying to do things all on your own. That's not what I've called you to do. I'm here to help you and give you the words. Stop trying to go on your feelings or thoughts of the past. My words are new every day. And don't worry how it looks or sounds to others. Learn to come to THIS place even when ministering in a group [with church] come here to hear my voice that I am speaking to them, through you.

The key to your ministry is hearing my voice above the noise. That's when you'll rise. And I don't mean in a haughty way. I'm saying that that is when your ministry will flourish. People will recognize your voice and that the things you'll be speaking are truth, because they'll know it's from me. We won't always be able to have this precious quiet time that we have in the mornings. I'm going to need to use you outside of the home—outside in this very loud and often doubting world. So you're going to need my voice to guide you but also to penetrate through their unbelief. You'll have to hear me clearly so when I speak the word that pierces their soul and their unbelief, you deliver it the way I spoke it. Do you understand that?

Yes.

Good, then get going in it.

Huh? What do you want me to do?

Practice. Stop being so timid when the Holy Spirit says to pray for those hurt people you see. Take your bubbly encouraging self and go talk and pray with them. Your time is mine. You can't operate the way you used to or are accustomed to. Your schedule for school is great, but when you walk out of that house, you're mine. You work on my time. At least you should. That's what I need you to do.

Stop looking at your past and what you call failures because you haven't SEEN me move. I'm moving. Your job is to deliver the message, not wait for the fruit to harvest. Yes, be happy planting the seed. But you put the seed down when I tell you and how I tell you. No fertilizer unless I say so.

But the ONLY way you're going to get this and use this the way I have for you is if you start listening for my voice and move when the Holy Spirit says move. Yes, he will tell you to move even when the people don't want prayer right then. And yes, there will be some who I don't heal in front of your eyes. Your job is to listen and obey.

Okay. Should I go out today?

You're not listening to my voice already. Yes, I said man in a red shirt.

[In my mind I see a taller guy with a red shirt and shorts on. Seems like he has a hat on because I don't really see a lot of hair.] Okay, I will look for him.

September 9, 2013

Well good morning. This definitely wasn't what I had in mind when you said I was going to have what seemed like an overwhelming year.

I know.

Well…

Well what?

Are you going to give me some deep profound word this morning to make sense of all of this?

No. That's not what you need.

What do I need then?

You need me. I'm all you need.

Huh?

You need to trust in me. Rely on me. I need to be your source of everything [this year].

But isn't that hard when it seems like we want for nothing? And are you upset about that?

No, I'm not. You have it so you can give it. Or share it. And I'm not looking for perfection, Jo. I just want your time. All of you. I want you readily available to give when I say give and go when I say go. Your confidence is not lacking. You have all that you need in me. I make all things new. I heal the broken. I cast things out. You just need to do what I tell you to do.

I am your source. I am your way. Follow me. Stay on course. Your source is in me and I'm all you need. No "thing" that you buy on earth can compare or measure up to what you need that is in me. And it's okay that you have stuff, because there are people out there who have stuff need to be ministered to and encouraged just like you. So be that for them. Pray that they hear my voice, and they'll know when to give and share.

My voice is what people need. They need to be guided by me. It's when people go their own way that they run into problems or find themselves "distant" from me. And really, people can't be "so distant." It's all a lie from the enemy, because I'm ALWAYS with you! It doesn't matter where you go or where you are. I'm there. My spirit walks everywhere you go, and we are one with Christ.

There is no such thing as, "You're too far out there, and God can't love or use you where you are." Those are lies. Sin separates people from me. So just remove the sin. Remove the lies from your head that tell you something different. I'm always with you.

Hey, so thanks for showing Sal to me Saturday. [A guy I played golf with who used to be a youth pastor and had back-slidden and left the church]. That was pretty cool. I hope that he comes to church one day.

He will come back to the church.

God, why did I hurt my ankle? Are you going to tell me?? [Right after encouraging Sal and giving him a card inviting him to our church, I stepped in a hole and twisted my ankle.]

This is your time to sit and watch what I do.

Are you serious? That is it?! Because so far this is not pretty. I'd love for that teamwork to magically kick in…but is that what this is for?

This is your time to sit and watch me do what I do.

Where? Everywhere?

WATCH ME.

Okay.

Anything else to say to me today? What do you think about Teen Bible Study? Should we move the date to Mondays?

You can move the date if it works for the majority.

Really? I thought you would give me a clear-cut answer. I feel like we're struggling with the group. Like their hearts or desires aren't in it. What's the deal? Are these our group members? Is there even going to be a teen's group here?

There will be a group here, but it may not have your hand on it. Your hands may be in it as a part of the process, but you won't get to be a part to touch it and be hands-on in it. And that's okay. I have other things for you. You

understand the call on your life to kids and youth, and as long as you walk with me, everything will be okay. I'll show you what you'll be a part of.

I am SO tired God [physically—I keep drifting off].

I know.

I really want to keep talking. Especially about Bible study, the house, a job for Wendell, etc.

I know you do, but it's not the time for all of that anyway. Just stay with me.

Yes sir. I'm trying my best. I love you.

I love you too.

September 17, 2013

I just want to talk to you today! Or rather just hear you talk. I miss you. I miss our times together. I miss times of quiet in my home! Okay, I'm talking too much, YOU TALK! I'm just so excited to be with you today. I love you and your presence. I've been missing it. Okay talk to me!

I miss you, too, daughter. And I love you more!

I know.

But I'm so glad you're here today too. I want to talk to you.

Ooo what about?!?!?

You.

It's always me, isn't it?

Yes. For now. I want to talk to you about your character.

[Big exhale.] Okay, what about?

I want you to open your eyes and look at yourself. Your actions, your thoughts, your words. And I want you to see if it lines up with my character.

I never went back and looked for your character like you told me to.

I know.

Do I need to do that first?

No, you'll be able to see obvious things that don't line up with my character as soon as you start looking at yourself. Yes, go back and study me, but you'll be able to start on this at the same time. Ask the Holy Spirit to open your eyes to see yourself in all honesty. Then ask him to open your ears to hear me better and to give his guidance regarding your actions and words.

Okay.

Wait for me. I'm not done showing you things [in regards to my foot].

Okay, are you showing me things about me or my family or what?

Just wait on me and see. I will show you things.

Okay. I think that it's just not what I thought it was going to be. I thought something great was going to happen with my kids and family, and this was going to pull them together but…

All you've seen was yourself and your attitude and actions, right?

Yes.

Good. That's what I DO want you to see. You have to be more aware of what you're doing and saying and how you're affecting these children. MY children.

Okay.

Stop trying to make them perfect. Stop trying to wait for them to be quiet to minister. USE YOUR KIDS. I keep telling you they are a part of your ministry. They're a part of THE ministry. They may not stand still and keep quite, but it's how YOU RESPOND to their actions. It's how you pass on the REACTIONS to those behaviors. Watch it. You're laying down bad foundation in my vessels. You have to guard your mouth and your attitude. YOU have to try harder. CALM DOWN. Stop expecting so much. Yes, let them be kids, but you have to stay calm in how you address them.

And yes, they need discipline. I have consequences for poor choices, and that's what they need. They don't always need physical discipline, because you give it out of anger and frustration, not a father's love. You have to look at me for your parenting guidelines. I don't care what others say or have written. I will tell you when to use the rod—if you seek me.

If you continue to go at this alone you will continue with what you currently have. Will you seek me during the day? Will you seek me BEFORE you get frustrated with the kids? Will you seek me when Gabi is throwing a tantrum and you don't know what her deal is? Because I DO. I know all the answers to your questions, but you don't ask me in a position to listen for my answer. You're like your children who walk out of the room [and you know that already—I've shown you that illustration and

you've used it]. But you keep ignoring the one who can help you.

Come to me. Ask me. Wait on me. Is Brianna under spiritual attack? YES. She's under attack. The enemy hates her like he hates all of you. Your family has a purpose that will destroy parts of his kingdom and his plans. So he fights those who are called to intercede and speak with boldness and pray for the sick. He wants to bind you all up. Make you busy. Lose sight of your purpose and calling because you're caught up in things of this world [her grades don't matter].

What??

Just wait on me and follow my instruction and lead. I will show you what and how to pray if you will follow me. STOP trying to do this on your own. Yes, she's smart. Yes, her grades will pick up, and you won't have to worry about math. But we have a course of action that we have to take together. READ. Read the book. [*Praying Circles Around Your Children* (Batterson 2012)].

You two HAVE to start praying. I know you're saying it and people aren't listening. Then YOU do it. You may not always have your fighting partner. He may be busy—whether it be my business or not. Until he lines up with where I've called him to be, it's your job to be obedient and follow my path. You wait on me, not him. YOU PRAY. YOU lead the kids. YOU get them back on track by your influence. Your family WILL be on its face again. My glory WILL come down in your home. You are not off in what you are sensing in your spirit. Your family HAS to get back to prayer in order for the conviction to come and

the refinement in their spirits to happen. You all MUST pray. Go now and be the parent they need you to be.

Okay. Thanks for today. I'm glad I made this time for you, and I'm sorry I haven't been taking time out of my schedule for you like I need to do. Please forgive me.

I do. I love you daughter.

I love you too. [Kiss my daddy for me today!]

He knows you love him.

September 23, 2013

Good morning, Daddy! I like days like this when I just can't wait to be with you. I feel like I just HAVE to spend time with you or please you or do anything WITH you!

I love that, too.

So I know it's been awhile we since met like this, but what would you like to talk about today? [I'm racing through my mind trying avoid all the things I think he'd want to talk about that I'm doing wrong…]

You.

How about a word for someone else today? [I draw a blank on which of my friends actually said they need to hear something…]

I want to talk about you.

Okay.

You're pleasing me.

Really? I feel like I'm making so many mistakes and failing—with my anger and attitude and yelling and not serving my husband…

Those things are going to require more effort on your part, but I'm pleased with YOU. Your heart is changing. You have not only a desire for me, but to see my kingdom on earth. You want to save the lost and disciple the new. You're passionate about things I'm passionate about. You please me!

Wow. Thanks Daddy.

You're welcome. Just keep doing what you're doing. Seek me and the kingdom first, and the other things will come. Bad habits will go. Just keep seeking me with your whole heart. Don't get caught up looking left or right. Just follow me and keep pleasing me.

Alright.

Teen Bible Study.

YES!

I know that you want to talk about it. To get my thoughts on what happened last week. I don't mind. I want you to talk to me. That includes your hearts and desires and even your deadlines. I'm not afraid of your deadlines! They don't move me or push me into doing something. I'm God. I can handle whatever your request is regardless of the time or size constraint. It's nothing to me. Especially when you're working for me!!!! I want to see these lives touched and changed; you're not out there on your own doing something outside of my will. This is for the kingdom. Of course I'm going to bless it. In my time… but I'm going to bless it.

[Smiling]

So was I put off by you asking that I bring the people there by October 8th? No. Will the people be there October 8th? We'll see. But until then, you keep doing your part. Your job is to look and wait and find the people my spirit shows you. Every time you step out, you're on a mission—not just the one your kids went on last week! But you're also on a mission for Teen Bible Study. Your eyes HAVE to be open all the time. You have to learn to stay in the spirit while living in the natural. You won't get much downtime.

Is that for me personally or "you" in general?

You personally.

Okay.

My spirit is on you and in you and it has to flow forth. You have to hear me in order to be obedient.

I think it'd be easier if you did something each time it was you so I'd know.

You DO know. EVERY time you get the thought that you should pray for people, that's not you. You've got nothing to gain. You're working for me. That's the Holy Spirit prompting you. If it impacts my kingdom, then it's me, and you should do it—regardless of where you are or how long it will take. No, not everyone will be willing to receive. You just keep trying and doing for those who will allow you. Your time will come. You will see the miracles; just stay with me.

Okay. [I started thinking about Teen Bible Study again and being in the room where we pray, and a black briefcase is in the center of the floor—don't know why. But it is still just the four of us meeting in there and him saying, "Build on your faith. Just build on your faith." So I don't know if the people are coming on Oct 8th, I didn't see them, but I know what he said. So I walk on, and with, that.]

You always want to talk about the house, and I just want you to stay with me! You can keep getting ready. I told you that before [for both you and Wendell]; just follow me to your house. I'll take you.

Okay. I have to get the kids up.

I know.

I love you, Daddy

I know. I love you more!

October 2, 2013

Daddy I really want to talk about the house today.

I know. What do you want to ask me?

You're funny.

I know.

I want to know if the answer you always give me to wait is the same answer you'd give Dell if he asked about it? Or were you just telling me to wait on him?

Okay.

Never mind. What do you want to say about the house?

I have a house for you.

Is it in Illinois?

No.

Sorry I don't like to wait.

I know.

So what do you want to say about the house?

That I have one for you, and I will show it to you.

Is it that one for $1000?

No, that doesn't have the yard you want.

Will the house have all those specs Dell wants?

It may. But you will know the house. It will almost call to you.

When we see it online or will we go inside to know?

You will know.

When will it be?

Soon.

Ugh….

Patience, my daughter.

Okay. Well, should we put this one the market?

You didn't prepare like I told you to. You said you were going to start de-cluttering and getting rid of things, and you did not do that. Of all the things you asked me that I said to wait on, I DID tell you to get your house ready.

So…does that mean it's too late?

No, but now you're not ready. Now you'll have to wait longer. This is the time and season for it.

What if I'm wrong in my hearing?

You're not wrong. Keep listening to me. You know my voice. Don't doubt.

Okay. So we need to clean our house?

Yes.

And once it's clean we should list it?

Yes.

Do we go with our old realtor?

No. I have someone for you.

Do I look for that person from friends, or do we let the bank pick it?

You may ask around. But you all are going to learn to operate by my peace. You will know.

Should we get an agent in St. Louis?

Not yet.

Okay. What about Dell's job?

He knows what to do.

Argh. Does he?

Yes, he does. It's been in his belly for a long time. He needs to let me do my work in him. He doubts, too. He needs to heed to my promptings. I've put those unctions in him. It's time to look elsewhere. This is the season. Don't wait on a sign to go. Just follow me. My peace is perfect. Spread out. Look for work. My peace will guide you. You will know. Pay, location, travel, benefits. You will know it's me and my doing and my plan for you.

There will be so much peace that you won't even need to check with Jo about it. YOU WILL KNOW.

But this IS the time. You may go. Don't look back and worry. No burned bridges to worry about. You'll be going in love and with the assurance of my peace. You've done what you were supposed to do there. They will be okay. You can even look today. That's how much I mean that you can go and it will be okay. I'm taking care of you. This is alright. You don't have to worry.

It may look like hard times around you, but I'm covering you. Shielding you from the worries of this world. Your purpose, your call, your house, these are in my hand. I'm guarding you. I'm watching over you. I'm getting you to your next level. Your next place, your next destination. You don't have to worry about anything, because it's almost like I'm picking you up and placing you there.

You may not have felt this kind of peace that I'm bringing to you before, but because of that, you will KNOW it's me. Just follow me. Do what I tell you to do. You'll know what jobs to apply to. You won't have to study and tarry long. YOU WILL KNOW the different jobs to apply for.

[I'm getting that you'll almost be amazed that you won't feel the need to do a lot of research after the interview. You'll just know and have a peace and joy and even a trust of what they say is what they mean, and you can trust that they're honest, and you can just move forward without all the research and mental consumption. I see you leaned back relaxing at the interview even, with your foot on your knee.]

My grace is sufficient. I will show you things that you do not understand. Things that will be out of your normal character are things that I'm going to do with and for

you so you will know without a doubt that it's my hand moving in your life. Your house? Yes, it's great. You will see it. Don't worry about your budget right now. I'm going to take care of you. Be wise in your spending, but follow me.

Seek me every day. Every morning. Get before me and seek my face and direction. You DO hear my voice, and I've called you to lead and to heal. You are my shepherd, and you will lead a flock. Don't get caught up in what you think that means, because I know. I know the people I have under your leadership. You don't need a title. You will be leading a flock and not even realize the impact you're having on them. They're not official. They're CHOOSING to follow you because of what I've put in you. I've called you.

[I KEEP seeing people who are just a little shorter than you. He hasn't said youth, but that is the impression I keep getting—regardless of their height versus yours!]

These ARE my children. You will lead and disciple and inspire and teach and empower my youth. This is MY call on YOUR life. And your house WILL accommodate both the things that you want and the things that will be good for the kids. Your attention to possessions and the stuff that could be stolen—you'll care less about those. You will not operate in fear of what someone could take. Your home will be open for service to me. MY HEART will be what fires you. Ministering to those broken kids. You will not be afraid for your family and your kids.

You will know how to operate by the peace that I will give to you. You will have to make choices, but you will know which kids to let in to stay in your home. Your house is for

MY work. That's why I've chosen it for you. There will be enough room. And no, you can't afford it. That's why it's mine. Just go where the Spirit leads you. Yes, you will go to some houses that are not it just because you all want to see them. And that's okay.

But don't be afraid when I show you your house that is not in your [price] range and there are overwhelming thoughts of not being able—but peace at the same time. Just trust me. Seek me. But trust me when I answer you. This is my house. And Jo won't have to worry about how it looks and having too much. Because YOU will be the one commissioning the house for service unto me. You will be the head [of the house] that reassures her that this is NOT for greed but for ministry. You will calm her because her head [Wendell] is aligned with the Father who ordained it. JUST FOLLOW ME. I will take care of you.

Now. Go and clean your house.

October 10, 2013

[I'm looking on Etsy at other sellers, how long they've been online, how many sales, thinking about how much money they're making and how I wish I made something that would sell and how I need to get more stuff listed and made and what are people making that's selling….agh…] Okay Daddy. What do I need to be making?

What I've put in you.

Ugh! What's that?

I've put gifts in you. Gifts to see what's in people's hearts, what speaks to them and ministers to them. Speaks to

their hearts, their hurts, and their pains. Touch their soul in the ways that I've touched yours.

So NOT yarn?? What's my medium?? What am I working with and on? I need help!!!

I know. But I've shown you.

I don't see it.

Stop and wait for me. You're getting frustrated, and I haven't called you to that. Now breathe and wait. Yes. You are seeing. I'm showing you that glass. What does it say?

You're chosen?

Yes. You are. They are. Go and speak to their hearts. What's in you is in them, too. Be free in who I've created you and them to be. My children. My chosen. My calling. My gifts. Go and walk in freedom.

Okay, I want details though. Stencils or free hand? Do I use the same shop or make a new one? Do I use the canvases? What am I good at? Why do I feel like you're leaving this to me? Ugh!

October 16, 2013

Oh Daddy…I love you. I love having you as my Daddy. I love these quiet times together. I don't know what I'd do or how I'd feel if I couldn't hear you anymore. What's the word for today?

It's love, my daughter.

I'm so glad you're there!

I'm always here.

I love you so much; I'm just amazed at you loving me this much. I'm so undeserving. I make so many mistakes. I'm always yelling at my kids! I get angry at my husband.

The word is LOVE.

Yes. It is. Thank you.

You're welcome. Let's talk about you.

Ugh. I don't want to. Let's talk about love. I sound like Gabi whining and complaining about what I don't want to do!

Yes, you do sound like a child.

Uh, thanks.

[Laughing.]

Okay. What about me?

It's time to change. Time to change your mindset about what you can't do and can't have. It's time to have.

Need help with that. What do you mean?

I mean that it's time to give.

Now you lost me.

Your possessions.

I thought you sounded before like we were to sell stuff we had to make money for the new house?

Not all of it. The things that are worth much, that's fine to do. But the small stuff that you're in control of, most of that should be given away.

Really? Even though we're also trying to make money for Miracle's trip??

Yes. Give your stuff away.

Wow. Okay.

You already see what I'm talking about. Go with what the Holy Spirit shows you that is to be given. Sell what your husband says sell.

Okay. So THIS is HAVING?

You will see how that plays out, but in order to have the things of the next level, you're going to have to rid yourself of some possessions you have right now. Not just to make room for more things that I have for you, but because you have too much!

I see.

But it's time to move, Jo. I see you all sitting and looking at things going on around you [economics, housing market]; I'm waiting on you all. Stop wasting time. I told you to get ready, and you're talking about the rebuke instead of taking serious action. Your time should be spent in preparations to go. Not looming bracelets. [No, there's nothing wrong with the bracelets, but you're getting distracted and losing your focus on what I said to you.]

Okay

TODAY. Get rid of some stuff. You know what's trash and what needs to be given. YES, some things can be donated at the store. But get it out of your house and garage. TODAY.

Yes sir.

Good. And walk with me. I'll make the provisions for your day. Yes, you procrastinated, but stay with me and we'll get all your work done together. Seek me for your help and timing and words to write. We'll get it all done.

Okay.

Your kids. They need to work. School and home. Make them do their work. There are things to purge in their rooms, too.

Okay.

You can't do it all. You DO need their help. But together, you all CAN have the house about ready when Dell comes home. You CAN do this by yourselves. Stop selling yourself short and using him or waiting for him as an excuse. These were your directions that you did not follow.

Yes sir.

Okay. Now. Get into your Bible study, then prep school, and find some things to get rid of. YOU HAVE TOO MUCH! Let's talk tomorrow. Make me proud today. Go get 'em!

[Chuckling.] Okay.

Love you, girl!

Okay! [Laughing.] I love you too, Daddy.

October 24, 2013

Hi Daddy. I missed you.

I missed you too, daughter.

I don't have a lot of time, but I just really wanted to talk to you today. Even if just to listen for a few minutes. How are you?

I am fine. How are you?

I'm better.

I know. I knew you would be. These little bumps can startle you, but you're always going to be okay, because I know that you trust in me…and you're seeing the bigger picture now!

So what's up for today? What's the word?

I can stop time for you.

Uh wow. Okay. Wasn't expecting that word.

You'll have the time you need to do the things that need to be done. But you put a lot on your plate that doesn't always have to be there, and you also waste a lot of your time on things that are not important.

Like Candy Crush?

Yes, but there's a lot more, too. I know you need a break from your day to play a game. That's fine. It's the other things.

I don't get it. Is this you talking or me thinking? I don't know the other things that I do to waste my time.

The Holy Spirit will open your eyes to see. Sometimes it's just nothing. Literally. You're doing nothing.

Oh….I still feel kind of made up this morning. I feel like I need you to say something that's clearly not me.

STOP WASTING TIME! [This was like a loud, scary bellowing voice that would've shaken everything if in a movie!]

Okay.

I've called you for a purpose. To be a leader, an example, and encourager, the one on the megaphone. Don't waste your time. I told you before that idle time is not your friend. And time to rest is not the same as idle time.

Okay.

I want you to lay things down.

Hmm?

Lay everything down at my feet and don't pick them back up. Everything.

Okay.

Your kids. Your house. Your clothes. Your needs. Your wants. EVERYTHING. I want you to lay them all down and trust that I will meet all your needs beyond your expectations.

But why would you exceed my expectations? Why would you bless us more than what we need?

Because I LOVE you. You can't understand me. My love is too great for you to fully comprehend. There are not earthly words for me and the love I have for you. But I want you to lay everything down for me. TO me. And don't pick them back up.

So then what do I do?

Follow me. You need to meet me here EVERY day. EVERY DAY. You need your instructions, because if you're going to fully follow and trust me—and keep those things down at my feet—then you're going to need to know what to do with that idle time you're not going to

waste worrying about those other things. I will sell your house. I will pay your bills. I will meet your needs. You have not seen what my love for you can do and what I'm capable of. I will show you, but only if your hands are not in it.

So will your orders every day contain CLEAR instruction, or should I be asking questions about everything that's going on each day?

I will instruct you, and you may ask questions.

May I start now?

Have you laid things down yet?

[I prayed and cried and laid down my marriage, kids, selling my house, bills, commitments (Upward, bible study, Teen bible study), obligations, school, daily decisions that had to be made. Asked if there was anything else in my heart to lay down. He said no.]

Okay.

Okay.

So I can ask questions too?

Yes.

Our real estate agent—are we supposed to use our old realtor, my friend, or do you have someone else in mind for us? [I don't know if I like asking questions. Feels like it'd be hard to separate my own thoughts.]

Because you're not trusting that when I give instructions I'll tell you EVERYTHING you need to know to go through a day.

Uhh. I guess not.

Lay that down. Lay down your trust issues. You have them with your husband, too. Unnecessarily. Lay those down.

Yes sir.

Okay. I do want you to use Janell. She's going to help you. She's got what you need. I have not shown you the agent for your new house yet. Just follow me on that. You want to know about the rest of your day. Just go through it as usual. Do you go to church? You can go to church if you feel up to it. It's not a requirement or necessity that you go. It's optional.

Okay

I know that you need to have that conversation with your husband. You will. And you'll be fine. You always are. You make it through those hard times. And you will get to a point where you can "handle" his issues. Don't let that concern you. That day will come. You WILL be fully on one accord and united as one. You just have a few more kinks to work out. And you DO need to work on talking in person. Technology is nice, but you two are communicating better in writing than you are in person, and that will have to change. That cannot be any longer. You must talk either by phone or in person. Not for everything, but about your issues is a must. No Jo, I'm not saying that as an absolute rule! I'm just saying that you need to get it under control and in order.

Okay.

Is there anything else you want to ask me about today?

Keeping things down at your feet…what that looks like throughout the day with my kids who fight and bicker and disobey all the time.

You mean like you?

Ouch. If that's how you see it.

You need to stop what you're doing, think about me and my words to you today, and parent like me. Yes I know to you that may look weak. Passive even. And Miracle can have her own opinion! She's in training; I talk to her about things to observe. She's been right in what she has said to you because I told her. But you need to look at how I parent my children and follow my instructions to you. Yes, stop yelling.

And yes, you're correct in your thoughts—you CAN control that and how you talk and behave with them. And yes, yesterday you lost it numerous times. I'm not saying it's going to be easy [as you thought yesterday]! But you CAN do it. Remind them of their errors and pray that their hearts change. It has to be in their hearts or nothing else matters. Their hearts will lead them back home. Your job is to submit all that to me. You teach, I'll change their hearts.

Okay. Thanks God. Daddy.

You're welcome daughter. I know you need to get those things written for bible study. Try harder this week to plan your daily time in your studies. It will make things a lot easier if you would set up a schedule and stick to it. Do not procrastinate. It steals what I have for you. The time together. The time in my word each day—you need that. So make it a point to do one day at a time.

Okay.

Okay. You have a good day. You'll get the ideas you need for bible study! [Wink]

Thanks Daddy.

October 25, 2013

Good morning.

Good morning.

[Waiting to feel or hear his presence.]

Your mind is not rested. Lay everything down.

Okay.

There. Now we can begin. You had a good time last night?

Yes.

But you have questions?

I did, yes. [Laughing.]

I don't know why you laugh. You know I know! [Laughing.]

[Smiling.] I know.

Okay, so prophecy is something that is given to someone who I can trust, and I can trust you. Yes, even when you were a child who was lying and stealing, I knew I'd be able to trust you, so you saw glimpses of this gift back then.

Okay.

What I'm going to do for you is I'm going to empower you to reach the people. You may not have a platform like you're envisioning. You're not going to be at a podium in a stadium, that's not what I mean. But I'm going to equip you to hear my voice and speak it. Wherever you are. We're going to deal with your fear of doing that. Yes. You have fear issues. Still. Stop being surprised at that truth and let's deal with it. You need to pray for boldness. You need to pray for boldness so that when I prompt you in a store you will immediately act and not get caught up in what they'll think or what will happen next. Just follow my leading.

Okay. I just don't know if I can hear you through the day when all the noise is around.

And that's what you need to work on.

Can you talk louder?

I can. I can speak very loudly. To even create a universe. But you have to LISTEN!

Yes sir.

Okay. Now I want you to picture what I'm saying to you as I'm saying it. Even this right now is different for you because you're on my every word. Did you feel that? [Some how my typing of his words was different than before. It was like slow-motion one at a time, but it wasn't. Weird and hard to explain. But it was as if I wasn't getting a whole phrase, I was getting one word at a time but fast enough to speak a complete sentence. Like the words just came right as I needed them.]

Yes.

Okay. Do you feel what's in your mouth? [This may be close to the feeling when you're about to throw up. My mouth was opening from the back and there was pressure on the back roof of my mouth.]

Yes.

That's me. I will give you your every word, and you will feel my presence in your mouth, and you will speak to whoever I tell you to speak to. Just like that.

Okay. Is there practice of that?

Yes, we're going to practice here. Are you ready?

No.

Okay, let's go.

Huh?

I want you to speak what I'm saying to you—keep typing for your records [book]—but I also want you to speak the words out loud. [Yes, you were right before when you thought of this as learning how to get comfortable praying out loud. You just have to get used to hearing your voice and it will develop. Love the Holy Spirit who teaches you, right? Big smile and chuckle.]

Okay let's go… Okay. You're not speaking.

Okay.

Let's go.

With that? With let's go?

Yes.

Okay.

You missed it again. I mean it. EVERY WORD! Type AND talk at the same time. Right now you should be talking out loud.

Agh!

Okay.

Go.

There you did it. And then you stopped. There you go. Now we're talking together. One voice. I'm speaking through you.

Wow.

Yes, wow. This is how you will hear my voice. Because I'm speaking through you.

Wow. [Tears.]

So when I prompt you at the store. Don't doubt me. And don't doubt the words coming out of your mouth. Come to this [and that's fine that you can't type because you're going to be speaking from now on]. Come to this place in your mind and speak what I give you to speak. Don't think. Just speak.

Wow, that seems crazy.

Sure it may. But you've got to trust in me who is speaking through you. You are just an open vessel, not the author. Trust my voice that you hear. Walk with me. I've spoken. And just like the woman at church said, you have the mind of Christ. You are one in the Spirit. So walk with us. Talk with us. Commune with us. Live with us. In the fullness we bring. And in all that we're going to do. Do you still feel my presence in your mouth?

Yes.

Because I'm present in you. I'm alive in you. We're working together. If you feel this you can speak as my representative. Don't be afraid. But wait for the Holy Spirit to prompt you. You may not go and pray for everyone and try to give them a word. The Holy Spirit will prompt you and show you who I want you to pray for and minister to and give a word to. You HAVE to be lead with this gift. It's not for your own use so that you don't get the glory. You won't get all the attention from others. When you speak it will be from me, not your own doing. This is not a gift for the masses. This is for who I give it to. Use it when I say use it. You *may* ask permission to use it for someone you know or who is hurting and may need a word, but if I don't come or you don't feel the Holy Spirit moving, then do not do it. You will be in your own will and not speaking as me.

Okay. So do you want me to start speaking these instead of typing?

I know you want these written out. And that's good. You're going to need them. Find an app that will transpose for you.

You're God…is there an app for that? The transcription I need? That I should even pay money for it?

You may. It's up to you two. Your husband will say yes, once you tell him that you have to practice speaking out loud, because he supports this and knows you're a prophet and wants to be supportive of your obedience. So find the app and then talk to him about it.

Okay, whew. A lot today.

Yes, a lot. But you can handle it. I've equipped you. Aren't you glad you didn't sleep in and miss this today?

Yes.

Okay today...do I need to keep talking out loud?

You should, but I know you'll type faster if we don't talk out loud. So your call!

Okay. Today. Go ahead.

Today I want you to clean your house. Not just because Dell is coming home, but because the agent will be by soon. Sooner than you're ready for because you didn't get ready earlier.

Okay.

So get that hard stuff done as far as putting things where they belong or taking things out to the garage. You're going to have to find homes out there though, too. This weekend you two will have to find time to work on that garage. I know you all need shoes, and you'll have time for that, but you have to get that garage worked on this week. Don't worry about the grass right now. Take care of the inside of the house and garage. That's what matters most this season. It's time to move; we need to act quickly.

Okay.

His job. Just ride this out with the telecommute option. Things are still going to change. Hear my voice; this is not yours. I have not revealed the company, but it will change. His job will change. Just be patient. I will show him. Focus on the house and what I'm telling you to do. Get those things done and in order and the house listed. That's the number one priority right now. House listed.

Okay, that's it? Clean house today? Does it matter when we go look for shoes?

No, either tonight or tomorrow night, but tomorrow day you need to work on the house and garage.

Okay. So do we still meet tomorrow?

Yes, you'll still have new orders for tomorrow, silly. I told you every day you need to come and talk to me.

Okay, I know. I was just checking.

That's fine! I know you're coming every day.

Anything else? I feel like there's more for today.

Let the Holy Spirit guide you. Invite and be aware of his presence. Wherever you go and who ever you talk to.

Okay.

You're going to have to change your whole life. Your mannerisms at home. How you speak to your kids, but that's going to come from how your heart and mind are changing. You're going to understand that in order to hear clearly, you've got to foster my presence, and you can't do that that with strife in your life. You're going to have to maintain peace and order in your life. Not saying the house will be perfect 24/7. But in YOUR life, your mind--—there will be order. You understand that difference?

Yes.

You need to go to Sam's Club to get those waffles.

Today?!

No, whenever, but you were thinking about them, so I want to make sure you go get them. [Chuckling.]

I love you girl.

That's my line!

It was mine first. Well, I didn't originally state it like that. But the love is mine. Mine to give. Freely to those who will accept it. Freely have I given. And, our time is up. [kid awake] Okay my dear, we will talk tomorrow.

You know I'm not always going to tell you when you're going to have an appointment during the day. I train you in the morning, then you practice during the day. I may give you a heads up sometimes but not always. Your job is to listen and work on your hearing of my spirit and knowing when it is time to speak. So always be listening for and to me. And yes, you can ask me questions during the day and totally expect me to answer you. Right then.

I want you to know that I hear you and I listen to you so you will more readily hear and listen to me when I speak to you. This is a relationship, and I'm totally vested in you. I want you to be a part of me and my spirit. I want you to abide in me. Yes, you need to read my word. Not so you know what to say, but so you won't doubt what I say as much because you would've heard it before in scripture. You doubt because you're unfamiliar with what I have said already. So read. Read. Read. Soak it all in. Yes, you may listen, but READ!

Yes Daddy. Okay. Gotta go clean up!

Yes, you do. I love you daughter.

I love you Daddy.

October 26, 2013

God I love you. I am so excited about this.

I am too.

Sorry that I didn't wake up early to meet with you today. I hope I don't end up being rushed because of other people awake.

It's okay. We'll finish what we need to get done. Let's get started.

Okay.

Today I want you to focus on me.

HUH? [I thought we were focusing on the garage!]

I know. But I want you to think like I think. Remember that I love people, and I want you to help them and love them and bless them. But I also want you to be a good steward of what I've given you. Remember the men and the talents and the one buried. Be wise in your decisions in the garage today. But also don't over think it. Be quick. Yes or no, sell or not, trash or keep. Be quick. The Holy Spirit is going to be with you both today giving you wisdom. Ask for it and use it.

Okay.

Also be mindful of the children. Don't throw away stuff you know they'd want to keep. You may not have room for it now, but you will. So don't hurt them by throwing away all of their stuff, Jo!

Okay…

I want you to worship me while you work. This more than just cleaning out your garage. This is preparation

for your blessing. So keep your mind stayed on me. Keep your mind in adoration and praise of me. Praise me for the things you've been blessed to buy and for the things you're blessed to give away. Remember, you CAN give to other people, but it's not a requirement for today. I don't want you to get caught up on who you should give something to and how to get it out of your house quickly that you end up wasting time on those things. Today is give, trash, sell, and keep if you so choose.

But you have a lot of stuff to get through in a short amount of time. The big stuff—put the dressers out and let someone come and get them if they so desire. Don't waste time breaking them down and calling around to find an owner. Let them go. Yes, you can sell the washer and dryer. Just move them out of the way to get past them. You WILL at some point need to clean out that storage, and most of that you just need to throw away. There are a few things to keep, but they're for maintenance, so you'll be able to get through that quickly with little thought. Again, that doesn't have to be today. But sometime this week while I've given you warmer weather.

Thanks, God!

You're welcome. I have to get you all ready to go.

Like, should we be packing too?

Not necessary right now. The books you had them pack was good. Minor stuff that can pack easily is good, but you REALLY need to focus on purging. Neither of us want all that stuff in your new house. So focus on purging and THROWING AWAY!

Okay. Anything else for today?

That I love you. You're doing a good job. You're going to do a good job today. Just don't stress about it. Stay in my presence while you work together. You can have peace and harmony in this. If something else arises, it should not be there. Cast it out and keep working. Stay focused. Remember the wisdom I've already given both of you.

You should get the trash can from the neighbor's house to fill that as well. Yes, three cans of trash should be filled today, and you should have another pile of stuff to trash as well. Get to work. Just focus. The kids can take care of themselves. Yes, Miracle can iron. Plan ahead today so you don't stress the kids at the end if you two work too late. You also need to plan out your breakfast early, because you don't have enough supplies.

[Smiling.] Okay! You're too funny. And too great. I love you. Thank you for healing my husband, too.

Oh he's not done. You just wait and watch! Big show!

Wow. I can't even imagine. I'm so excited!

Me, too. You are all great servants. There are big things ahead for all of you. Okay. You've gotta run. GO.

October 27, 2013

Good morning. Sorry that it seems I have to rush today because I'm getting breakfast.

That's okay. I understand. At least you got up when your alarm went off, right?

Yes. Still dizzy though.

That will pass.

Okay good. So what's up for today?

I'm giving you peace.

Okay.

I want you to walk in it. All day. At some points it will seem difficult, but do your best. You already have it; you just have to walk in it. Think before you speak. Calm down before you speak. You speak too fast, and it can get you in trouble. My peace doesn't speak quickly. It waits. Waits for my words, my answers. Remember, it turns away wrath. Speak slowly today. Not comically, but be slow to speak.

Okay. I'll definitely say that I'll try my best!

Good. That's all I ask. But you CAN do it. And at some point you will. And the slower you speak, the less you'll get angry.

Well I'm sure we'll all appreciate that one.

Yes, they will.

So what did you think about the garage?

It's good. I know you'll get it finished. I want you to be quick in your sorting still. Don't tarry over what should be an easy decision, but think before you throw away [in regards to bins of paper].

Okay.

You can get that area clean. It can get done today with your car back in the garage.

Okay.

His car will come after he moves his sell pile.

Okay.

Your kids are beautiful.

Okay…

[Smile and chuckle.] I love them.

[Confused face.] Okay…

Yeah. I just wanted to say that to you. I love Brianna a lot, too.

I know. I'll try to show love more.

You can't show more and reach her hidden parts of her heart because you still have anger and bitterness and hatred in your heart towards her. You have to let that stuff go. Truly forgive her for the things she's done to you, said to you, stolen from you, and all the lies. You have to let her go when she wrongs you, because that is hardening you, that affects your relationship with her—even though you think you're over it. You HAVE to deal with that hatred in your heart. Anytime you can spit out, "I hate her," that HAS to be dealt with. You need to bring those things to me and ask forgiveness. You need to lay those things down at my feet, and you need to make those things subject to what I say in my word. Those things do not line up with scripture, where you want to go in your relationship with her, and where I need to take you in ministry—those things MUST be dealt with and put in your past. Like, NOW.

Okay. [Asking forgiveness. Realizing I have a lot to repent for and it's going to take awhile.] Okay. My people are up and I have to get moving. Dell will ask what today's assignment is and I think I heard that its finish the garage and be slow to speak, is that correct?

Yes it is. Have a peaceful day.

Thanks I'll try my best. I love you.

I love you more.

I love you, Jesus.

I love you too!

[Me laughing.]

October 28, 2013

Good morning, Daddy. I just smile when it's time to talk to you.

I smile, too.

I love you.

I love you more.

Sorry that I slept in today. I shouldn't have stayed up so late. I hope we get things done for the house today. Everyone keeps saying we're not ready, but I think we can be. So will you show me what needs to be done?

Yes. There are more things to be done, but it's not so much that you can't do it all in one day if you set your mind to it and just focus on the house. It will take longer if you try to do school every day.

Okay. So what do YOU want me to do? I actually have a few questions for today…if we have time.

Well, I always have time.

True. Okay. Well, let's start with today. What to you want to share with me? Mmm, give me wisdom today. Please!

Of course. I want you to follow me. The peace you carry, you're going to have to work at controlling. Your temper rises and it will feel like what you've strived so hard to maintain all day you've thrown out the window and failed. Just keep resting in me. Ask me to handle it for you. I know this may seem strange at first, and even out of what you believe is your responsibility to control, but just try me. Listen to what I'm saying and do it. When your kids make you frustrated, JUST GIVE IT TO ME! You can't control everything. But the one who does control the universe wants to handle these things for you. Just let me do what I do. Your job is to what? "Listen and obey!" So don't lay your things down at my feet and then pick them back up. I told you to lay those things down and leave them there.

Okay. Yes sir.

Okay. On with it.

[Thinking about the deaf lady I prayed for at the doctor's office Friday. I felt God in my mouth, like what we practiced, and felt the Holy Spirit get my attention. I asked what I was supposed to say to her and he said, "wait." It was then that I noticed she was deaf. So before I left, I put my hands on her ears and prayed for her ears to be open. Nothing happened. She then gave me a paper asking for money. I gave her the change I had ($3) and Brianna and I left. Pretty bummed out since I knew I felt him. I expected something to happen and was glad that Brianna would've been there to witness it—thought it'd do something for her. But nothing. So I've been thinking about that the past few days when we talk.]

Yes, the lady. You let me take care of that, too!

Ugh. This is hard.

It can be, while you get used to it. Or you can think of it as your daddy taking care of you and handling the things you don't need to get wrapped up in, right? Those things aren't your job. You can't change the situations you keep trying to have your hands on. Those are for me anyway, so just give them to me! It doesn't make sense for you to continue trying to pick up things that I'M the one whose job they are, right?! That's silly, isn't it? To say you're trying to do MY job?

Yes, it is.

Exactly. So keep remembering that when you're picking up those cares and concerns that you are trying to do MY JOB. Leave it alone. It's not yours!

[Smile.] Okay.

I've noticed you're not talking out loud.

I know, but I just want to get this done [faster by typing].

Okay. You sound like your son.

Ugh.

Well, what's your job?

To listen and obey?

Correct.

Okay…I think I hear kids. Can I just keep typing so I don't get their attention?

Yes. But not tomorrow. Tomorrow we talk out loud.

Okay.

So make sure you get up on time so we have time to work.

Okay.

You had questions for me.

Well yeah, but I don't think you told me about today, did you?

Just that you need to work on the house and get some school graded and done. We are going to have to have a change about your kids and school. You're right that something is not working, but we don't have time for that one right now.

Okay.

Your questions.

Do you want to tell me when we'll list the house or what our goal should be?

No.

Huh?!

It will happen. Just don't be lazy or slow down. You get too discouraged by your husband's comments and actions. You need to stop that. Be who I've created you to be. If I give you an order then you do it until you finish or I say otherwise. Stop cowering because of other people's opinions.

Okay.

Is Ann supposed to be our realtor?

I have not shown you your realtor yet. Nor your house—you were right about that. That is one of those houses you COULD go look at, but it's not yours. It's missing something you need [something that was on our list].

REALLY? Missing something?

Yes. As nice as that house is, and it IS pretty, that's not what you want.

Hmm. Okay. So when are we going to see our house?

When you see your realtor. It will happen in my timing.

So should I stop looking on the websites?

You can. It doesn't matter. You have not already seen the house though, and you're not going to see it until you have an agent. So you decide if you should continue using your time like that.

Okay. Should we use our bank's movers program to buy?

Yes, you may do that.

Is that what you want?!

Yes.

And you'll provide the right agent?

Yes.

You know this is so hard for me to trust my hearing when we converse like this about personal future decision stuff.

I don't know why. You know my voice, Jo. It hasn't changed. You can trust me for the small details of your life and your character and your habits, but to ask me for wisdom in your financial and life decisions you back away?? THIS is what I want from you. I WANT you to seek me for wisdom in your life. You are doing the right thing.

Okay. "The fruit of my labor is your reward." (just popped in my head. Wasn't in His voice. Maybe Holy Spirit? I don't know.)

If you hear something and you don't know whose voice it is—1. Does it line up with the word? Does it glorify the Kingdom? 2. Is it something you would say? 3. Is it negative, evil, does it come from darkness? So if the fruit of MY work is YOUR reward, does that sound like Satan? No. And it's not something you've said or would say, so it then you can determine that it was one of us speaking to you. You can take that phrase home and marinate in it. See what it means to you!

Okay.

[30 minutes later...] Well it seems I need to go now.

I know. Remember to give your worries and concerns to me, okay?

Yes. I'll do my best.

And remember communion today, too!

[Smiling.] Okay! I love you.

I love you more.

Oh. I'm going to ask you about my family one day…

I know.

[Me laughing.]

October 29, 2013

Good morning. I'm so tired.

I know. You keep going to bed too late. You have to do better in order to have the rest you need for the day.

I know…I think I'm too tired to hear.

You're not too tired to hear.

Okay…

You may need to open your eyes so you can stay focused on me, though.

Okay.

Or you can talk like you're supposed to be…

Mmm…I know, I sound like my son now.

Yes you do! Yes, you can lay back down when we finish, though not for long.

Okay. Is it going to rain so we don't have to go to that field trip?

You'll see.

Do we have to go to that field trip?

No, you don't have to go. That's up to you. You have a lot to do in your house, with school, Bible study, getting to the store—I understand that. You can decide whether you go to the orchard or not. But you do have a lot of friends going, so it may be fun for all of you.

Okay, I'll decide later.

Alright.

So do I have an assignment for today?

You do. I want you to wash my people.

WHAT? I know I didn't hear that right!

I want you to wash them, cleanse them. With the communion you take.

OHHHHHH. I get it. I guess I need to look up the correct words to say for communion, huh? Do you get upset if it's not a certain way?

No. They just need to know that the bread represents his body and the juice is for his blood. But there needs to be a time of repentance.

I'm not sure that we have time for that with the field trip [I'm envisioning the kids laid out on the floor crying, like they do in other countries…not that my kids EVER weep in repentance anyway!].

No you don't have to do all that. I'm just saying there needs to be time given for them to confess their sins—like you did yesterday. You saw the effects last night when Gabi apologized for riding the car like a surfboard, right? The greater spirit of conviction that you pray for will arise from time in communion. For all of them. They may feel like it's routine at first, and you can study it out and make it deeper for them, but it's going to impact your household. So do it. Keep track of it. Write the dates and how things begin to change and flow around you. There is power in communion. You tell them that. NOT to be taken lightly at all. The giggles have to end. You tell them, DADDY SAYS!

[Smiling.] Okay will do. I want to know you more.

I want you to know me. I want you to fellowship with me during the day. You'll learn how to shut things off and hear me—like that guy said. It'll come. You'll see. Keep meeting me here every day and you'll see things change.

Okay.

You have questions today.

Well, I just wondered if I did. But I don't have a list! What about the realtors?

They're good. I like them.

So go with them?

Yes.

Okay......Don't ask when the house will sell?

You need to go ahead and pack. You all still have a lot of stuff. Even with purging, you have a lot of stuff to pack up. Pack wisely. Don't over-stuff the boxes and label well!

Okay. I like that part!

I know. Don't hang it over his head though. That would be wrong.

I know! So does that mean we're moving soon?

It means I said you can pack up boxes so you're ready. [You love hearing your parenting tone, don't you?]

Hmm.

Exactly.

Okay. Too bad we missed the neighbor's boxes.

It's okay. You'll get some more.

I wish we could have movers.

You could. If that's how you want to spend your money.

Umm...that wasn't a green or red light. I want you to say yes or no.

I don't always say yes or no. Now if you ask me a direct question, I'll answer that. But you just made a statement about a wish.

Okay. Should we hire a moving company?

No.

Ugh! This is a lot of stuff. And we don't have any friends!

You'll have what you need.

I'm going to ask you about the moving company later. I really want one. One drive over there?

Okay. Call around and check the prices, then let me know what you think.

Okay.

Okay!

So what did you say about today?

You just need to keep working. You have plenty to do and a lot to get done. Just list it out. Write it down and plan for what you're going to do when. Then DO it!

I need to get up, huh?

Yes, there are beneficial things you could do right now, but I know you're tired and how you behave when you get that way…so lay back down for a few minutes, and when you get up, BE UP. Stay working towards one of your goals.

Okay, thanks.

No problem.

Love you, Daddy.

Love you, too.

October 30, 2013

Hey. I'm not doing good at this. I'm so tired that I never want to get up to talk. I know I need to go to bed earlier...I'm just not doing it.

I know. You'll get better. Or I could start waking you up in the middle of the night like Ravi!

Mmm...that depends. Is he rested in the morning? Do you give him supernatural rest to function after that? I think for now I'm probably just going to try harder to go to bed earlier and wake up on time!

Okay. Today your assignment is simple. Work. On the house, on school, on Bible study, on the journals, on everything. Yarn, too. Just work today. Get your work done. Don't worry about those clothes right now. There are other things more important than the clothes that HAVE to get done.

God, what do I do about Brianna?

You just wait and watch. I've got her.

But I'd sure like to know when. She gets so frustrated and over the top, and we're just trying to help her or get her to communicate!

I know. But like I've said before, when you lay those things down to me, don't pick them back up.

Okay. It sure seems like that'd make me a passive parent, though.

Hmmm. Maybe it could LOOK that way. But I see it as you being an obedient child.

Mmm...okay.

I'm really not going to talk long to you today. I need to you get up and get focused and get things done. No, you're not going to have a formal day of school...but you need to get some subjects done. And yes, do school with Gabi!

[Smiling] Okay. Thanks for being understanding of my tiredness and my short amount of time here.

I'm not condoning or saying that the bad habit is okay, but yes, I understand that you have an issue to address and work on. You'll get better. Your priorities have to change.

Are my commitments outside of the house okay?

Yes, I'm talking about your priorities at home, in your own private life and time. You still have things sucking up your time that should not be. I know it may be a process for you, but you need to change some of your habits [and TV shows].

Okay. I understand. Oh, off topic. Thanks for working on my ankle. I love that it's getting better. I'll be glad when I can run a little. And I need to start working out. Unless you want to take the weight off of me?

No, you can do it. Priorities, remember? They have to change...

Okay, okay. So we'll talk tomorrow before bible study. Actually, we have to talk again today because I have to write my devotion for tomorrow, and I want you to write it!

You want ME to write it?

Yes.

Or I can give you the ideas and then YOU can write it.

I guess. I just wanted it to be from you, that's all.

I understand. I like that, too. Thanks. Okay. We'll talk later today then. Don't put it off too long though. You have A LOT to do today.

Okay, I won't.

October 31, 2013

[Yesterday I didn't make time to sit, talk, and write *with* Daddy. So I asked Him what He wanted me to do yesterday while getting ready for Bible study. He said to be fruitful. He had also given me the devotion for yesterday's bible study that I had to do. He gave it to me Wednesday, October 30th, but I'll type it here so it's in with this date since they want me to do it again in January for the whole group. In my preparation, I asked Daddy, "What do you want me to tell them?" The following is what He said.]

[Tell them] that I love them. That I want them to walk in my peace. My peace that passes all understanding. I want to wrap my arms around them and take away their pain and sorrow. I delight in their presence. I want to spend time with them. I want them to feel my presence. I want them to hear me, see me—in every area of their lives.

I want them to know that I give the joy that they seek. I know those secret places in their hearts—and I love them dearly anyway. Their scars don't scare me. Their

sins don't scare me. [Then his tone changed and he started talking directly to them through me.]

Your past doesn't scare me. I want relationship with you. I want you to know me like I know you. I want to spend time with you. I want to talk to you. I want to be the best thing that's ever happened to you.

But in order for that to happen, you have to put me first. Yes. First. Just like there's room in your heart to love multiple children or people, there's room for you to put me first. But you have to choose to give me that place.

Choose me. Seek me. Love me. Serve me. Honor me. Obey me. CHOOSE ME, above all else. People, places, statuses, houses, things, and stuff that all passes away. Choose me. Choose to serve and work in my Kingdom for me. Because you love me and want nothing else other than to please me.

Choose me. Above all else. I'll take care of you. I'll meet your needs, I'll shelter you, clothe you, feed you. Make your requests known to me. I have all that you seek. But you must choose me. For I've already chosen you. You're Mine. My prince and my princesses. I've chosen you. You're beautiful. You're complete – yes, complete. Because I complete you. I fill all those holes and gaps and pains and cracks – I FILL YOU WITH MY LOVE AND THE HOLY SPIRIT. Nothing else and no one else can fill you, complete you, make you, adorn you, cherish you, wash you, purify you, love you like I have and always will. Because I created and chose you.

So now, choose me.

November 1, 2013

Okay. Good morning, God. I'm dragging today, but I'm here.

[Smile/chuckle.] I see. Yesterday went well. Good job delivering the message. It's always good to be obedient and just deliver the message, whether you get a response or feedback at all. Just be obedient.

Okay.

Today.

[I'm trying to quiet my mind so I can hear clearly. Don't feel like I'm hearing well today.] I want to be like you. Not like that, but I want to be in your image. I want to make you proud, to make you smile, to make you happy with my life. I want to please you in everything that I do. I want you to be able to use me and trust that I'm going to do what you say. I don't like failing. I don't like the guilt I feel when you say go and I look at the situation around it or around me. I don't like that sometimes I'm so busy or rushing that I just don't listen. I hate that by being a child of God I still have moments where I'm acting like a real CHILD! What does it mean?

What does it look like to be obedient all the time? To walk in your service as a lifestyle. As a conscience choice to obey your every word and command? WHAT IS THAT? And can I actually do that???? With a husband and four kids and commitments and obligations and us rushing to get in and out of stores so we can get on to the next one or just come home because we're tired or someone is cranky and acting up in public. What does it look like to serve and follow and please you ALL the time? I can't even imagine what it looks like, let alone try to figure out how to do it. Wow. I'm talking in big paragraphs like you!!!

You're funny. You can do it, Jo. Every time you step out. Every time you speak. Whether it be to others or to your children. EVERY THING YOU SAY AND DO IS A REFLECTION OF ME. Whether you do it intentionally or not. People see it all—whether they say anything or not. And you ARE doing a good job. When those people come up to you and say how well-behaved your children are—those are affirmations for you that you hear me, you're doing your best, you're training your children in the way they should go.

Does that mean I'm saying your goal is to please people and man? No. But what I'm saying is that the light that's in you and Dell, you are passing that on to your children, whether it always looks that way or not! They're getting it. They know how to behave and speak. Yes, they're still kids and they're going to make mistakes, just like you do, but the light that you're putting in them and shining in them—they'll get it. It will all come in time.

Just don't give up. Don't get discouraged. Keep doing what you know is right. You will see my hand on all of your children. They WILL ALL serve me. You will see.

Well that's reassuring—that even I'll see it. Thanks for that hope.

You're welcome. Keep it in front of you. You do not labor in vain, but you will reap what you sow.

Ahh...thanks. Both hope AND a warning! Gotcha! So is there a word or direction for today?

Yes. Be fruitful.

Again? Be fruitful?

Yes.

Okay. Was I not fruitful yesterday?

You can do more. I want your hands to be fruitful, too. Put them to work. Be diligent in what you touch and do. Don't procrastinate. Get to work and get it done. Monday should be all about wiping down, not working. You work this weekend. Paint today. Move things out tomorrow. Start prepping the rooms Sunday. Wipe it down Monday. Don't stress about boxes and what you don't have. Work with what you do.

The list seems long, but you have most of what you need. Pick up the shoes and mulch today so you can split up and work tomorrow. Get inside work done today so most of tomorrow is happening in the garage and outside. MOST of tomorrow, not that you'll be outside all day. You'll still have work in the house tomorrow. But the bins and kitchen stuff and above the washer—that's all today stuff.

Yes, you do have some school to get done. Mostly grading because you've gotten behind. And you really need to work on that yarn today. Don't keep putting it off because you think the house is more important. It's important too. You have to get your projects done AND put online to sell. I'll take care of you—but you have to do YOUR job. Don't get lazy now. This is your "go" season, so you MUST be ready.

Okay.

Do you have any questions for me? Concerning directions or the house?

I don't think so. It just seems so hard to maintain!

That's why a lot of it has to be cleared out. Yes, box up as much as you can from the school area shelves. It IS messy and cluttered. You'll need to take out your glass, too. Don't worry, Jo, you'll have time for your crafts again!

[Smiling] Okay, good. I'm glad you know my heart's desires!

I love you, sweetie.

I love you too, Daddy. Tell my other daddy hello.

I will!

November 3, 2013

[Yesterday we were working in the house and outside and what he said to me was just to stay focused on what I was doing and I'd be able to get it done. We didn't sit down and talk.]

Good morning, God.

Good morning.

I got up today!

Yes, I see. Good job.

Thanks. How are you today?

I'm well.

Well that's good. I missed you yesterday. Even though we've had some days that are short, I missed sitting down with you yesterday morning. I could tell the difference, especially when Wendell cut down that tree and it seemed like everything was going awry. I wished I had told him clearly why you had said Friday. If I had sat with you, you would've given me verbiage for him before we started or given me a heads up to stay calm about the tree and that it wasn't time lost or WASTED. I just really needed those moments with you.

So I'm here today. With food to cook, dishes to clean, and house to work on—I want to spend my first moments with You. I love you. I need you. You are my air. You are my life. I need your direction and your wisdom. You are the world to me. I love you.

Awww. I love you too, daughter! And I, too, want this time with you in the morning, every morning. We both need it. You want direction, and I want to GIVE you direction. It's a win for both of us! So you want to hear about today?

Yes!

Okay, well today I have planned for you to church and come home and work!

Ahh…that's what we were thinking, too. Is there anything more specific you want to share with me?!!? Or—we were going to stop at Target to get a rug and three shirts for Miracle. Is that okay?

Oh yes, that's fine, but don't be in there an hour. You get in and get out. No tarrying or mindless shopping. Yes, I know the boy wants to see stuff. You may walk through QUICKLY to let him see the prices, but that's it. Be kind and loving as I am with you when you want to look at needless things, but be firm and quick. In and out.

Okay, yes sir.

When you get home, I want you to start in the kitchen. Then I want you to go into the family room. Work in there all together. You can do the kitchen while the kids are changing and "straightening up" their rooms—though you'll have to go back in there to clean their rooms later.

Okay.

You're going to look at the walls and stuff that's out of place. Someone needs to dust with the cloth and wipe down those shelves. I'll let you decide if you paint them. But arrange this room and take a picture so the kids can see how to put it back. You've done the hard work in here, now it's just time to arrange it and wipe it down.

In the living room—same thing. Check the walls, wipe it down, dust it, put it in place. If there are electronics, then he will pack them up.

Upstairs—check the hall walls. Have Brianna clean the bathroom, then you check it. If the floor gets cleaned today, you won't have to do it tomorrow. Just eyeball the linen closet due to sleeping bags.

Girls' room—you should just have to check the closets and have them put their stuff on top away. While you shouldn't NEED to check under Brianna's bed, for your peace of mind you will, and it will be so minor that you won't care much.

Well that's good.

Her closet is not the same way! But her bed is good enough for tomorrow. She needs to work in her closet. You may need to pull the clothes she knows she's not going to wear. She just has no need of them.

Okay.

Same with your other kids—there is needless stuff in their rooms. Just pull everything off their shelves, and it should have a home neatly on their cubbies. There IS enough room in there for their stuff. No real need for their room to be messy. Get rid of the clothes on top.

Your room—clean it. Fold and put away the clothes. Move his nightstand. Figure out where you want those jewelry boxes, and remember what Dell said, "It's only temporary!"

Oh! Does that mean that you're going to tell me about the new house?

Noo…we need to get this one ready to sell first. One thing at a time. This is not the time to multi-task. This is the time to focus.

Okay.

[Smiling.] Don't work more than four hours. So once you are ready to start, set the timer. For real, this should not take your entire day and night. Be diligent in your work. Okay, so WHEN you finish this evening, you need to finish grading and do your lesson plans for school, then put everything back away. I want your house set up how it will be tomorrow—today. So put the books back the right way and put the table and chairs back out.

Yes, you need to call about the water.

Oh you saw that?

Yes.

Well, can we just tie it back down tighter or change the way it drains?

You can, but if you're going to have it removed, you need to call about it quickly. Also call for your home inspection.

Okay.

Actually at this point, just double check with the realtors to see if they want you to have it done for the listing.

That sounded like it could've been me.

Yes it does. May've been…

I have such a hard time trusting my hearing.

I know. You always have. You'll get over it. But that little bit right there is because the more time you spend with me, and the more you ask for wisdom, don't you think you're going to get it? You are my child. Ask me for the things that I want you to have. Don't you think I'm going to give them?

Yes.

Well then, don't act surprised when you start sounding or behaving like me. THAT'S the goal, right? To be like ME? You're made in my image; shouldn't you act and talk in my image, too?

Yes…

Okay then, stop doubting what I'm doing with you. I'm training you up to be who I have called and want you to be. So just walk in it, my daughter!

[Smiling.] Okay.

Okay, then. Now go make breakfast and clean as you go! Have a great day, sweetie! You can do it!!

[He's reading my thoughts about him not saying anything about the garage.]

Yes, garage. It's not your focus today. Today get the inside of the house ready. If he wants to work in there when you're DONE today, that's fine. But it's not your area as a couple today before you're done INSIDE. Do you understand?

Yes.

Okay, then. BYE! Go get'em!

[Laughing.] Bye Daddy!

November 4, 2013

Good morning. I love you Daddy, but today I am short on time!

I know. You didn't get finished yesterday.

Yeah…about that. Dell was really upset. Well, upset. He wants me to ask you what you think when we don't finish what you tell us to do.

Well…it's about choices. You were right in what you thought. Just like you give your kids a list of things to do, they choose whether they complete them or not. There's either a reward or a consequence for their choices. Same with you two. You're not always going to make the mark—and that's okay. I understand that. You're human, you get distracted easily! You'll get better at this—listening, following directions, obeying, making the mark—and the better you get, the more reward you'll see. It may just be as simple as being able to rest and have peace in your home, but I know for you—that IS reward!

Truly!! I think we did spend a lot of time in the family room, and once it was done-ish, it did feel really nice to just sit in here.

That's okay, my child. Your time of rest is coming soon. But right now you have to make up for lost time!!

Okay!

What I'm not going to do is tell you how many hours or what time you should be done and concern you with calling the realtors to come early. I've given instructions, and you know what's left to do. So make the choices necessary to get the stuff done. Keep planning the kids' school and hopefully they can keep focused to get it done while you work in another room. That's your hopefully, not mine!

I already know your day. Start the morning peacefully. Take communion. Explain what YOU need to do today and kindly ask them to help you by doing school, unless you ask them otherwise. Try not to involve them so much so they can stay relaxed, get school done, and you can work quickly on your own. This is GO time all day for you, though. There won't be a lot of sitting time except for when you're helping with school. But readers need to come and read with you in whatever room you're working in.

Okay.

Now, here's what I want to say to you about the rest. Yes, call the bank, and I'll provide your agent. Ask them for the list of foreclosed homes. Give them your price range. Do you want me to give you the number?

Yes!

You already know it. I'm not going to take you above your means. I'm going to take care of you. You just have to trust me. So play your cards as you normally would. Be smart and wise and trust that I'll do what I want to do with you. You still need to work on your budget, though. Your spending is a mess. Both of you. Get it together.

Okay. Yes sir.

I know you're tired. You're going to have to push through today. And Teen Bible Study is going to make for a long night. You can make it, though.

Okay.

Alright, get going. You have a lot to do.

Does it matter where I start?

Well, finish M's school and then either the kitchen or your room. You still have to paint, too. So hurry up!

November 5, 2013

Good morning. Am I going to get it all done??

You will.

I don't know how I'm going to finish that yarn stuff. I need your help. I don't even know how you could help me, though. Crochet faster without my knowledge! [Laughing.] I'm SO tired. Was I supposed to have Kay come over today, or did I over extend myself? I just felt like if she was feeling that she was supposed to ask me, I shouldn't put her off another week. Was that right?

It's fine. It'll be fine. Yes, I put you on her heart, so that part is right. It doesn't matter *when* you meet, it's just important THAT you meet. And don't worry about what to say, I'll give that to you. Like last night—was that awesome?!?

It was! It was amazing! That's how you do it? I loved it! I really loved it. I want more of that. I wish I could've seen Sondra's face [I was driving at night]. Did she get it? Did she like it? Was it completely out of her realm of thinking? I don't even know how she feels about ANYTHING, and I just put everything out there! I didn't know if it was too much for her to handle or process in one night!

She'll be fine. What's important is that you delivered the message I gave you for her. THAT, she got.

It was so cool. I like working with you!

Oh, I like it more, trust me! [Laughing.]

And the lady at the grocery store…even that was like, simple and fun!

Yes. And stop worrying about how it's going to sound. Don't explain anything before you start with the message. You do that with Wendell at home, too. Don't apologize for the story before you give it. Cut that out of everything you do. No stories before the story. JUST SPEAK! Deliver the message. If you feel the need to talk or explain afterwards, that's fine [in relation to home]. But when you're out and I give you a message for someone, just deliver the mail! If you lead with telling them that it may sound crazy, then guess what? It's going to be crazy to them. YOU'RE going to sound crazy to them. Just walk in the power and authority that you have and deliver the message straight!

Okay.

Good. Now with Kay, I know you've been thinking about this meeting, and you've thought you need to plan and prepare and have books handy. Just be my servant. Just listen to me. Just say what I tell you to say, and follow my lead when you talk to her. You have what she needs already in you. You don't have to know what EVERYONE

else says or has said. You need to know what I say right now for her.

Okay.

Do find your GFC stuff, because that's what sparked her interest the first time. You *could* start with that, or you *could* just let her talk and wait for me to lead you.

Gotcha. I'm gonna follow your suggestion and lead!

Good. Hey. You have to go. Your son is all over you.

Yes, I know. Thanks, Daddy. I love you.

I love you more.

Oh wait, what about the house?

What about it?

Are you gonna tell me how long its going to be on or when it's gonna sell?

No. You'll see!

Aww…

Just keep your house in order and wait for my timing. Do contact the bank today to get your new agent assigned over the river so you can begin looking over there. And call for your inspection.

Okay, cool. Thanks, Dad.

You're welcome. Love you. 'Bah.'

[Laughing.] Bye!

November 7, 2013

Good morning. I'm sorry about missing yesterday.

You're forgiven.

Thanks. I don't seem to be getting better at my time management. I keep going to bed late and am too tired to wake up in the morning.

It will get better. You have to make ME your priority. You enjoy having that "alone" time when the kids go to bed, and what happens there is that I am no longer your priority. I don't mind you taking pleasure in doing things, but you have to know what time to cut it off. You can't be up all night doing selfish things that don't even matter. You have to choose to do what is best for you, me, and the kingdom. The shows aren't it.

Yes sir.

Having said that, I want you to know what I have planned for you.

[That thought was out of the blue and random. So not me—even though I doubt the voice based on what he said. When will I learn??]

So, since you doubt, sit back and close your eyes.

Okay.

Edit later. No backspace, just space a few and rewrite if you make a mistake, I need you to listen so you get this all—since you still doubt.

Okay.

I want to please you.

Huh?

Just listen. I want to please you, give you the desires of your heart, but you must work for me. Me only. I am your God. You are my servant by choice. You take delight in working for me, but there's more you can give, and I need you to give it. Don't hold back, don't be timid and scared. Just do as I say and as the Holy Spirit leads and prompts you. You just take that first step. The things that come out of your mouth when you're talking/coaching others—that's good stuff. Now take it and do it. Take that first step of obedience. Say that I love them, I'll give you more words. I DO want to see if you're a willing vessel or not. So just follow my promptings and do what I say to do.

Okay.

Now I want to tell you about the house. Don't doubt me. I told you to call the bank and use who's assigned. I told you that. Don't worry about a thing. You were right; it's in my hands now. You just live every day for me doing whatever we tell and prompt you to do. The houses are no longer your concern. Just roll with me.

[Me laughing.]

I'm going to bless you. I'm going to take care of you. I'm going to meet all of your needs. And I'm still going to blow your socks off! Yes, your fancy socks—I'm gonna blow them off because I have big plans for you. Sure this may be hard to believe, Jo, because you have limited reasoning. I don't. I see all and am all. Your scope is finite. So just stick with me, and follow me where I take you. Finish looking at those houses. Though you'll know when you see it. She's even going to be amazed [the Realtor].

So what about this house here?

Just wait on me. MY timing is perfect—not yours.

Okay. So nothing, huh? No special intel or…

Nothing.

Okay, fine.

It's fine. You can't see what you can't see. So just trust me, who sees all.

Yes sir.

Well listen, I know your time is precious today. Get your work done. Maintain the look of the house. When you get this house down and can keep it tidy, you will have learned a very valuable lesson. I look forward to that. Okay. You're tired and you have to keep moving. Go now. Have a good day!

Thanks, Daddy.

You're welcome.

November 8, 2013

Good morning. I'm running behind again.

I know.

It's going to get better, I know. You tell me; I believe You!

It will. I love you, Jo. Nothing can stop that or separate you from my love. I know you make mistakes and you stay up late and you don't want to get up in the morning to talk. Not because you don't want to be with me, but just because you're tired. I know. I get that. And I forgive you of those mistakes because I'm a loving God. I don't want to harm you or oppress you. I want to love you and

forgive you and have relationship with you. THAT'S what matters.

Thanks. Hey, I'm really thinking about my friend.

Do. Keep her covered in prayer. The enemy is trying to take them down, but he won't because of the army of women surrounding her and covering them in prayer. Keep her lifted up. And keep praying for him. It's going to happen. She has to stay strong and remember who she is in me. She's not fake. She's chosen. To wear my garment of praise. Beauty for ashes. Weeping may endure for a night, but joy comes in the morning. MY JOY that only I give. She's got it in her because I am in her. She's mine. She's covered. She's going to be okay. She can make it.

Tell her to stand strong and firm on the word because that's what I've given to her. Use the tools that are in it. The warring scriptures, the declarations, the promises of mine, the gifts, the tools in there are endless. Tell her to make a list of what she thinks she needs right now, then study through the scriptures to find the tool for her to use for that thing. She'll find it. It's all in there. Just keep her covered, Jo. I know you want to rescue everyone from everything, but this isn't one to rescue. She will make it through the fire coming out as my gold. I love her; she's mine.

Thanks, God. May I share this?

Yes, she needs encouragement today. I love her so much.

I know. You're awesome.

I am! Go. Your car is warm. We'll talk later throughout the day. Listen for me today. I want to instruct you and get you to see some things.

Okay. Cool. I love you.

I love you more!

November 9, 2013

And good morning!!! We'll see how well this goes with my son already down here with me. I've asked him to try to stay quiet! Hahaha. We'll see…

We'll be fine. Just stay in my presence today. Work on really keeping your mind stayed on me. That "always being in prayer." Try to do that today. When you're not in conversation with anyone else. Be in conversation with me. See how that affects your day today.

Okay. That sounds easy enough.

[Smile/chuckle.] We'll see… People read the scriptures and act as if its impossible though they know nothing is impossible for or with me….funny, isn't it?

…Yes…though I'm sure I've been one of those people who think, "How can I pray all day when I have life going on all the time???"

Well sure, I understand that. I created you. I know you. But I also know what your true abilities are. You all cut yourselves short, and that's really from believing the lies of the enemy…whether people believe that or not. ANYTHING that contradicts MY WORD—is from the enemy. ANYTHING. So if I said you CAN—then YOU CAN. Don't doubt it.

That's why it's so important to be in my word and learn the scriptures and promises and tools in your belt! You need those things to stand on. When times get hard and you go through the fire—you need my word! And YOU need

to learn more, Jo. Your mind IS blocked. You need to be praying about this daily. When you all take communion, pray for your health and the mind of Christ.

Okay.

And you've got to do it every day. You all may not "see it" and what it's doing for you, but I know. Just keep at it. Yes, with your husband when he's available. Health and mind of Christ. It will change things. For all of you. Not just to keep you healthy, but mind blocks—at home, school, work, scriptures, memory, words to songs! Who you are in Christ, the authority you have—pray it. EVERY DAY!

Yes sir!

Check on the women you spoke to this week. Ask how they're doing and if they have any questions for you. You already know the answers, but always pray and seek me first. That's what you keep forgetting today. Invite the Holy Spirit to be free wherever you are and call down an army of angels. You can do that. They're at your disposal in a sense. If they're tools you can use, then USE THEM!!! You have to know my word and what I've given to you or you will be the generation lost because of lack of knowledge.

Wow. God, what do you want ME to do?

Be my vessel.

No, but I mean like, what's my purpose? What am I going to do when I grow up?

Tell and teach my people who they are in me and what they can do in me, through me, because of me, with me. The tools I want YOU to use, I want them to use too.

You're going to help them to see that and teach them what they are and how to use them.

That's cool.

Yes, it is. Your people will NOT die because of lack of knowledge. I will show you what you are to say and teach and who and where to show it. You will be effective where I send you. You will speak to the people, and that's why I'm preparing you now. Do not take any of this lightly. I've chosen you to be my messenger. Learn this now so you don't fear it later. I'm teaching and preparing you so you can teach and prepare others. You just have to keep following me and my directions.

Hey, do you think I'll ever hear you audibly?? Sometimes I feel weird saying, "He just talks in my head."

Why? This is how I or the Holy Spirit speak to people, and they dismiss it because they think it's them or crazy voices or –"SOMETHING." "Something" will NOT continue to steal the credit for MY voice. YOU will teach the people that!! My people perish for lack of knowledge…not on your watch. Be that voice in the darkness. Awaken my people to live in me. I AM the one who calls them out. My Spirit draws them and my son saves them.

You are called to be a voice crying out to them to show them the way. Be a leader of THE WAY. Point the people to me in all that you do. Whether you see the change or not, you WILL be one who plants, waters, and sees the harvest…at different times, in different seasons, in different people. Just do your part. Follow me and the Holy Spirit and do what we tell you to do. Do YOUR part in the process of life. We handle the rest. Take comfort and joy today, for I am with you. I love you my daughter.

It's time for you to go. [He's saying this RIGHT as my son is getting up from the table and putting his stuff away in the kitchen! He's so awesome! I love God! And now my son is asking when my Jesus time is over!]

November 10, 2013

Good morning, Daddy.

Good morning.

Are you well today?!?

I am!

That's good. I love you. I miss you, really. Though I know that's on me. Oh, and I didn't do too well on the "praying all through the day thing." It's hard! I'm used to just doing life, you know? I'm guessing that's something you want me to continue working on, so it's okay that I didn't master it yesterday, right? Keep trying?

Yes, you're correct.

You ever just feel like this is all made up? All in my head?

No, just you feel that way.

Yeah. I guess. Okay. I DO like that normally when I think this way you show me something or say something that clearly isn't me or that comes to pass. Ooo, like today…can you reveal to Dell about the job? He wants to hear it himself, so I said I was going to pray that you would send a messenger to confirm that he should seriously consider this job. This is the most he's ever been offered, and he wants to know if the telecommuting part that keeps him at Avaya is just a temptation and keeping him where you don't want him to be. Can you send him someone to tell him what to do?

I CAN…but if I don't, that's not because of YOUR hearing. Do you understand that, Jo? Your ability to hear me doesn't mean you can ask me for anything because you doubt, and then I do it for you. I'm not a Genie that's convenient when you need me. I'm GOD.

Yes, I see the difference.

Good. Because your hearing doubts are the enemy. You talk about hearing and believing, but you, too, have struggles believing sometimes. And that needs to change.

I guess 'cause I feel like it's all in my head. It'd be cool to hear you audibly or see something. I really want an encounter! I want to go somewhere and see something AND REMEMBER IT!! I sound like my son—I want more than what I already have.

You do. You sound unsatisfied with what I'm already sharing and doing with you. You shouldn't be that way.

Okay. Help me, Lord. Help me to believe, and trust, and follow, and serve, and obey. And NOT DOUBT.

I can help you with that! But it's also on you. YOU have to silence those voices and shut down those thoughts. REMEMBER—communion! Health & mind of Christ.

Yes sir. Today. My word. I won't forget!

Okay, good. Is there anything else you'd like to discuss today?

No.

Good. So let's talk about what I want to talk about.

There's more???

Oh yes. I always want to talk about more!

I have no idea where you're going to go.

That's good! That means you HAVE to follow me! Now trust my voice and what I'm about to say. Clear your head—mind of Christ now!

[God, give me the mind of Christ.]

Good! Now let's go! I want you to serve me with your whole heart. I want you to follow me. I want you to love me. With your whole heart. That's going to take time. It won't be overnight. You will have to focus on me every day and follow what I say and do.

Okay.

I want you to love me, and from that love comes a love for people. All people. People everywhere and from everywhere. Compassion for my kids and those who are still lost. I want you to pray for them earnestly. I want the lost to burden your heart. I want them to consume your heart—still in a healthy way, don't worry about not taking care of your family—but I want your heart to feel what mine feels when there are lost sheep out there. I want you to be bold and daring. It will look almost crazy to others the boldness that I want you to have. Pray for it. Just as they had in Acts. They faced persecution, they prayed for more boldness. They go hand in hand! Pray for it. For all of you.

Okay.

I want you to have peace. I give the everlasting peace. I am your Abba father who takes care of you, so no doubt

and worry should come. EVER. I have you in my hands, I will not let you go. Just follow and serve me.

Okay.

You're going to have to learn to clear your head when there are all kinds of stuff going on around you. You have to stay focused and in tune to my voice. At all times.

Okay.

God?

Yes. You're distracted. I'm waiting for you to clear your mind.

Okay.

[I see an image of Pacman!]

Okay. Just as Pacman was to eat, yours is to eat my word. Be so hungry that all you do is eat my word and it will produce fruit. As you eat the word, fruit comes. And with the fruit and the benefits/powers/tools that they bring—you can devour the enemy. He's no longer a threat to you because of the character shaped in eating the words and the production of fruit that gives you the ability to defeat the enemy. Do you follow?

Yes, I follow.

Okay good. I need you in my word MORE. You're not in there enough. It needs to be every day. It needs to be out of desire, but that's not something I can force. It's beyond the job of getting your bible study done at the last minute. You need to be in there every day. Hear me though. I'm NOT saying that doing your bible study EVERY DAY is not okay or enough. I'm just saying that you need to be in

the word EVERY DAY. PERIOD. Just get in it. Book is better, but as you get there, iPad is good, too. Faith comes by hearing. Take advantage of every tool and system you have. Just get in it.

Okay.

Now, just go get into breakfast! Start moving so you can get out on time!

I'm ready to move closer. Is someone going to come see the house???

This week.

God was that you?

Yes, that was me.

I hope so. It's hard when I hear you on "my side." Not like how that sounds but because that'd be an answer that I WANT to hear...you know?

Yeah. How about you just keep your house ready so whenever someone needs to come, you're halfway ready?

Yeah, that's supposed to be the plan...we just keep failing at that. Okay, gotta go.

I know. I love you, Jo

I love you too, Daddy. Kiss my dad for me!

I will!

November 11, 2013

I love you, God.

I love you too, daughter.

I really am enjoying our times together.

I am, too. They're building your character, though you don't see it. You're being molded and shaped into who I want you to be. I'm loving this!

That's a little surprising.

What is?

That'd you'd love this. I mean I guess it makes sense because you love your children and want intimate relationship with them. It just sounded weird to hear you SAY that you're loving this.

Hmmm. Okay. It's still all a part of my word though, you know?! Nothing's changed!

I know. I'm just saying!

Well, okay then. How about today? Are you excited?

[Confused.] About what?

About this day that I made!

Oh...yes.

GREAT!

Wow, you're REALLY excited, huh? I didn't think you'd be that excited about a day when we have no plans to go anywhere or really do anything. It seems like you would see it as an unproductive day—for the kingdom, you know?

Ahh, Jo, you've got it all wrong. Your mission is not always and only outside of your house. The mission INSIDE your house is just as important as the mission outside. Your family is VERY important to me, and I don't take anything that you or your family does for granted. It's all

important to me. AND EXCITING! The seeds you're planting in them, the watering, the pruning of their fruit trees—that's all exciting AND important. You're building the army right there at home.

Don't take that for granted. Don't despise it. I've given them to you. You're right for always bringing forth the message and the lesson. This is their training ground, too. You're equipping them with the tools as well. And the family time you'll have…it's great that it's somewhat of a day off. You're together as a family! I LOVE THAT!

[Me laughing.]

I DO! It makes my heart happy when my children are unified together. And don't keep worrying about the sibling issues, it IS going to work out. Keep loving and encouraging them individually, and they'll come together for one another. Brianna is missing that special one-on-one. When she gets it, things will change. She'll change. The dynamic in the house will change!

Well, aren't you going to tell me what her sweet spot is? What is it that she needs? Why won't she tell me? Why won't YOU tell me? All these years and I feel like there's just one little thing that opens her heart and breaks down her walls. One key. And no one is giving it up. What's the deal with that?

You will find it. This task is yours. The Holy Spirit can help guide you, and he will—but I'm not going to give you the answer. She wants it to be sincere, and she will know that it's you who discovered it.

You know this is not cool, right?

[Chuckling.] Not everything is fun and dandy, Jo. You know that.

Yeah, I know…ugh. This ten year journey really is for a reason, right? Are we almost done? Will we see the benefit of it?

The end of it depends on you. Finding that key is only the first part. Once you're in you've got to maintain your position there. The enemy is not going to go easy on you once you get through the door of her heart.

ARE YOU SERIOUS? We're not even going to be done then? Come on! PLEASE tell me this is all worth it 'cause this is beyond—not fun and dandy—this is miserable. I feel like she's the one who ruins everyone's life.

You can't look at it like that, Jo. SHE doesn't determine your attitude and behavior—or those of you around her. That's all of your own responsibilities. You all keep blame shifting and putting your emotions and lack of control onto her—but tell her—not to blame shift. YOU all need to wise up and do better. You're not practicing what you preach. Get it together.

Ugh. Okay. I hear you and I see that. Help me, Holy Spirit, to do better.

I will.

Ahh! Weird.

[Chuckling.] I told you that we're all here.

I know, it was just weird to hear someone else speak. This could get really confusing on paper, you know?

I know. But YOU know who's who. That's what matters for when you read back through these.

Mmm…this is sweet, you know?

Yes, it is.

So, should I be talking to Jesus and the Holy Spirit throughout the day?

You can.....but are you ready to discern the different voices?

Okay, that sounds like I'm crazy, right. All the voices in my head?

I can see that, but that's not right. Anyway. I think that because your relationship with them is going to be different than ours, you will not only need to learn their voice by spending time talking to them, but you'll learn when to use those relationships to help you work. Are you following?

Umm, I'm thinking—because their roles are different, our relationships are different, and therefore I will need to learn WHEN to use our conversation and relationship to do my work. Well, *your* work.

Yes. Because your power comes through Jesus, then you need to know how to use Him (you understand what I mean—not in a negative way). And because the Holy Spirit teaches and guides, you'll use that relationship to guide your words and actions and give you revelation. Woo! I love this, don't you?

Yeah...but I didn't know you loved it this much!

Yes! My child getting understanding of our purpose and roles and how to use them to build the kingdom and bring knowledge to my people? Jo, this training is amazing! This is not the stuff you get in regular books—unless of course, I've given it to someone already and they've written the book for others to learn—which is fine and they have But you don't read, so it's so good that

you're coming to the source to get the information! I'm so excited! For you, for me, the kingdom, the people you're going to encounter and teach and inform and train! THIS IS SO EXCITING!

WOW. I really can't believe how excited you are! I hope I'm not being a "Debbie downer" to you…

Oh, you're not. You just don't get it yet. But I do because I see your future and I'm so excited that you've made it to THIS POINT TODAY! THIS IS A GREAT DAY!

This is why you were excited earlier?

YES! Now. Let me tell you want I want you to do.

Okay.

Pray.

Pray?

Yes, just pray. You need to get in my presence today, FOR REAL, in addition to continuing to work on the prayer throughout the day. You follow?

Yes.

THIS is when you're building your relationship with the Holy Spirit and Jesus. Mainly the Holy Spirit, though. I do need you to pray in tongues more to build up the intercession part so he can do his work between us and build your relationship with him. But right now, do your best. I know you still doubt with your tongue, too. Yes, you did hear a different tongue at VOA, and, yes, I'm doing things in you. Just let it flow out of you and stop worrying about it. You HAVE to go to bed earlier so you can rise earlier, because you're going to have to spend

more time with us. I know that doesn't excite you right now, but you'll get over it!

Okay.

Okay. I need you to go right now, though I'd love to keep talking to you...you want to come back later?

Uh...yeah? Why are we leaving now?

Because I have so much more to say, but you need to meet with your husband to email the realtor about the houses.

Yeah, 'cause you know I want to talk about houses, right?

Yes, I know and we will because I want to, too!

And you're still so excited?

I am. I've got great things for you, I told you, Jo. And you are going to be amazed! But you've got to be with me every step of the way, so whatever I give you to do, do it. To the best of your ability. Just be obedient. NOW is the time to not look back, only look forward. Don't worry about your budget, and don't get discouraged or depressed. You know I have you. And you're not a worrier, so stop worrying. Go look at houses and email her back. We'll talk later. I love you "bah!" [Laughing.]

[Me laughing.] Okay, I love you too. Bye!

November 12, 2013

I really hope we have places to watch the sun rise or set. Even inside the house so we can see it every day. A nice view. Are you going to tell us about our house? And DO know that it's probably going to be hard for me to trust your voice versus mine!!! But I just wish you'd go back to telling me every day what to do—rather, I know you do. I wish you'd tell me what day someone was coming to see the house and when we are going to sell and what house is ours and when we're going to move and how much it's going to cost and how we should be looking for it…ugh. So. Good morning, how are you today??!?!?

I'm well, thank you. Have a lot on your mind, do you?!

A little bit!

Well, I understand. It's a lot to think about. But dear, the thing is that you don't have to. You don't have to worry about all of that. I've got it all under control. You just need to go with me.

I know, but…it's hard. The realtor wants to know what we want and what our price range is…is she even the right one??

[Chuckling.] Yes, she is. You just need to relax. Answer her questions. Let her know what you like and dislike. Then let her do her job. And let me do mine!

Mmm…so have we seen the house yet?

I'm not going to answer that. You're getting ahead of yourself. Just look at those houses. Tell her what you're looking for, and leave the rest to us.

Okay…but what about this house? What's going on with that?

You are worrying.

Am I? I don't feel WORRIED about it. I'm just wondering. Curious. Thinking about it.

And what SHOULD you be thinking about?

You?

Yes. Me. The kingdom, the work, the glory of it all. Those are the thoughts that should consume you. Not the house, his job, the work. You need to change your focus. Just like the job just came to him, you need to stay busy about my work, and things will come to you.

Ohh! Does that mean you sent that job? Is he supposed to take it? Interview? You know he really wants to hear that directly from you, right? I'm asking, but I don't think he necessarily wants to get it from me.

Yes, I know all those things! And, yes, I sent the job. Whether he takes it is up to him.

Really? It's optional?

Everything is optional, Jo.

True. But if you sent the job, isn't he SUPPOSED to take it?

It may not be for him to take.

Huh? Come on God…what?

He should go to the interview and then make a decision. I'll be with him. Guiding him. Helping him discern. But the choice to take it will be his. He needs to press forward, though. Definitely interview for it. And, yes, to him that means that he needs to start looking out instead of trying to figure out his current job. It's time to look for a new job. The telecommute is just to ease with the transition, but it's time to go.

Okay. I'm cool with that, but I hope that works for him, too. You STILL have to show him this though. He's not asking me to ask you and report back to him. He wants YOU to speak to HIM.

You don't need to all caps for me, Jo. I know all these things. You're stressing them like I need to get it—I'm not human!

I know. And I mean no disrespect.

I know.

It's just that if I stress it in our conversation, wouldn't it be like praying it over and over?! Like, "I REALLY want this so I'm going to keep praying until I get it" type of thing. You know what I mean?

Yes, I follow. Not necessary, but I get your point and where you're coming from. You're funny.

….So…are you going to talk to him?

JO!

Huh?

STOP WORRYING ABOUT IT!

Okay…I'm trying. I didn't think I was worrying about it, though.

Then you need to look up the definition of worry—no, not now. Then look in the bible for the word and its origin so you can see how it would've been used in its original text. Then see if you're not worrying.

Okay. So, are we being productive today?

Yeah, we are. You're learning that you need to relax and let people do their jobs. That your hand doesn't have to be in everything. And to let me do my work. You just lay things down. Your brother [Jesus] told you a long time ago that he would carry your bag for you, but if you're

carrying it—he can't. So what are you going to do? Carry things or lay them down and let him carry it for you?

Lay them down.

Okay then. DO THAT! Yes. We're being productive. You just need a day to look in the mirror at your issues and thoughts. You don't have it all together yet. You may not ever until you get here. But until that point, every day you need to assess yourself—am I carrying things that I don't need to? Am I being obedient in my thoughts and actions? Am I lining up with the word? Am I pleasing my daddy? Am I honoring God in all that I do? Am I serving others with a joyful heart?

Ouch.

Yes. These are questions you need to ask yourself EVERY DAY. You do your job; we'll do ours. You handle what is YOUR responsibility, and we'll handle ours. You stop trying to do our jobs and just focus on yours—because if you do that—if you focus on those questions and make the changes necessary—you're in a kingdom mindset.

Don't get confused and think your focus will be on yourself. It's not. Those are questions to ask to get, and keep, your mind in a kingdom mindset. Read them again. See that? Those are KINGDOM. If you're doing those things, then you're already serving me and representing me well and shining the light in a dark world. But if you're NOT doing those things—then you ARE focused on yourself or things that don't really matter. And it's not that I don't care about what you care about, it's that your focus has shifted off of what is truly important in order to carry out the call. You follow?

Yes.

Okay. I DO think this was good and enough for today. You have a lot to think about. Memorize those questions. Someone else is going to need them too [wink]!

Okay, I will…though my memory is bad…

Mind of Christ, Jo. Mind of Christ. Pray it every day, throughout the day. Speak it over yourself. Take your communion. Take this all very seriously, because I do.

Okay.

Okay. Now go close your eyes until your next alarm. I know you need a boost! I love you, daughter.

I love you, Daddy.

November 13, 2013

Hello.

Hello. You're not quite in it this morning, huh?

No. Does it make that big of a difference where I am? [I'm in my in my room on my bed.]

For you it seems to. Your mindset is still one of going back to bed, and your mind is wandering because you looked around on the computer first. You need to quiet your mind before we can effectively begin.

Okay. Hey so how come I keep running into situations where I feel BAD about not having all these problems and issues that other people have and go through?

You want problems?!?

No. I'm just saying, like how people say that if Satan isn't attacking you it means that you're not a threat.

Do you think that Satan is NOT attacking you??

No, it's just not like everyone else's.

You need your problems to match?

No.

Because your calls and your testimonies aren't the same. They're on different roads than you are. It doesn't mean that one is "better" than the other. It means that you're called to minister to a different set of people, so you have to travel the road I have before you in order to minister to those people. Stop looking at others and wondering what's wrong with you or that you're less than those other people. Or even that you're not working for the kingdom because Satan isn't attacking you like YOU think he should! That's ridiculous. Dear, you've had your own personal struggle for ten years. I think that's a long time for you to be carrying the same issue around, don't you??

Yes.

Now. Because your calling has to do with your family, the place where you get attacked is your family. Your kids. Your cohesiveness. Dear, please don't look at others and compare yourself to them. Ever. For any reason about anything. THIS is the life and the situation and the issues that I've put you in in order to accomplish what I need accomplished from you. From you all. These are lessons for your whole family. Stop selling them all short because they don't "look" big. They're big in your house, are they not?

Yes.

Okay, then. Stop it.

Yes sir.

I do not want to hear comparisons. You live your life according to the way you're supposed to live it—PERIOD.

You want to still talk??

Yes, I want to still talk.

Okay.

I need you to wake up. Both physically and mentally. We meet every day, I give you tools, instructions, things to do or say…it's not for naught, Jo.

I know.

Okay, then act like it. I've got purpose for you. And for these writings. It's almost time to start looking back at them. But you have to be ready. You have to be awake, alert, vigilant. I'm not saying that we're not going to meet, but you're getting close to being released, and you need to be ready. You need to begin training like an athlete trains for an event. YOU HAVE TO GET SERIOUS ABOUT THIS, JO. Right now you're not. You're just doing it every day. Some days, because you have to, not because you're awake enough to fully choose it and have a desire to do it on your own.

YES. You need to start reading back through these. Pay attention to the many things I have told you to do. And pay attention to the things you STILL HAVE to do. It's like taking notes in class every day but not going back through it to study. That's what you're doing. You've

got to wake up. Get it together. And yes you CAN get it all to fit into your day. Even your hobbies. You need to prioritize, make a schedule, and stick to it. There are plenty of hours in the day. What you lack is consistency, and you've known that for a VERY long time. What are you going to do about it?

Uhh…

Yes, dear. It's almost time to arise, but you still have a lot of work to do. Get it together. Wake up. Fully. You cannot fully rely on our time together. There needs to be homework, there needs to be prayer and intercession and you working alongside Jesus & the Holy Spirit. You're in training. You come to class every day, but you're not studying for your tests & exams. You're not doing your homework. And I know that you completely understand what I am saying to you right now.

Yes, I do.

Good. So let's start seeing some changes, okay? Starting today. And take communion more seriously. Look it up for real. And yes, take time to get the things done that your husband needs, too. Part of serving people joyfully is doing the things that are important to them. If those Christmas lists are important to him right now, then do them. The birthday party, plan it. Yes, I know you want to wait on him so he feels a part, but if he thinks you're dropping the ball because of your lack of interest and that you're not valuing what he values—then you need to take the time to get those things done. Do you understand?

Yes sir. Wow. It's been awhile since you've spoken to me like this…

Well, you need it. I know where you are and what's up ahead. Because you don't, you're living your life as if there's nothing else to do but talk to me every morning. This alone is not going to make you what you're called to be.

November 17, 2013

Hey, good morning. Sorry I haven't felt well and haven't been here for a while. Will you forgive me? I know it's not an excuse, but I just wasn't up for getting on each morning and then yesterday was just too rushed.

I know. And yes, I forgive you.

Thank you.

You're welcome. You excited about today?

A little, I guess. I'm hoping people come, hoping that the buyer comes, hopeful that we like the new realtor though I don't think these are any of the houses…what are YOU excited about today?

That this is the day I made! Remember that day last week when you thought I was really excited?

Yes.

Well that's how I feel every day you get life to live. It's a GREAT day! I'm excited to see what you do with every day that I give to you!

You're so funny.

Why?

Just that you get excited about OUR days that YOU give us and you want to see how we use them...like you don't already know!

I know. But I love you. I'm excited for you. I'm excited to see where you're going. I care about you and the things that you do.

Just seems funny that's all. Since you know all.

Hmmm...okay!

So you want to tell me about today? Or the house we're going to buy or if the house is going to sell soon or all the things I've missed in the past three days?

Well, you said I'm funny, so...I'm not going to tell you when your house is going to sell. You keep asking, but I haven't told you. That's fine, I'm not mad that you keep asking, I'm just not telling you right now.

Ugh. Okay.

I want you to rest in me. Fully. Completely. In my arms. Stop thinking—worrying—about the things going on around you, and just rest in me. Do your work [bible study], take your time, and live your life as you normally do. This house stuff is just going on around you, it is not you. Be careful how you treat this time, and change your life according to it.

I think that's why I keep asking when we're moving. So we can plan things accordingly.

I know. But I'm telling you to keep your focus on ME. MY work. MY things. And then, MY plans for you. It's ALL going to work out, and you will all see that. But

right now, today especially, focus on ME. Get back in line with ME.

Yes, Daddy. I'm sorry.

It's okay. But that's why we need this time together to help keep your focus straight.

Okay.

I love you so much. You don't have to get down in my presence, you should never walk away lowly from our time together. Our times should leave you uplifted and encouraged, full of hope and positive things to change.

Okay.

It's all good. You'll see. So your word for today is—get back focused on me.

Alright.

Now. Let's talk!

Huh? Oh, I thought you were done. With that recap, you just sounded like it!

No! I want to tell you about your house!

Really?

Well yeah, a little bit!

Wow, okay. I may need help believing it's you and not me…

As you often do. As you wish! It's going to have trees…

God. I need help. I'm not going to believe this.

Just write.

Okay.

It's going to have trees lining the back. You're going to have land. Not a field, but land enough to satisfy both your husband and children's desire to explore!

That's cool.

You're going to have rooms. Rooms to spare, really.

Bedrooms.

Rooms you can do what you want with. They may not be technical rooms for coding purposes, but people can fit in there to sleep!

Really?

Yes. So yes, you two will have room for your crafts!

YAY! [BIG SMILE]

Dell is going to have an office. [I think he said pretty much set up already.] See? Aren't you already glad that you did NOT sneak into Dell's file and read what he wrote?

Yes.

Mmm hmm...that was not for you to go into. That was a boundary that HE needs to open up to you. Good choice, but watch your temptations. That was too much, and you should've shut that down earlier than you did.

Yes, God.

Okay! House!

[Smiling, shaking my head!]

Your kitchen is nice. I almost don't want to tell you about it, because I want you just to be amazed when you see it. You will love it. It will almost make you want to cry—in person, not from the pictures. And cry because of the reality of it being yours. Not during your thoughts of not being able to afford it and that it could never BE yours. The kids will have room to play upstairs and downstairs. You will have plenty of space for school and a library with lots of room for shelving—if it's not already there!

Nice.

I really don't want to say too much, Jo. You'll know when you see it. There's lots of room, and it's beautiful, and you're going to love it.

Have we seen it yet? Because we really liked that other house.

You're definitely NOT going to see it today [at the showings]. And you're right; you've set your parameters too low. I AM going to blow your mind.

But I just don't get it? HOW are we going to be able to do it? I can't think of any way we can afford a big house like that.

JO. YOU'RE NOT LISTENING TO ME!!! JUST FOLLOW ME! Raise your search limit, and follow me. YES. It's OKAY to fall in love with a house when you see it. When a house seems like too much for you, too much to afford, too much to DESERVE—you follow me. Your tears are okay. I love to give good gifts. You can argue with me all day about not deserving it, but you didn't deserve my son, and I gave him to you. Don't argue with me. Ever. You're always going to fail. You will never win in a race against me. I'VE got this, not YOU. YOU just FOLLOW ME.

This is SO hard.

I know.

'Cause I just don't see how you're going to do it. What if you're just describing my home in heaven, and I'm getting my hopes set for down here?

Really? Heaven? That's what you wanted to compare this to? Really, Jo? I'm not going to describe your home in heaven for you AND your KIDS! No dear, I'm talking about earth. BABE, I've got this. I've got you. Trust your DADDY! Trust our time together. You want to doubt our time and the thoughts in your head—then just watch, but stay with me while you're watching. Remember. Stay with me. Focus on me. Follow me.

Okay.

Now. Go look for the real house. If you find it, when you leave the realtor today, go drive by it on your way home. That's IF you find it [wink]!

Hmph. Okay [shaking my head]. Daddy?

Yes.

I love you.

I love you too, princess.

November 18, 2013

Good morning. I'm like, tired. Of houses. I don't want to talk about a house today or probably for a while. It's probably silly to feel burned out about a house after only one day, huh?

Yes, and you have to listen to what I say, not anyone else, unless you know I'm speaking through them. Go back to your old recordings and follow my voice on there. You've gotten so many words, Jo. It could seem almost silly for you to ever be discouraged, because I've shown you my hand throughout every step of the way. I've given you all words into your futures; I've told you about your pasts. Just follow me, stay with my words, and when you feel low, remind yourself of what's been said by listening to or reading them over again. Yes, reading them or listening to them every day IS good. Not necessarily mandatory, but it's good. You need to be reminded, you need to be focused, you need to keep your eyes stayed on me so I can keep you in that perfect peace.

Okay. I'm going to try and get my life back in order [school/ life/responsibilities wise] today AND keep the house clean. Maybe it's time for that person deep down inside that I always talk about to come out and stay. I'm going to need your help staying calm and not getting anal about it, though!

Oh, it'll be fine. You can do it. This is your time to shine. It IS a new day for you. I'm taking you somewhere new. In me. In you. In your household. EVERYTHING. This IS a new day for you. Enjoy it, celebrate it, embrace it, *become it.* This is new and it benefits you and everyone you come in contact with. As you walk into this, and it becomes your lifestyle, not only will it be contagious for your family, but it's going to affect others. People are going to see it. They are literally going to see your peace that you have and that surrounds you. It's almost going to sit on you, like a cloud all around your shoulders and head, you're going to just be in it.

Now things will still get you upset and even rattle you a little, but with this peace, you'll be able to quiet those storms quickly—though not always easily. You'll have wisdom in your actions and words, and that will help to guide you through the processes ahead of you. Use your wisdom. You've asked and I've given it to you. Be wise in all of your actions. ALWAYS think first—before you speak and act. Let my spirit guide you. YES, ALL of the time.

You need to slow down your speech; it's still too quick—especially at home. Watch your face, too, because while your mouth is not speaking, your face IS, and that will get you into trouble. In a place where even though you were thinking wisely, your face negated everything you said. So this peace cloud that is around your head and shoulders, let it guard and keep your face pure and peaceful, as well.

Let my spirit transcend upon you like a dove. And let it just rest upon you. The joy they speak of—it'll come. That's not a dull word, that is coming to pass too. But first you will get peace.

That's cool. I definitely need that.

Don't I know [chuckling]?! Your children will enjoy of it, too. Not just from you, but they'll start to pick it up themselves. You WILL have love in your house, Jo. Don't worry about it. Just stay with me, and follow my directions, and you'll become the woman I've called you to be.

Okay. That's good to hear. The kids and love part.

Oh, of course. It's all going to come together…but in MY timing, not yours.

Yes, I see that for sure.

Okay, I want you to go and get your work done. Bible study, school, house, yarn—all of it. You CAN get it all done. But you HAVE to focus. Keep your priorities straight, and start to seek us during the day. We're here to guide you. Use your wisdom and get peace. You can do this! I'm proud of you, dear. You're growing up [like a grown up to a kid while pinching their cheeks]!

[Smiling.] Yeah. Thanks, God. It's all because of you. I love you.

I love you more. Do good today.

Thanks, I will. Try to do my best.

You can. You will. Stay focused. Timers are good [wink].

November 19, 2013

I'm so proud of my husband for talking to you. I'm really happy for him. I hope that he keeps it up.

Me, too. I enjoyed our time together. It's going to take him awhile to get used to it and the fact that he CAN hear me.

Yeah, I know! He's funny. Well, I guess you probably are saying that same thing about me, huh?!

[Chuckling.] Uh, yeah.

Okay, okay. I'm funny, too, then [laughing]!

Your hair is pretty.

Thanks.

You're pretty. You don't look like a man just because you look like your brother...

Okay.

Why don't you pray for him every time you "see" him? Don't you think that would be a good idea and a good use of your time instead of lamenting over the fact that you look like him??

Yes.

Good.

Hey, God. I don't know what you'd have to talk about today, because I can't think of anything 'cause it seems like we talk every day and we'd run out of things to talk about I'm going to hate this conversation later, I can tell. Do you want me just to sit and see what you want to talk about?

I was going to ask about my sin and ask you to show it to me. But I bet you DO want me to just shut up and listen a little bit, huh? Stop running my mouth when it's listening time?? And I'm going to Kay's house today. I don't know what you want me to say over there…or why I'm going really. I don't know what's on her mind to discuss today. I guess I really need to spend some time in prayer today before I go, huh? Stop talking??

Lil' bit, yeah.

Okay. Sorry.

It's fine. You were just going on for a while, and it's a good time to listen.

Okay.

Today. Today as always, I want you to REST in me. Seek me. Follow me. That's the number one thing for you today and every day. Seek me, follow me, rest in me. And

yes, you can share that [I know what you're going to be thinking next]!

I want you to worship me with your actions today. I want the things you do to be a service unto ME. Do things joyfully today, without complaining or murmuring. Ah, you caught it…so you're not like them in the desert for forty years…nice. So worship me today with more than just your mouth. I want to SEE your worship of me. And it's easy; it's not hard. Love what I've given to you and treat it as such. Those children, that husband, that house, your things—are all blessings from me. So worship me in your use of those things. Change the way you think and look at them.

And if I have to discipline??

Do it in LOVE. Not anger. That didn't change. I always want you to love those children, and love is an act of worship. So if you have to discipline them, stay in love, and you'll stay in worship. You're shepherding and teaching and guiding and training—those ARE acts of love and worship. Anger is not. Don't do it.

You want to see your sin? It's your lack of self-control. It's YOUR outbursts. Even when you think you're controlling it, but then you speak of your spazzing out for something being not done right or in its place. They are STILL seeing and hearing it. YOU HAVE TO CONTROL YOURSELF! Stay calm on the inside, and it will reflect on the outside. Self-control is what you need to work on. The uptight stressed mom needs to go. Permanently. Forever!

Okay! Okay! Gotcha. You're not fond of her!

No, because she affects my children...and your children. You're shaping them, and I need you to be more careful. You may not have the sin issues that your friends have. Yours are in your home with you kids. You feel and see the heavy mantel you carry with children. You HAVE to be an influence and an example that they don't get in other places. You ARE going to be *that* example that they *choose* to follow.

Yes, I'm speaking of more than just your kids. Your influence spans across yours, other kids, and other parents. And you & your husband *will* be in this together. You're going to impact many families *together.* Yes he will have more time when he's at home more. I'm not going to get into the job scene right now! But just do what I tell you to do, and you'll see it all unfold.

Okay. Anything about or for Kay today?

Ah...she's on the right track. The Holy Spirit will guide you with her today. We don't need to talk about it right now. Just be praying this morning and when you get there. Alright, my love. It's game time. We'll talk tomorrow. I love you. Stay peaceful today and use self-control!

Yes, Daddy. I love you, too.

November 20, 2013

Hello. I'm up a little bit earlier today...

Yes, I helped with that. [Dell called home phone because alarm wouldn't set from his phone.]

I see! So how are you today?

I'm well. And you?

I could be sleeping….and I'm starting to feel a little hungry, but I'm going to go to Sam's Club anyway.

Well that's good. You need to get some things for your family.

Any good books there???

You shouldn't be tempted buy anything today!

Well that'll make Wendell happy! So what's the word from you today?

Same. Rest in me. Find peace in me. I'm all that you need. I will take care of you. I will provide for you. Just come to me. Lay it down, and I will give you rest. I have all you need. My cup runs over, and I want to pour out onto you. I want to fill you with my peace, my joy, and my love. I have all of this for you. Just come and get it. It's yours for the asking; it's yours for the taking. Drink and enjoy all that I have and pour out to you. My love and my grace are sufficient. Go in peace and carry what I have given to you.

What runs out of me and into you is for you to now pour out onto others. My gift is for giving. It's continuous. It's not for holding onto; it's to share and continually give away. I AM the gift that keeps on giving. There is nothing like me, better than me, superior to me, above me. I AM ALL THINGS and NOTHING ever changes that. I AM. I AM. I am.

Now, go in peace and share the love which I have given and shown to you. Do your best. Make every moment count. You're here for purpose and for destiny and for great things that I have not yet shown to you. But follow me now, and see that my hand is upon you and everything

you do. Rest in me. Walk with me. And watch what I do in and for and through you.

I love you My child. I want what's best for you—however that may look to you! I know the plans I have for you, I declare. Ahh...I love you, girl. I really do. I'm proud of you, and you make me smile.

I've heard that before, but I can't say that I understand why. I don't feel that I do much—in terms of outside the home.

Ahh, but you do. You're working for me; you're spending time with me. And see the real problem is that you still look at these children wrong. You still see them as burdens, and they're not. Not only are they gifts, but they are assignments. What you do INSIDE this house is just as important as what you do OUTSIDE this house—because your kids and the kids you teach are PART of your assignment.

Everything you and I do and share together isn't just for you or for us. It's for THEM—the ones who follow behind us and hear what I've said to you and through you. This IS one of those experiences people talk about as part of their testimony that excites and builds faith.

Don't discredit this OR your children. You have to stop seeing them that way, and you have to start seeing them as part of your assignment and purpose. Watch what I'm doing. Do you see Brianna???? I'm working in her. Give me praise for that and encourage her and pump her up. Celebrate what she and I are doing together. There's something being birthed right now. Continue to support it. And now pray for it—and for her as she leads. She's at the beginning of fulfilling her call. This is an awesome time. And don't take communion lightly or for granted.

I told you that you may not see the effect of it, but it's already working. DO THIS EVERY DAY!

Yes sir.

Okay, I know you've got to get to the store. I'm going with you.

[Me laughing.]

You're funny. It was just a peaceful reminder.

I know, it just sounded funny.

Please start talking to your brother [Jesus]. You need to start getting with him and the Holy Spirit so you don't get behind.

Okay…

Alright. Let's go to Sam's!

Okay, let's go.

November 21, 2013

Good morning, Lord. How are you today? I'm doing well.

Well, I'm glad to see that. I am doing well too. Full day ahead…

Yes. Another bible study Thursday. I'm looking forward to being off next week, though!

I know. But you'll be fine. These are good times for you and my children. I'm glad you're serving here.

That's cool.

It is.

[Chuckling.]

I just want to let you know that I'm proud of you, Jo. I really am. It doesn't matter that you haven't all the way "arrived"—you never will until you get here. But I'm pleased at what you ARE doing now. I see the commitment you have both to bible study each week and to our communion here. I see it all. The things that go unnoticed at home—I see it. And it's not going without reward. Sowing and reaping, right?!?!?

[Smiling.] Yes, that's right. It's everything.

It IS everything! You're right!! I love you, girl. I really do.

I love you, too.

My peace is here for you, and it's coming to you. Just wait and see. Your family will see and experience a whole new person. It's going to be great. Just watch. Just STAY WITH ME! I know your kids miss the Christmas show, but just stay with me. Keep on the plans that I have for YOU. For YOU ALL. My plans are higher than yours. I see and know all, and I know what I have for you; so don't get distracted by the shows and productions around you. This is a new place for all of you, and I have you here for a purpose. So get what you're supposed to get right now out of this place. My ways are higher and I know all. Just follow me.

Yes, Lord.

Dear, this is sweet time, but you really need to get moving because you're behind.

Uh thanks…not going to stop time for me, huh?!?!

Nope. You just need to learn to be a better steward of it.

Ouch, yes sir.

Alright now, go. Love you.

Love you, too!

November 23, 2013

Good morning. Sorry about yesterday.

It's okay.

Sleeping in was so nice, though. I just thought I'd have time to get us in there, but everything was already in full swing. It's amazing what three hours can do!

Yes.

So do you want to talk today? You seem quiet.

Oh, I always want to talk, dear.

Okay, so what's up?

I'm quiet today because my heart is heavy.

Really? I'm not sure I heard this right…

My children. They are not seeking me and coming to me for wisdom and direction in their lives. They are just doing their own thing. Some of them are praying, but it's just one-way communication. So few are listening for and to me. It hurts me to see my children in this way. I want so much more for them.

Ohh. You want me to get on FB and say something?!

I want you to pray. I NEED YOU TO PRAY MORE. We talk every day, but I need you in communication with the others. I need you interceding with the Holy

Spirit and praying through Jesus. I need you to seek their counsel concerning your friends, their situations, your conversations with them. <u>This</u> relationship is good, but I need you to work on those other links more now, because that's where you are weak.

[Sitting here thinking about my friends and meeting a lady today and what I should be saying to these people.]

And THAT'S why you need to pray. Those words of knowledge or encouragement or direction that you're wanting to be able to give to people—those come through the Holy Spirit, and if you're not praying and in tune with HIS voice and unction, then you'll miss what you could be giving. I'm not saying you'll never get anything, because you're only listening for MY voice—-if you ARE seeking and listening—which you often DO NOT. But the Holy Spirit is going to give you the words that he hears from us so you HAVE to be listening for HIS voice. Jo, you have to start communicating with him more so you know his voice. Do you get it?

Yes. I get it. I totally get it. [Thinking that it'll be interesting to see Jesus' role and relationship when I get to that point.] I know I don't pray enough…or at all really. Not a dedicated time, just when it's "needed."

Yes, well, for both of us—you need to start dedicating time to prayer like you dedicate your time with me in the morning.

Okay.

YES. You keep thinking about it, the answer is yes. It's time to print. There's too much here for you to take the time to come to your computer and open and close. You

need to be able to flip through it. Yes dear, I know you. I know you like paper! You may print these. And I know your family will be interested in them, that's fine. Your family may read these. They're not for public use…not yet. You'll see how all of that will unfold.

But the book/journal/record that you will print from home will be for your home use. I'm not saying you can't refer to knowledge given when talking to people, I'm just saying that the book is not to be handed over to someone [outside of your husband or kids] for them to read. Follow?

Yes, I follow.

Good. You're going to have a fun day today. Try to enjoy it! Get some yarn in and finished. Have fun at the game and party. AND PRAY! Set aside [go to a room] time by yourself and PRAY. Preferably this morning before you meet that lady for the scarf.

Okay. But the timing is mine?

Of course. You always have a choice…I'm just giving a suggestion…

Okay. I love you so much. [Thinking about how I've been singing A LOT the past two days. Just happy in worship to Him.]

I know…I've been enjoying your singing the past few days. Something new is happening, isn't it?! I see that you're joyful and happy in your praise. It's a beautiful thing. Change IS good, my dear…

I know…but some change is hard and it hurts.

I know, but we'll deal with that when the time comes.

There are so many people and things that I want to ask about…

I know. But you really need to pray and pray about those things. I'm telling you—that's the key right now for you.

Okay. I will.

November 25, 2013

Good morning Lord. How are you this morning?

I am well.

Good. I am too! Just a little tired….which is no surprise, I know…

[Chuckle.] You'll get better.

Thanks. Didn't realize he was going to be a distraction. [Dell in the kitchen getting food.]

He isn't. You just need to focus on me.

Okay. So what's up for today?!

Well, I liked you're reading last night.

The book or that I was just reading?

The fact that you were reading at all!! [Laughing.] Good for you!

Ha!

Well, I know that's different for you, so I'm proud of you actually doing it.

[Smiling.] Okay…

That is a good book, though.

Hmmm, I was wondering if I should get the study guide that goes with it?

You could. Or you could just read the book.

Mmm, that was no help.

That's a decision you can make on your own. But it doesn't make sense to buy anything and not use it, Jo. Anything. Book, something in the house, clothes…that's just wasteful and not being a good steward of what you've been given. If you buy something—use it. Plain as that.

Okay, I will…do better than what I have been of that. I'm not sure how saying I'm going to read books is going to go for me…

I understand. It all takes time.

Cool. So what's up?

I want to talk about you.

I don't want to talk about me. [I don't think you said that.]

I want to talk about you.

I just got sleepy; let's not talk about me. Let me just close my eyes for a minute.

Are you done?

No, I keep getting more and more sleepy. I just want to lie down.

Are you done goofing off and ready to listen??

Yes…no, I'm really sleepy, and Dell is a distraction…

Jo.

Yes.

Wake up. For real, to everything around you. Wake up. Now listen.

Okay.

I'm giving you information that is not just for you. It's for others. It's for the people. It's for your kids. Your job is to take this information and share it. Give it away. Teach it to anyone who will listen to you. You cannot push it on people, though. They will come to you. You feed those who come to eat from what I've given to you. Do you understand the difference?

Yes.

Good. So I'm glad that you're going to start reading more; you need that. You need more understanding, because the people you talk to need more understanding. Keep getting it so you can give it. That's how it works. That's the cycle. I need you to stay on point. You have to know what you're taking about. You have to stay in my face to get wisdom; you have to stay in my presence to receive what I have for you—so you can give it! It's not just for you. Gifts are for others, not self. Wake up.

Sorry.

You need to get before me, in my face, in worship. You need to get yourself to a place in worship—at home—that you feel my presence in your pure worship of me. Your tongues need to flow at home. You have warfare to do for self and others at home, and you need your prayer language to get it all done. There are things you don't know or understand, and the Holy Spirit has the tools for you to pray with, but you have to get in tune with him.

I don't mind your yarn, I get that, but you have to be careful of your idle time. You have to be diligent about watching your time and filling it with things that should be done. Don't procrastinate; get things done. Don't just sit around during school. Keep busy while you're doing school. Yes, I said that, you can you be engaged in school while doing something else and still give school the attention that it needs.

Okay. [I rubbed my hands together with fingers interlocked, but not tight—which I've never done before. They got super hot quick.]

Your hands are made for my glory…use them wisely.

Give me wisdom.

I will. I am. It's yours. Just keep asking, and I'll keep giving.

I liked Pastor's message yesterday.

I did, too. You can't predict when or how I'm coming. But you know that I am. Just seek me and ask me what to do or what to say. That's where you miss it, Jo, and ultimately, miss me. You don't stop and ask in the moment. You just try to do it yourself. And I know it's not because you're trying to steal the glory. I know and get that. But it's just a matter of you not remembering the right way to do things. You HAVE to remember.

Throughout the day, too? When we're just at home, you mean?

Yes. Throughout the day, even with just your family. Solomon asked. That's why he was so wise. Okay Jo, you're in and out too much to listen. I'm done anyway. You close your eyes and rest and get ready for your day.

It's because I didn't take my spark! That's the only difference...

No, it's because you're not getting enough rest at night. Don't blame your band-aid for the root problem. You know better.

Okay. Okay, I'm going to get off here.

Alright, love. Get rest and be well. I love you.

I love you, too. Oh, so Larry. He's good?

[Big smile.] Yeah. He's good.

Okay, cool. I really was surprised, though. I just really thought you were going to heal him...

I know. Many people did. But many people saw the man stand in God's presence and continue to worship, even in the face of adversity. He stood for me until the end. He's not going unrewarded, for sure.

Okay. Thanks for sharing. Please take care of his family, his kids.

Oh, I will. They're not forgotten or forsaken. I've got his kids. You pray for their mom.

Okay.

Alright, love. Scoot along!

Okay, bye.

Good morning. I'm sorry about not meeting or wanting to meet. Sometimes I just get tired of talking about me. And I can't imagine how you don't get tired of talking about me. Not the way that sounded, but don't you get tired of talking to me?

I keep expecting you to run out of things to say, and that's not happening.

Jo, you don't have to be here if you don't want to be. It's a choice, remember?

Yes, I know. But I need to be here.

Well, that I know. But you still have a choice. I'm not going, and I can't MAKE you come every day. But the benefits of coming surely outweigh the inconvenience you feel of getting up early each morning.

Yeah. And I feel bad about rolling over at the right time and STILL not getting up until now…

Don't worry about that. You will decide what you think is best for you each morning. I know that we're going to miss some days for various reasons. But guilt should not drive you here, LOVE should.

Yeah, I hear that. I'm sorry.

For what?!

For love not driving me here every day. Some days it DOES feel like obligation, but other days it's that I'm so excited about our time and just longing to get down here and talk to you!!

I know. And THAT'S what I want EVERY day…but I can't make you do that. It's all on you and how you feel about and view this relationship.

Got it. It's on me. I have to work on it—not in a WORK kind of way. But our communication depends on our relationship—and that's on me. I get ya.

Good. I love you.

I know. I love you, too! But you love me more!!!

Yes, I do!

You have big plans for today?

Just shine today. Shine my light wherever you go. I long for people to feel My love and see how present I really am.

Okay.

You were going to ask me about someone…

Yeah, but I forgot who. I know I have to give something to my friend next week…

But we'll do that next week. You need to be praying for her in the meantime.

Okay, I will. More than I am now. All my friends, really. I need to get better. Hmm...God is there anything else that you want to say about anyone??

My mind and my heart are set on everyone. I love my people. Whether they obey me or not. My love abounds, and I want them all to come home and feel the fullness of me and my presence. I want everyone to feel my love. It's for all people. But my children won't listen and come to me and seek me. Those who follow me don't seek me to learn and hear my voice for wisdom and for counsel. So they don't talk and witness to others and tell them about my love because they're not experiencing it themselves.

If I'm not exciting to people, if they don't let themselves experience my love and my grace and my forgiveness, then they're not driven to tell others of my goodness, my faithfulness, my love and my mercy. My own people are selling me short.

Experience me so you can share me. I'm not to be kept for yourselves; I'm to be shared with others. With ALL. I want ALL my children to be saved, not just the select few who want to keep me a secret for the people they like and think "look" the part of a believer. My children are dying with no knowledge of not just ME, but of ALL that I entail. My faithfulness, kindness, forgiveness, laughter, joy, true, unconditional love. I WANT MY CHILDREN!!

I need my people to stand up and speak out. Not judge the masses, but LOVE the masses. I want my children to COME HOME!! They've been gone and astray too long. I want my babies back in my arms. I miss my children.

Go and find them. Bring them home. Set the church on fire. Tell them what I'm saying. Tell them to refocus and remember what they've been commissioned to do. Tell them to set their hearts on fire again for me and not let it burn out. Tell them to catch others on fire so they can live. Tell my people. I want my kids back. Get to work. Let your light shine and work for me.

December 2, 2013

Good morning. I slept in way too long today.

Same thing…so I don't need to say it.

I know. I'll get better some day.

I know.

So what's going on, what's the word?

Still that I love you. That'll always be my word for you!

That's cool. I like that. Especially on these days back from a long absence and I feel ashamed for not coming to meet. I need to not just know that you love me, but accept your love for me.

It's a different thing, for sure. That's where people miss it. The head knowledge versus believing and accepting and receiving it for themselves. Just what your pastor said yesterday.

Mmm...are you pleased with him?

Oh yes, I am. He's obedient and he listens for and to me.

That's where I need to be, huh? Listening FOR you. Like, OUTSIDE of this time, huh?

Yes. And yes, I saw your heart. I know what you were about to ask. I know that you feel like you can't trust this or ME because of the house. Listening and trusting me are choices YOU have to make. I can't make you believe. YOU have to choose to do that yourself. Now what you got upset about—I didn't say when and I didn't say how AND you said you didn't want to talk about the house anymore. You didn't come back to ask for clarity or understanding. You took it into your own hands, made your own assumptions, and chose to believe that you heard me wrong because it was all a lie. You can't follow directions because YOU can't figure it out—how I'm going to work and do things. If I said raise the limit on the house, then raise the limit. You WON'T see your house on that list, because you lowered it back down to what you could afford.

I still don't know if I want to do this. I get hurt. I don't like to want things that I can't have. It hurts my heart. I feel let down and disappointed. I don't want to be like that again. Even though I can see why we didn't move in Illinois, I still wanted that house, and I don't feel like you answered my prayer when I said to take the desire away.

Maybe because your desire for that house wasn't bad or a wrong one. The location wasn't the right one, but perhaps what you liked about the house you can still have....do you see what I mean? Plus over time you DID start to dislike things about the house. You didn't like the basement.

I know.

So what, Jo?? Why do you feel so let down about something you can look back on and be happy about not having?

I don't know.

You're putting me in the category of your husband who has let you down and disappointed you, so you try your hardest not expect anything from him so you're not hurt again. I'm not that person. I'm not a husband figure. That which you have with/about your husband, you need to deal with. But right now I'm talking about us.

I'm God. I'm not a husband, I'm a father. I don't let the bride down, I take care of her. I know what's best for her...even when she doesn't see it—or even if she doesn't agree at the time. I know all, I see all, I take care of my people. So if something doesn't line up with what YOU want, then you have to decide how you're going to deal with that, because I'm taking care of you. I know what I have for you.

Those bumps in the road that you're on are just bumps. They're not defining of who you are and what your purpose is. They just create new ways for you to get where

I have you going. It's bumpy. There are ups and downs. Sometimes people get upset or their feelings get hurt. BUT I KNOW MY PLAN FOR YOU. You have to choose if you're going to stay with me or not.

Okay. So what do you want me to do about the house?

You can look for a house. You, personally, have to stop letting things—your desires—upset you because you can't have them now. Dear, that's a tantrum, do you realize that?

No, I guess I hadn't. I felt like if I wasn't jealous of people, that was good enough. I didn't realize I actually still had an issue. I feel like I'm like that in shopping, though. I'd rather not know what I don't have or create wants, because I'm out there looking around at stuff.

Right. The "stuff" isn't bad. It's what you do with it or what you do to get the stuff. Where is it driving your heart? You remember when Jesse Duplantis was describing his home [in Heaven], and it had those things in there that he liked so much?

Yes.

Well, dear, if you don't have desires on earth, do you think they'll translate to desires in heaven? It's OKAY to want things! But again, it's what you do to get them, and what you do with them, that brings the problems. It's okay to go to the store and see nice things, and even make a wish list, as long as you're still content with what you DO have. It's that unhealthy drive that gets people in trouble.

Just control your emotions, your drive to get the things that you see. You still have to make wise, sound choices with your money. That's what's an issue for you all now— your

spending. It's out of control. You all see something you want or like and then buy it. There is no self-discipline going on in your house. You all seriously need to work on that. I'm glad you have set up money to go into your savings each period, but you all need to get on a budget because you're just wasting money each month. And YOU need self-control with the grocery and food bill.

Yes sir.

You still feel unsettled. Jo, what do you want to know?

I want to know when we're going to sell this house? When we need to have it cleaned so we can be ready for a showing!? Where the house is? How much is it so I know where to look? Is it a house we can actually afford? Are we going to be outside of our means so we struggle and have to rely on you for a house?? How much are we going to pay for the house? How will we know when we see the house? I just want to know everything, that's all. Yes, I can hear the tantrum in my voice, you don't need to ask.

Well, here's the deal. IF I sat here and told you all the answers to those questions, you wouldn't believe me. You'd doubt you heard right because things look to be the opposite. So do I tell my daughter what she really is asking to know? Or do I tell her what she needs to know to give her some kind of peace and rest right now? Because if I tell her the answers, it's not going to bring her to a place of peace—not because IT can't or I can't, but because SHE won't let it. So what would YOU do???

If it was me?

Yes, if you were in My shoes and your daughter was asking all of these questions, how would you handle it?

I wouldn't tell her. We do this all the time, huh? We let our kids know we're going somewhere but never tell them where we're going. Oh gosh. Is that this mean? Should we stop??

You think it's mean?

Well, we do it for the surprise effect, but when you do it, it doesn't feel that fun. And yeah, surprises from you are nice, but our trips to get to the destinations are a lot shorter than your trips…

Hmmm. I guess so…to you.

So you're not going to answer anything?

Well, like I said, are you going to believe any of it?

Probably not. But I could use it as a method of confirming something. I think the difference is that the drive to make what you have knowledge of come to pass takes control and takes over. It's driving you to make something happen within your own power. And by NOT knowing what's in store, you're relying more on the Holy Spirit to be in control and for God to do what he wants to do. Did I say that right?

Yes. You try to do it with your own hands instead of mine. You said it. So what do we do, dear?

Mmm…I think you should tell me what to cap the house search at.

I already did.

I know. I don't know if I said it out loud on here. I think it was talk during the day, wasn't it?

Yes.

So that IS what you want me to do? Take the search to $500k?

See, you're already doubting even though that WAS confirmation of what you got before. You hadn't written it out; you remembered hearing my voice for that—during the day. And you STILL question and doubt it's authenticity…

Well, what do you want me to do? Trust everything in my head???

We've already talked about this. And that's why it's time to print and go back and read, Jo. We've talked about the voices in your head and how they will line up. I don't need you to say it; I know what you're thinking—that you're not qualified enough. You haven't had enough time with me to trust what I'm saying to you. You're not sure of yourself and if you know enough.

Jo, do I need a list of your limitations? No. I am God. I created you. I gifted you. I called you. I'm using you for my purpose and my glory. I don't need you to tell me what's wrong with you or what's not right. Stop comparing yourself to others. Recognize they started somewhere. They didn't just appear at the forefront. I have a plan for you; just go with me. But when I give you something—a word or an answer—I don't need you to question it.

Your husband doesn't question it OR you or your hearing. He believes. And you don't even know what he has to base his belief on. He just does. And that amazes you because you don't feel like you've proven yourself to him. Or anyone else for that matter. But I don't need that. I need you to be the willing vessel that you say you are. So when I speak, you speak. Without hesitation. Do you understand?

Yes.

Good. Now raise your search parameters. Take it to $500k with five bedrooms. The location is south of 64. You can search, or you can wait, but I suggest that you print or at least look back through these communions, because I've given you other indicators of your house. You just have to believe it. We must both leave now. We will talk tomorrow. Please go to bed at a decent hour so you can get up before your children and talk to me. This is too late in the day to be apart from them. I love you. Don't get down from anything today; just let it soak in and change your thought system. I love you.

Thanks. I love you, too.

December 3, 2013

Good morning.

Good morning.

Are you well this morning?!

I am.

That's good. I like you!

Well *that's* good! What are your plans for today?

I'm going to work on Etsy, make some bracelets, do my bible study, and then YARN because I'm behind!! What are *your* plans for me today?!?!?

Oh…I want you to do what you have planned. I want you to feel productive today. You need that. That sense of accomplishment.

Yes, I know that I do appreciate that feeling.

And you *do* know that it shouldn't drive you because you're not ALWAYS going to see the fruit of your labor, right?

Yes, I know. But it's hard still. That's why I like crafts, because you can see your fruit right away. AGH! My friend's gift. I need to work on that today! I need your help.

I know. Would you like to ask me or do you just want me to start?! What do you want from me?

Well, it's supposed to be scriptures, but my track record with scriptures is not that good. I don't hear well. I think I'm hearing references that don't even exist!!

So what if I give you words and then YOU find the reference that goes along with it. That way you get your hands in the homework as well [wink].

Okay, that sounds like a good plan.

Well, of course [chuckling].

Okay. Are we ready now?

I'm always ready.

Right. Okay.

Daughter: I want my desires to be your desire. I want only the best for you. I want your cup to run over. I want you to feel my spring of life, living waters. I want you to feel my presence and know that it's me AND that I'm ALWAYS with you. Even in those dark places when you feel that you're all alone. I am with you there. I know you know I'll never leave you, but I want you to know that my heart BURNS for you. I am so passionate about my relationship

with you—OUR relationship. I don't want anything or anyone to get in the way of that.

I want you to be hungry for me. To seek me. To FIND ME. I want you to come to me first. Not just for the big things, but for all the little "small" things...because I don't think they're small. They involve you. I want to be apart of your every move, every thought. I want to you to come to me for discipline issues, for anger, for love, for wisdom....anything that you deal with, I want you to come to me first. Ask me, I'll show you. I'll answer you. You'll know my presence and the answers that I give freely, but it takes time. It takes relationship. And yes, you DO HAVE TIME! I give time and I take it away. And to you, I give my time.

I'm here for you all the time. I'm waiting on you. Come to me. I'm here. I'm waiting on you. I'm hungry for you. My heart is for YOU. I see you in the back, in your room, on your knees, seeking me there, but I need you to seek me in the front. Out. With people, with friends. Let me guide you with words to speak. You've got stories. You've gotten these words to share, but let me guide you and tell you who, what, when to share.

I love that you share your testimonies to help my other children. I am so proud of you. But I want you to experience my love and relationship and presence in a deeper way now. This IS your new season. I want to take you to higher heights and deeper depths with me. I'm ready to take you places you haven't been before. Are you ready to go with me? I want to take you back to that place where you were young and carefree and happy.

Do you remember that place? It's far back. It's in me. I am those happy thoughts and feelings. I am what has carried you through. Let me carry you now. Yes, come and REST in me. My presence brings the joy and the peace that your soul longs for. I give that. I am those things. Come now and find REST in me. Remember, I am the one who gives time. You do have the time. Give it to me. Make me first in your life. Seek me first. Every day. Set life aside because you know it will be okay. But these new levels in me require a new thing in you. I'm ready. Now come and seek me.

1 Kings 9:1-3
Psalm 23:5
John 4:14
John 7:38
Rev 7:17
Matt 6:33
1 Kings 22:5
Deuteronomy 6:4-5
I Corinthians 8:3
Ephesians 3:17-19
1 Corinthians 2:9-10

December 4, 2013

Good morning.

Morning. Yes, I said it's time.

Ugh…I sure hope I'm not hearing you correctly. I hope that you're NOT talking about the house and someone coming this week before Friday. Please tell me I'm thinking about the wrong thing.

You said you wanted a heads up.

Umm....I'm going to choose to doubt this conversation. I don't think I have time to look silly [and bossy] trying to clean up today when I'm supposed to be doing all this other stuff.

Okay. Why don't you just schedule your time and stick to it. If you do, you'll see that you DO have time to clean your house. It may not be as good as Dell would want it, but it'll be clean. You'll at least be at peace when you go to bed at night.

Ugh. Seriously? Is this for my own peace of mind or is someone coming?

I don't need to answer, because you already said that you're not going to believe.

UGH! I want to say let's talk about something else, but I have a tendency to ask about the house and "when are we moving..." argh. Okay. I'll straighten up. Hey, you want to tell me about the weather then...are we having bible study tomorrow?!?!

You should keep all of your preparations the same. I'm just asking you to clean your house at the same time.

Okay. I have a lot to do that I haven't written down. This month is going to go quick, and I'm just focusing on this week.

That's okay. It's all going to work out.

Now you have me looking all around the room at things that I need to deal with. I'm distracted. Probably too distracted to sit and do this AND my bible study work.

Well, take everything off of your surfaces so you can see it all and then put it where it goes. That will help your

house immensely and lighten your stress if someone calls before you're ready.

Okay. So is there anything "real" that we need to talk about? This doesn't seem like a very polite conversation from me.

I can handle your real emotions, Jo. Just like a dad would. I know life is frustrating at times, and you feel overwhelmed. But come to me, that's what you're supposed to do. Cast all your cares upon me. Ask me for help, peace, guidance. That's what I do. That's what I give. So just come to me and ask for those things.

Okay.

Okay. I'm actually going to let you go early today because I want you to get in your word and get your bible study done. I want you to finish ALL that you want and need to do today. So go, but go in peace. You can make it. You can get it all done—WITHOUT stress and fussing at the kids. So write it down, stick to your plan, and get it all done, okay?

Yes sir.

Good. I love you.

I love you, too.

December 7, 2013

Morning.

Hello.

How are you?

I'm well.

Good. I'm sorry about the past few days. Bible study and then I slept in.

I know you enjoyed some extra rest and your snow day.

Maybe I cannot do these always early in the morning. Maybe I could do them at night like those other ladies.

If you'll come, yes. It's not a problem with me what time we meet. It's that you don't come later in the day or at night. So it's up to you, really. No me.

Okay. So what did I miss the past few days?!?!

Well, you know I love you.

Yes!

Okay. I was just going to tell you about a few people.

Really?

Yes. And now I see your head falling back so much that I'm not sure you going to make it today!

Oh, I'm sorry. I'm awake.

Mmm hmmm. Yes, I wanted to tell you about some people. [At first I saw a woman in a kitchen in front of her cabinets. I think it was a black and white scene. Maybe it was early in the morning, but her back was to me, and it was like she was getting a coffee mug out of the cabinet. The second time he said it, she had turned around and looked as if she was setting it down on a table. But her arms were apart as if she had a whole serving tray that she was setting down, not just one mug. And in both scenes it felt like it was the same friend we just talked about, so it makes me doubt I can hear… especially after taking days off, really.] **Okay, if you're done….**

you can hear just fine. Let's go. I said I wanted to talk about people.

Is this for my benefit or theirs? Am I supposed to share these words with them? I hate that I AM so tired…

Told ya! Jo, if you would come back tonight, we could do this tonight. Or even before you leave for the game, which you'll have the time. But without rest, you're really no good for yourself or me—or the kids! You need to get more rest!

I know. Am I one of your "persons?"

No, but I'm going to talk to you while you're here.

Okay. I do keep drifting. I'm going to come back after breakfast. That's my plan.

Okay. We will see you then. You CAN do it, Jo. And you know it's better that way because you have the tree this afternoon.

Yes. I'll do it.

Okay then. Later.

December 9, 2013

And good morning. I failed. But I guess you knew I was going to, huh?

I knew you weren't going to make it back, but I'm not calling you a failure, Jo. Listening to and obeying my voice is a process. You are not ready to drop everything for me yet. You may get there, but when you don't come when I'm waiting, I still don't call you a failure. You're human. I know that you make mistakes and get caught

up by distractions. They're all choices, remember? It's a choice who you're going to serve—and when. What you need to do is say what you need to say when you come back and allow us to pick back up where we left off. Don't carry that weight of guilt once you've been reconciled to me, do you understand?

Yes.

Good.

I'm sorry for not coming back the other day, will you forgive me?

Yes. But understand that it wasn't a sin; you just didn't choose to come back. I didn't order you to come back. I told you I had a message for you, and you were going to come back later to get it. Do we need to keep going with this?

No, I get it.

Okay, good. Then let's get started. I love you. Always have, always will. You can't change that. I created you, I love you, I want to spend eternity with you. Yes, you make me smile, too! I chose my son to die for you. He loves you, too. We both want what's best for you. Even if it's something that doesn't line up with what you want. We all agree that you need to change the order of your day. You could be so much more productive if you would just focus on your task at hand. Whether it be school, craft, cleaning or meals—you need to set the time and stick to it. Get it done. Then you'll have more time to spend with us. But you waste so much time with useless things. You must choose differently in order to get where you need to be with us.

Okay.

You're going to be okay. I don't say these words to upset you or get you down. It should motivate you to want to do better since it's actually quite easy for you to improve.

Okay.

Okay. So do better today. Make a list of things that need to be done. And get back to planning your meals; you've gotten sloppy with that, as well. You can do better, Jo, so do it!

I'll try. I just feel so unmotivated, tired, lazy…

Well that's two-fold. One is because you're not getting enough rest, and two is because you're not taking care of your body. Both your physical and spiritual body. You need to work out and spend more time in prayer and reading. You're not taking care of yourself. If you will do those three things you will be better all the way around. It IS that simple. You just have to choose to do it.

Okay. And of course, I'm going to put off until tomorrow to do it because I've started so late today…and I need to get my kids back to school.

Yeah. Why don't you catch up on the school stuff today, write the list of what you need to do and get outside the home, work on your meals, and then plan your schedule for tomorrow. Today you need to grade and make their schedule. I want you to start fresh, and that means going to bed tonight so you can get up refreshed tomorrow and ready to hit the floor running. Literally. For real.

Okay. I'm tired already just thinking about it!

Yeah. That's because you went to bed too late last night and hit snooze all morning. Go and take care of Josh and get started on today. You can do it. I'm with you. I love you.

December 10, 2013

Good morning. Going to try to get a lot done today though I'm super tired. Kind of feel like being less ambitious and going back to bed after this. I can exercise another day and not get the kids up so early for school…I need to be awake to be a good teacher today, right???

Mmm…. I'm not going to answer that the way you want me to.

I know.

Okay, good. So let's move on then so we can get more done today.

Ugh k…

I want your light to shine, Jo. It's not shining the way I created it to. I need you lighten up.

So you mean my light of faith or don't be so serious??

[Almost like a smile/smirk.] Mmm…should I let you just figure that one out on your own?!? You need to be my example at all times…and you're not always doing that. Hello. Jo.

I'm too tired. It wasn't all my fault last night. All the kids were up except one. I'm so tired. Can't I just go back to sleep???

It is a choice.

Ugh… You make it sound so bad to have a choice.

Well, you have to remember that it [a person's choice] doesn't always lean in my favor! When the choice is to go my way, then of course I like it.

[I'm so tired.]

Yeah. Don't think you're going to do things the BEST way today. You may make some good choices, but I think you're going to fall into some other temptations. And though I'm saying that, I'm not saying that you're a kid or a mistake or you're going to sin with your choices today. I'm just saying that they may not line up with what I think is best for you. Do you understand the difference?

Yes. I think I'm going back to sleep for a while. Is there anything else you want to say to me?

Sure. Always. But you're right, you're not being a good listener right now…I need a willing and able vessel, and right now you're lacking a bit.

Sorry. Okay. Bye, Lord. I'm so sorry. I don't think I can do it right now. I'll try better tomorrow.

Okay, dear. Bye.

December 11, 2013

Thanks for helping me wake up this morning.

You're welcome.

It *is* making me think that something is up today that I had to be up early for…even though I keep reminding myself that I asked you to help get me up this morning. Was I supposed to get up in the 5 o'clock hour before I actually did?

You could have, but I was just getting you ready. Your days do need to start earlier if you're going to get your things done.

I need to learn how to focus more, huh?

Yes.

Right now it's like I have to get up early to allow for all the time I waste, huh? That picture with thirty-seven hours left for working your dreams really has me thinking. I guess what matters is figuring out how many hours I'm with kids since I don't have a regular forty hour work week. I probably need to look at and get with my schedule too. Maybe just stick to it.

Yes. Your time IS scheduled, but you're not working the schedule. I'm glad you pulled it back out, though.

I really feel like I need to pray. Is that the case?

Yes, it is. I need you to pray more. YOU need to pray more. You can't just be limited to our conversations. The Holy Spirit has things he needs to work in you, too.

Okay. Hey, how's Denise??

Hmm...she's fine. Just keep praying for her. She's felt some opposition, so she's trying to be wise. Plus it's the holiday, you know.

Yeah, I know. It just seemed really strange. Feels like it just dropped off...I didn't know if she got in "trouble."

It'll be okay. She'll be okay. This is her time of awakening, but she'll make it through this and come out strong in the end.

Okay. That's good. I need to read more too, huh?

Most definitely!

Miracle's bible is gonna be cool. She's going to know more than I do soon, huh?

She does know a lot already. They're doing well. Encourage them; don't push them. They're reading their bibles. That's good.

Okay. What am I supposed to be doing right now?

Praying. I want you to pray—in tongues, too. I want you to pray throughout the day. You need to learn to stay in my presence, my spirit, my atmosphere. Learn to stay with me. Walk with me—all day long. Not just in the morning.

Okay. Will I ever have an encounter and see Jesus?

[Laughing] You will see what I have in store for you!

Awww...okay! I'll go pray, though the sleepy bug has caught me again.

[Laughing.] Goodbye, Jo. [shaking his head.]

Bye Daddy!

December 12, 2013

I don't have much to say today.

That's fine. Your job is to listen.

Uh, wow. Okay. So what's up?

I want you to listen to me more. The Holy Spirit revealed to you that YOU have self-control issues more than you previously thought, and I'm glad that you were able to see that. But I need you to listen more. To ME. You're still not getting that you can come to me anytime, with anyone,

anywhere. You're not seeking me when you should be. When people are talking to you, most of them need or could use a word, but you're not coming to me to get it. And it's not just about you not wanting to or feeling like it, it's about you keeping them from receiving what I have for them. You ARE being selfish. In more than just your home with your husband and children. You're being selfish with others. You're doing what you tell people NOT to do, and that's keeping me to yourself. Do you see that??

Yes.

Okay then. You need to get it together, Jo. I told you to print these out and start reading them. I told you to come to me. I told you to listen to me—but you're not doing it. And these are the SAME THINGS you fuss at your kids about, and you're doing it to me. Now what?

I don't know. And maybe I need to just stay here in this feeling so I can see what my kids feel. So just give me a minute to feel bad about myself.

Okay.

It kind of reminds me of when my husband is always fussing at me 'cause I'm not doing what he says or REMEMBERING what he told me to do, so it seems like I'm never doing right.

It's easy to feel like you're stupid or less than, isn't it? Now you know better than to stay there, though sometimes you struggle with that. But imagine how your kids feel who aren't as easily pulled out of that pit of "less than?" They need help don't they?

Yes.

Okay. You need to change both your method AND your cleanup process [and yes, this does apply for when you're in the church]. You may give a harsh word or rebuke, but if you don't encourage them with something after cutting them, you're going to leave them there to bleed out. So get it together, Jo. Learn what you need to learn. THAT'S WHY I SAID PRINT THESE OUT!! There's wisdom in these times together, and you don't catch it all in one go. You need to keep reading.

So what about my kids?

It's not even that you need me to tell you what to say and how to say it. It's about you thinking before you speak. And part of that thinking is coming to ME and asking me about a situation. If you're going to pause to stop and think, why not get my wisdom and counsel in the matter? That way your words are wise, and you can better handle the situation. COME TO ME! I believe I've been saying that for awhile too.

Yes, you have.

Okay then.

Okay. Dare I ask if there's anything else you want to say to me?

You need to take time for me. More than this. You need to clean up your afternoon & evening schedule, and you need to make time for studying these, reading my word, reading books. Something beneficial to your spiritual body.

One problem is that I can't do yarn and read at the same time.

I understand. There are other things to watch that are beneficial to you. And you notice the difference of playing

them [the DVR or DVD recordings] and NOT playing them, don't you?

Yes.

You need to put Sid Roth back on.

Yeah, I know.

Good. So do it tonight.

Okay. Are we done?

Yes, we are. But remember, these are not one time messages. Take the time to come back here and do what you need to do to best print them out. Yes, you're going to have to put in a lot of time to prepare these and edit them. SO BE IT! Get over it. Do it because I said so!!

Yes sir!

Okay, I love you. Now go!

I love you, too.

January 3, 2014

Good morning. I know it's been a REALLY long time. Not only do I feel bad, but I feel far. I feel guilty about it, I've missed it but recognize it HAS to be something that I GET UP EARLY to do. I can't sleep in with kids AND get this done.

I know. It's been hard on both of us. I missed you, too!

You're not mad, are you?

No, I'm not mad. I'm just glad that you're back. Any place you want to start?

My sister wanted me to ask you what you thought about the wedding.

Why doesn't she ask me?

Well, I don't know! That's what I'd like to think, too!

Hmmm....well remind her that she can come to me, too. It's just a matter of her training her ear to hear me. Then SHE can ask me all those questions she has about her kids instead of asking you to ask me!

Oh that sounds great to me! [Smiling.]So, did you want to say anything about the wedding?

I gave it to you. [When we first started, my mind wandered out of order.] **They're covered. They were already married. It was all for show. If she wants more than that, then she can come to me about it.**

Okay. Fine with me. I don't know what's upsetting her so much. I must have missed it, because I was just relaxing and not working a function for once.

That's fine. She can come to me.

Okay. I don't think I have anything else right now. I'm gonna need your help with the other assignment I have for someone.

Oh yes, that's fine. How about you sincerely pray about it and see what the Holy Spirit gives you for her, too,

Okay, cool. Okay now...what do YOU have for me?

Well, I do want you to print this out so you can go back and look through it. Look for words that ministered to you, homework and assignments you were given, and just simply re-read what I've spoken to you. Despite what your husband thinks—you need to print! For you!!

Okay.

And I know you enjoyed reading, and I saw you looking at all those books in the bookstore and wondering about what and when you'd write. That's okay to do; don't feel bad. There is a book inside of you, Jo. You just don't know what it is right now. But you will. You'll know it when you see it.

God, I need your help this year. Right now in this seeming month of consecration. I feel like we worked and fought so hard to get out of our previous church, and now that we're in the next place we don't know what to do anymore. Like we're in our own wilderness, by our own hands. The big, organized church isn't telling us what to do, and we've forgotten how to function and operate and maintain on our own. We've forgotten how to keep our own spiritual man and lives up without being told what to do each step of the way. This month pray over the windows [banners of topics that hung during consecration], this month build, this month sow, work at this event, practice for this show. Now we have free will, and we don't know what to do. We've been programmed to be reliant for eleven years, and now it's like we're falling apart because we forgot how to think and operate on our own. Wow. I DON'T want to be here for forty years though.

Good. I'm glad you see it that way. It's in your hands. But now that you see it, you're responsible for it. I'm not going to bail you out or give you step-by-steps. You know what you need to do [pray]. And whether you go at it alone or you wait for your corporate body—that's a decision you'll have to make. But looking at your past, waiting hasn't proven fruitful for you. You've fallen apart; sin is running throughout your home; your kids are disrespectful and

mean to each other; you're not happy with your family and how you ALL are operating.

So choose this day who you will serve and rise up and follow. Don't wait for everyone to get on board and rearrange their schedules. They may not be at the place of desperation or even care enough to change or see there's a problem within your home. If you see it, you're responsible for it. So take action. Stop being lazy, stop putting things off, stop waiting for the "perfect" time. It's always perfect when you're with me. Don't wait on the others, Jo. You've been waiting too long and it's tearing you up inside.

Just do what's right; things will change; they will follow. I'm not telling you to override your leader—I'm telling you to do what's right for you, your relationship [with me], and for your family. Things will fall back into order. But I KEEP telling you and sending people to tell you that you HAVE TO PRAY & WORSHIP me. You feel weighted down with the burden to pray as a family. I know this. I'm telling you—just start. Don't take over, but just start doing it. Watch how it unfolds.

Okay.

Okay. Think that was enough for our first day back?!

Yes.

Okay, good. So are we month-to-month now, or will I see you again soon [smiling]?

I love you, Daddy.

I love you too, dear.

I'm gonna see you soon.

Good! Now get that room cleaned so we can get the rest of the house in order!

Yes sir!

January 7, 2014

Hey Daddy, sorry that I'm short on time today.

It's okay. I'm going to have you get some work done downstairs today. You're going to work on your book.

[Not sure I heard that correctly. I thought I was getting that I was going to work on getting my print out together/combined. I guess that would be a notebook/journal book for me, huh? Okay I get it now.]

You doubt your hearing so much. I don't know why!

You know that's not correct, right? That YOU DON'T KNOW something [laughing].

Right. I bet you know that I mean you should get it by now since we keep going over this same thing over and over and over. YOU'RE the one that doesn't get it!

Yeah, I guess. So we're trying to go back to school today WITH Daddy at home….not sure how it will go.

Well number one, don't stress the kids with your time schedule. You're not a classroom. You don't have a bell that's going to ring regardless of whether everyone is done or not. Be relaxed. Today at least…while you learn to relax a little bit every day. You're too uptight. You make yourself stress out whether YOU realize you're stressed or not. Your body pays the price for what you're holding onto. Your family does, too.

You need to focus on the things that REALLY matter. I think your idea of redefining success is a great thing for you to do. I think your new book will help with that, too. You've got to put things in order the right way—then let everything ELSE fall into place. You need to take care of US [our relationship], then you [spiritually & physically]—the rest [mental/emotional]—will fall into place with those two in place, and then your family. I'm talking about cleaning, planning meals, being a good steward of what you spend. THOSE are the things that are important in your home.

And when you do those in THAT order—those things you THINK I left out—like devotion and praying with your kids—those things will automatically be in there, because they'll be running off of your personal life.

Okay. So what about if someone asks how I/we do it. Do I need to write it all out for them?

YES. And you should be. I DO want you to work on that homework for Kay. And I know that seems hard for you to remember how it all began and what you do here, etc. I will help you. We're going to work on it together because I want you to get it done. You're not finished with her, and she's not the first and only one that you're going to coach along. You NEED to get this all written out and in order.

But like I said, I'm going to help you because I want these to be MY words that flow out of me to you and through you. You will not misguide them if you speak through me. That's why OUR relationship is so important—because it's not just for you. It's for the other women that I'm bringing up behind you.

Okay. And there is TIME for all of this right?

Yes, because you're going to learn how to MAKE time. You're going to readjust, re-analyze, rediscover what's truly important in your life, and you're going to let other things go. On your own. Without kicking and screaming!

Good. Okay. I'm excited.

You should be. It's exciting to follow me. You Christians ARE too down. You're right for noticing all the rejoicing in the Bible. You should ALL be excited about me and my work and my kingdom. THIS IS AWESOME!!!

[Smiling.] Okay.

I know you have to go. I'm releasing you now. But you need to be back on your computer with me today. Don't let the day slip away from you.

Okay, I won't.

January 8, 2014

Morning, Daddy. I love you.

I love you, too, dear. My eyes are on you. You make me smile.

[Grin.] That's cool Daddy.

I want you to know you're just at the beginning. I have things coming for you, and you're on the brink. We need to tighten up your schedule. Your day has to be more structured. It can all fit, but we have to get it in line and then work the plan. We can't have big gaps and lulls of time, because you're going to have to be productive in all that you do. Now there will be times of rest, you'll get

that. And you'll get your time with your yarn! But we have to get our work done. First things first.

Okay, I get that.

Good. Today I need you to pick up what you didn't do yesterday. Even with school and Bible study tomorrow, you should have time to work on putting the book together. Copy and paste is all I'm asking you to do right now so you're a step closer to printing it out. Go ahead and confirm with Dell that you have the ink that you'll need. You know you're on your last ream of paper, and you will need something to put it all in once printed out.

Okay.

That's it, Jo. We're doing baby steps right now. You need to be thinking about Kay and when you can meet with her regularly and also on the questions that she asked you.

I almost feel like I need YOU to answer those! I don't think I know all the answers.

The Holy Spirit will help you remember what you need to remember. Put on the mind of Christ, and ask the Holy Spirit to help you with them. We're not going to just GIVE you the answers, though. The answers are yours, and they're already within you. You just have to figure out how to pull them out. It's going to take time. Put it in your schedule!! It's not lollygagging to do things that are benefitting the Kingdom, Jo. I know it's hard for you to sit down and "rest" and do work on your computer because it LOOKS like nothing. But it IS. It IS something. And it's for my kingdom and for my glory. You NEED to take the time to do these things. How do you think a book is

ever going to come out of you unless you learn to sit and write?!

I don't know!

Well I do. I keep saying you're in training right now. But you probably forgot that because you haven't printed out our past sessions yet!

Ha ha. Okay. I hear ya. I will work on it today.

Good. I know you will. Okay, shower up and get back down to get your workday started. Love you!

I love you, too.

January 10, 2014

Good morning. I am a bit distracted today.

I know. But you're here.

[Smile.] Thanks for being understanding.

Always.

I need to ask you about this mission trip. Before we go through this whole process with the visa and all…we never even ASKED you if she should go or if you want her to go. We just jumped in because it just seemed like an obvious thing to do. She wanted to go. I wanted her to go. It's for your kingdom. So why not?!? So what do YOU want?

This is why I don't like asking direct, personal questions. I hear things I either don't want to or sound too easy or sound like something I'd want to hear. AGH!!! Okay. I'm going to try again [I took a break and bite of food…mind clear now]. Do you want Miracle to go on the trip?

Yes.

On THIS Missions trip? With Global Awakening's Youth Power Invasion?? THAT missions trip?

Yes.

Well, who is going to go with her???

You'll see.

Ugh. This is not cool. Can I ask around to try and find some people?

You can.

Errr… is my niece going? [I think she's going. First I got "you'll see" and then two yeses, but I doubt.] So we need to press with the visa application?

Yes.

Okay then. Let's talk about the house, shall we? Since I realize I've been avoiding all these important questions and discussions.

What do you want to ask, Jo?

I don't know, but Dell is getting frustrated now, so that makes it little uncomfortable, you know? And on one hand I feel like we should pack up, and on the other hand—we need our stuff. It's just frustrating with the unknown. What are we doing?

You're waiting. And while you wait, you get ready. So get ready. For a showing, for selling, for moving. Just get ready. YOU be ready when I release it. Don't do all this complaining and then spaz out when the time comes because you're not ready. Get ready. Be ready.

Okay.

I see your baby steps, but it IS time to pick up your pace.

Okay.

You want to ask about that other house before we get off of here?

Oh yeah, I guess.

Pull it up.

Well that was silly. It's gone already. I don't get your point. See how this is NOT fun to me?? Ugh. So we're starting over AGAIN, huh?

Yes. And my timing is perfect.

Ugh…just temper tantrum day…fine. I'm done with this. This is why I don't talk about it. It's just plain frustrating.

YOU just be ready to go when it's time to go. Don't think you have to know where you're going in order to be ready. Abraham had no clue, but he went. You be the same. Ready to go when I say go. Now go. Start your day. Do your work. Be productive. Bye.

Bye.

January 13, 2014

Good morning. I don't know what to say today.

That's because you let shame and guilt get in the way. I don't do that to you. Just come to me. As you are. Mistakes and all. I accept you.

Okay. Hmm….give me some more lyrics!

[laughing]. You're funny.

You know it! So what's on your mind today?

Well today I want you to rest in my peace.

Really? It's a Monday, school day, and I have to go out in the middle of the day…plus practices tonight. Doesn't seem really restful and peaceful.

Noo…..resting in my peace is something you do anytime. It doesn't fill a block of time on your to do list. It's what you do AMIDST those things. Resting in my peace means taking all those things you have to do—and resting IN them. Not letting them stress you or get you down but just living and walking in my peace that I'm with you, I care for you, I'm going to take care of you. Just resting in the knowledge that I've got you!

Okay.

Yeah. So do that today.

That's it?

Well, you have to work on your schedule. You've got to get your life back in order—planning meals, planning your OWN cleaning schedule, planning time just for you and just for us. You need down time, but you also need to keep your work time productive. You're slacking too much. I want you to SEE the benefit of all the hours you have in the day. You have plenty of time to get done what you need to get done. You just HAVE to stay focused and not get distracted or lazy.

Okay. I will try to do better today.

Okay. Start now. When you close this, delete fifty emails.

Really? That's what you want me to do?!?

It's part of cleaning up your life, your workspace—so that you have better productivity.

Okay. Cool. What else?

Then I want you to consolidate ten more days of your book.

Okay.

Then I want you to plan the meals for the week. Then you should get some computer work done--mails, typing out notes that are lying around—then you get to throw away paper trash!

Yes! Okay. I can do all those.

And you can do them quickly. It really should NOT take you thirty minutes to do all that. Here. Set a timer and then start. Okay?

Yes. Okay.

Great. GO!

January 14, 2014

And hellooooo! Thanks for letting me do my bible study first. That helped me a lot.

I know. You need more time in your word anyway. Like, on your own, not just because you're doing bible study.

Yeah, I know. I'm really bad about that. I really need to memorize more scripture too, but it's so hard. Hey. My memory. What's up with that? Why is it so bad? Is it normal, really, or do I need to get it checked out?

You don't need to get it checked out. There is a bond between you and Brianna. A connection in your timing.

Well is it something I need to identify before it can go away? Or what's the deal?

You need to fast that out.

Uhh…seems like that would take a LONG time since we've had problems for so long. Like it's deep rooted and won't want to leave right away…like in a one or two day fast! Ha ha.

You are right. It's not a short one. You're going to have to be dedicated to your cause and your focus. And I'm not sure who's going to want to join with you. This is something you may have to do on your own.

Uuuuggggghhhhh.

And THAT'S why it's not done right now. Your willingness, or lack of willingness. You're not at your point of desperation. Which I can't see why you would choose to NOT better yourself and your daughter. If I tell you that the breakthrough you need is a the end of a fast, why wouldn't you do it?

Because I don't know how long the fast is going to be. And what KIND of fast. You want to tell me the parameters???

Why? So you can decide when it's convenient for you and your schedule? So you can pick the "best time" for you to get your breakthrough? That's crazy! No. When you're serious and you start it, then we'll talk. But until then, I've already given you that it's not short.

Hmph. Fine okay. I'll be praying about when to die to myself.

'Cause that's what it is.

Yeah. So now I'm going to feel guilty all day, huh?

No. You don't have to feel that way. It's just a matter of how bad and how soon do you want the change you SAY you've been wanting? It's all up to you, Jo.

Yeah. Okay. I feel like all I do lately is throw tantrums and get upset with you.

Yeah. Like Gabi, huh?

Yeah.

But the good thing is you're still here. Many of my children get mad and throw tantrums and walk away; some never come back. So I'm glad that you're at least still here—even if you are grumpy because you can't have your way.

So what's the deal with this weight?

You're doing good.

Are you okay with me doing the side job? I'm sorry I didn't ask you first [OR my husband].

Yeah. You handled that out of order. And even though it was okay with him in the end, I don't want you to do that again. You knew it was wrong, and you did it anyway. It was very sneaky, and I don't like that at all.

Yes sir.

But I do like the side job for you. I know you're looking at people who need the help, not just because you're trying to make a sale. Focus on HOW to address them so you don't offend them and put them off. Use WISDOM, Jo! You have it; so use it!! Do work on that cheat sheet you're thinking of. Keep studying the product. It will all come together.

Okay! I want to do that now!

I know. Go ahead. Just remember today you have to die to yourself in order to see the change you're looking for.

Okay Dad. I hear you. I'm going to try. Harder.

Good. I love you, babe.

I love you too. Oh hey—the dancing stuff?

[Smiling.] We'll talk about it later.

Okay. Love you. Bye.

Bye.

January 15, 2014

This isn't fun anymore. Is it only for a season?

No, it should be a lifetime.

Well what's my deal? This seems like a burden and didn't used to be that way.

You need an attitude adjustment.

Mmm…I don't want to get on punishment by you. I think that'd be too harsh. I'll try to work on my attitude myself.

Oh no, you can't do that. You can't do it on your own. You need me.

Well, yeah.

No, I mean you NEED me. You need TIME with me. Serious time. You're back in school; you have to wake up early to meet me; you feel like you don't get to do the

things YOU want to do. You're whiny. And you need ME to help you change your perspective.

Okay. So are you going to just do it?

Nope. You have to WANT it enough to come and get it.

What?!

Yes. Yesterday we talked about your fast for what you really wanted breakthrough for. So you can look at this as punishment, or you can just see it as me letting you carry one more thing on your back—since that's what you're choosing to do anyway. You want to carry it all—so go ahead. And when you see that that is NOT working for you, you just come back and let me know you're ready to take this to the next level. Because right now you're not ready.

[Silence.] Hey, can I use this on MY kids?

Sure. But you already saw this coming and said something to them about it with their school work. They didn't have enough work to keep them focused and take their work seriously, so you said you were going to give them more. Same type of concept. You're going to work better when you have more work because you're going to focus on your tasks. But that's AFTER you give it ALL to ME.

You've taken your load back from me, Jo. That's why you're starting to struggle with OUR relationship. You don't want to come before me every day because you know you've got things that you THINK are "hidden." As if! So that's what's really going on here. You don't think of them as being sins that you're hiding, but that's really what they are. You need to cast it all at my feet, and then leave it alone.

No. I DON'T move in your time. You're still in your house, and you haven't found a new one. Yes, that makes you upset and frustrated. You can't have your way. So you get mad. And you think you're going to hurt ME by putting those things in your back pocket and carry them around—as if I don't know they're there? Really? No, dear, you're not hurting me. You're hurting yourself. Now who does THAT sound like conversation with? Funny, huh?

No.

Well then, get it together. Because that is what you'd say to her right there too. Get YOURSELF TOGETHER, JO, 'cause right now you're not. Lay your issues out on the floor and ask ME to pick them up. You keep your hands off of them. I do things in MY time, in MY ways. You wait on ME. Stop trying to do things on your own. Stop trying to push people. Stop trying to blame ME for everything that goes wrong. It's not ALL me, Jo. It's not. You all are responsible for a lot of your own issues.

Okay. So I need a minute. I need time. And now I have a headache, so I want to lay back down. When am I supposed to think? This, to me, is like homework, and I have that other homework I'm supposed to be working on. But when am I supposed to get quiet time to think and write??

What is this time?

Different. I'm here with YOU…and my bad attitude and all. I can't do homework this early in the morning. I hate that I'm mentally awake when I have to do things for everyone else.

Yup. You've got a bad attitude. Take your little nap. I hope you feel better when you wake up. You act like you're

not getting enough sleep...like a baby or a toddler really. That's how you're behaving.

Whatever. I have a lot to think about, and I need to be able to go deep, and I need quiet to do that, and I don't want to keep getting up earlier to do work because I'm TIRED. Ugh! I sound a mess. I need to go.

Yes, you do. Go. Go back to sleep. And when you wake up, you better be ready to get it together for the kids' sake. Don't take any of this attitude to them that they didn't deserve—and you shouldn't even be acting this way. So get it together!

January 18, 2014

[Just re-read January 15th.] Wow. That was good.

Yeah, you always did like the rebuke!

Yeah. I'm not sure why, though. I don't like it from my husband, that's for sure!

Well, that's different. That's really personal, or at least you take it really personally.

And you're my daddy…but you're God. So even though it's still personal, it's still different.

Yes. So is there anything you want to talk about today?

Mmmm…I don't know. We're going to see houses tomorrow. I'm pretty excited about that. I kind of want to ask you about the houses, but I don't at the same time. Maybe a little afraid.

You've expressed that about your husband, too. You need to think about why you're afraid to ask an authority figure

for something. Find the root so you can pull it out at its source.

Okay.

Because you've expressed this fear of asking Dell in front of your kids, and that's not a fear you want to pass down. They should not be afraid to go to their earthly OR heavenly father EVER. With ANYTHING. So you need to make this right and get everything back on track.

Okay.

You shouldn't be "afraid" to ask me if you're going to see your house tomorrow. I'll respect your wishes and not tell you, but I have information that you want and need. If you don't come to me and ask, I can't help you like I could. It's really simple. You just ask, and I give the answer you need from me.

Ahh, there's your catch. You don't like my answers. You want them to be clear and to the exact point. And I give some questions back to you. Or I don't answer them the way that you want or like. That's your deal. You don't want to ask so you don't have to deal with my responses. Plus, you're still upset about that house I didn't give you on Preswyck. You didn't like the way I didn't take away your desire for that home like you asked me to. And it still amazes me that you can realize the how and why of things, explain them to others like it all makes sense and I'm so good for my provisions, and then you still come home and are upset about not getting what you wanted or getting it your way. [Get it together...]

Well, I just don't want to get my hopes up for anything anymore. I feel like I'm always let down.

Those are the feelings you have about your husband, I know. Is that how you feel about me, too? Is it just because of that house, or do you know of it going deeper and further back than that?

I don't know. I may need to think about that. My expectations of my husband are too high and I feel like I need to lower them. But you…you're God. There's nothing you CAN'T do. So it's just a matter of me ACCEPTING that you CAN, you just DON'T all the time. Like accepting that you're sovereign, and you can do what you want, when you want, to whom you want. You don't HAVE to answer every prayer the way I want it answered. You'll just answer them. According to YOUR WILL…exactly like I've prayed for you to do! Ha. Just round and round, huh?

In a sense, yeah.

I want to write…

I know. So you're done with this last conversation then? We're done with the house?

I just wandered, that's all. Sorry. It'll be neat to see if we played with those scripture references and it works out, huh?! [For fun, we lowered the price of the house based on my bible study scripture references and what was going on in those scriptures.]

I speak, Jo. My children listen. Just stay with me. In everything, in all things, stay with me. Stop getting caught up and distracted by what's going on around you. Keep your eyes on me. I will provide all that you need, no one and no-THING else.

Gotcha.

So what do you want to write?

Music, books, articles, anything that will help people [and bring in a few dollars to help out at home].

Do you feel you need help at home [financially]?

No. But if we made more, we could have more, so we could give more, you know? A bigger house so we could house people [though I know no one who comes in town and needs a house to stay in…but still]. We could give more away, or at least I would. If I had my own money I wouldn't have to check with Wendell first. I could just give it away freely! I would love that! Not having to be accountable to anyone else with it. Just bless whoever and however I want to bless! AGH! Sounds too exciting! I need a job!! [Laughing.] Just kidding! Please don't make me work outside the home in a 9-5!

You'll see what I have for you…but it's my timing, not yours. It will all unfold, and you'll see the fruit of your labor, and you will be pleased.

Yay! Sounds fun.

Oh, it won't ALL be fun. It will still come at a cost! Don't be mistaken. What success is to you and me is not success to the world. You will face opposition, but you've already overcome. You stand and stay with me—you'll be pleased, regardless of what you will have to go through. You'll make it out—golden on the other side. It will be good.

Okay. Sounds like I died…but okay. [Laughing.]

I can help you write. You just have to get back with me, you know? Get back in my presence, spend time together. Open up your heart again. We can write together.

Okay. I'll do that.

Cool. You done?

Yeah, I've got to get some yarn going for this thing next week.

Okay sounds good. Love you, girl.

[Shocked laugh.] That's mine!

Well, it was mine first, right?!

Uh…yeah…but…weird. [Laughing.] I love you too bo—no, I can't call you boy! I love you too, Daddy!!

Have a great day, sweetie.

Thanks. I will. Thanks for being patient with me and allowing me to slowly get back into my groove to meet with you and enjoy it! I really do miss you.

I miss you, too. Don't stay away so long.

Okay, I'll work on that, too. Love you, bye.

January 20, 2014

Good morning, Daddy.

Good morning.

I want you to be pleased with me. I hope that I had a better weekend this week.

[Smiling.] You did. I enjoyed yesterday, too.

Yeah, it was nice. I can't wait to see what joy looks like on me. I keep thinking it has to be something great or so totally different from what I look like and am right now, because people have been talking about it for so long. Like it's going to overtake me and be so obvious to everyone else.

You're expecting a big hackle?!?

Yeah, I think so!

You know that it may not come like that right?!?

Yeah, I know…

It's so much of your perception and outlook on things and on life…sure, you may laugh a lot more and a lot more loudly! But it's your state of being that will be different, and to some, that WILL be just as obvious as a loud hackle in service.

Yeah, that is true…and those are the people who NEED to see joy on me, huh?

Definitely.

Hmmm…that's cool.

Yup. So what are your plans today?

Just school. Work on the house somehow. Try to stay caught up on my week's schedule. Oh, yarn when it comes in today! Do you want to talk about yesterday??

Yes, we can.

So were you telling me to lay down my TIME to you? Is THAT what I need to sacrifice? Is THAT the most important thing to me?

Well, when you start to do all of your complaining, it all boils down to YOU. What do YOU want? You want to be able to sit and yarn, or watch TV, or sit in the quiet and think. You want time to yourself, but you feel like you give and you give and you give. And the only giving that you seem to enjoy is the ministry part. When people need to talk to you and you stop your world for them, that's what you get pleasure out of. Being available for other's needs.

But the needs of your family seem like a burden to you. You don't enjoy giving them your time. You feel like they suck the life out of you and all that YOU want to do. So YES. I did say give ME your time. I gave you that family and those kids. I expect you to take care of them in the right way. With the right attention and same attention that you give to others. That's why your joy is so important. Your kids will see the same smile you gave to those kids at children's church when you looked at and talked to them. THAT'S what THEY need. THEY need to see you happy—but not happy, actually joyful [because you know the difference between happy and joy].

Right.

So I need you to sacrifice your time for me, do what I ask of you, and I'll give your time back to you. Though after a time of this, you'll see that your desire for your time will change. A shift in your perspective and desires. Kind of like your shift in your TV habits.

Yeah. So, yarn?

Yarn. There are different parts to the yarn. Right now you're selling to raise money for Miracle, which I get.

I don't think I can talk about this right now. I just had to second guess myself on my hearing, so I think this section will be skewed. Can we talk about it later? Either throughout the day or maybe tomorrow?

Yes, that's fine. But you shouldn't be second-guessing.

Then why did I think you said I hadn't prayed about Miracle going, but you and I just discussed it recently??

Because you ASKED me about it. You still haven't prayed about it, Jo. That's what you heard me say, "You still haven't prayed about it yet."

OKAY…this is NOT the same as when I'm asking you about something? Does that mean all my questions I ask here, I need to pray about, too? You mean I need to be praying about the house because our conversations aren't sufficient? Ugh, right? You know that? UGH.

What you think about and don't act on is what you know—this IS NOT your prayer time. We're conversing, communing, fellowshipping. This is NOT prayer. There is no worship here, and the Holy Spirit isn't doing his normal job here. You still need PRAYER TIME! This is not it! And that's where you're lacking. That's where you're failing on the whole process and what it COULD be. There's so much more, Jo.

Yeah, I know. I know there's a ton more because I still haven't figured out how to use any of this.

Oh, but you have. You've used some of the things you've gotten from me here to help and encourage people. You're doing what you do know how to do, and that's good. There's just so much more to it.

And it'll come through prayer?

It will come through prayer, and it will come when your time is my time. Lay down your time to me. You will see how it all works out. And if you need to talk to me more during the day to make it work or to check with me on a time-taker, that's fine. Do that. Just give me your time. Yes, ask about yarn time, too. I know you have that show this week. Do your best in your preparations. You'll get

done what you need to get done. Don't stress this week though. Because really, that would show that you didn't give me your time! Lay it down; I will bless it. You will see. Love you girl. Get on with your day now.

Okay. Love you, too, Daddy.

January 21 2014

Good morning, Daddy! How are you today?

I'm well. I see you're in a good mood.

Yeah. No special reason though. Just glad to get started with our time…what do you want to talk about?!

Well, I know that you really have the house on your mind, but that it's also a sensitive subject for you….so….what do YOU want to talk about?

[Chuckle.] Hmmm…I don't know. You start!

Okay. Last night you asked to see something about the house…

No, No, No! I don't want to talk about the house. Talk about something else!

Okay……so what DO you want to talk about?

Well, we've tabled a few things recently. Like the dancing and yarn. I didn't know if you wanted to talk about Sunday at all…just wanting more of you. This joy that everyone keeps speaking of. Or the words I keep getting for my healing hands and prophetic voice. I have no thoughts about any of these things, so this is a good time to talk, because I shouldn't question anything you say! Hahaha! Oh, and you know I have to come up with something for Thursday night's class, too. So whatever you have for that would be good, too.

Okay. You've given me a lot to choose from. Are you ready to listen and type exactly what you get?

Hold on. Okay, now I am. [Eyes closed!]

Okay. We're going to talk about your mysteries of life. The ones that intrigue you and sometimes keep you unsettled in your spirit. What do I mean? What do others mean by the words that they speak to you through me? Let's dig into one and see what's going on, shall we?

Yes. And you sound really mysterious right now. Like a John Paul Jackson show or something! [Laughing.]

[Laughing.] Okay. Let's go then. You want to know about your life. What's keeping you down, what's holding you back, what's plaguing you. What's holding you back is <u>you</u>. Your priorities are wrong; you waste a lot of time. So you're missing what I have to show you.

HUH?! This is OLD stuff! You've said all this before!

And you haven't changed anything, Jo. So until your time aligns with mine, I can't reveal everything to you. I can't even reveal most of these things to you because you haven't given me your time. So we must start at square one. Maybe every day if you're not getting it.

Ugh. Really?? Well maybe you need to tell me in more detail what giving you my time looks like? Yesterday all I did was school. Didn't do any yarn, though I'll have to do it today when it comes. What do you want my day to look like??

YOU HAVE TO PRAY, JO!!! I said it yesterday and you didn't do it. You really do need to enter into that secret

place where you're coming to me in prayer privately and speaking in tongues. You really do need to pray in tongues every day. That's where your increase and intimacy is going to come from. That's where we need to be. This is one level of intimacy, but you need other areas, too. Your worship, your prayer life, those are all different areas that I need to inhabit and be a part of on your daily basis. And THAT TAKES TIME. THAT'S the time that you need to give me. Do you see it now?

Yes. I see it. I get it.

So if you're not giving me your time there, this isn't all for naught, but this isn't all of me. This isn't all that I want to show you and do with you. This is a good starting point, and I know many people think they can't get here, but this is just your launching pad, dear. We have way more to go and to cover if you stay with me. But I'm going to need your time to take you to that next level—that next dimension.

Okay. I get it.

Good.

So do I need to fast?

I really want you to give me some of your time first before you start the fast. I don't want them to coincide so you think one hinges on the other. I want YOU to come to ME on your own—in prayer and worship, and not just because you're fasting.

Got it. I understand that. Well! I'm glad I let you lead today! That's funny.

'Cause I should be leading every day?

Yeah. [Laughing.]

Yeah. Alright, then. Let's get to it. Get off here and get to work. You do have a lot to do today. And you need to get your house ready.

Okay. Yes sir. Love you, Daddy.

Love you too, babe.

January 22, 2014

Good morning. I didn't get up early, but I DID come and pray today!

Yes, you did. Thank you. Baby steps. We'll get where you need to get. It's all good.

Good. Hey, do you have anything for Kay's family today? Anything I need to do or say? Or that you want to do or say for today?

Just invite me in when they come. Let my presence fall in this place. My fresh presence and fresh anointing. I also want you [or Miracle] to pray for each of them. Just let my anointing and words flow through you.

Okay.

What you're "teaching— you're not, really. Just be you. Just talk. Let it all happen. Yes, you should record it. It would be good for YOU to have since you think you struggle with remembering things.

Don't YOU think I struggle with remembering?

No. I think you struggle with understanding your power and your abilities. You don't have a bad memory at all.

Use what I've given you [gifts, strengths, abilities, power], and you'll see things more clearly.

Hmmm…okay.

So today when she wants to role play, just go with it. The kids will be engaged, but do pray over them before they arrive to cover your children. Invite me in, I will send my presence. As long as you keep inviting me and making room for me, Jo, I'll come. I'll be there. I'll fill you and use you. But when you don't give me the room and space to infiltrate your life—then I can't fill it the way I want to.

I long to shower you with my gifts that I have for you. The gifts of blessing people, healing people, encouraging people…all those things that you already love to do. I want to do those things for and with you and through you. I want you to see people blessed and healed by your hands. But you HAVE TO INVITE ME IN. YOU CANNOT keep trying to do everything ON YOUR OWN!!!

Yes sir.

And you heard my heart there, right?

Yes, I heard it. [Smile.]

Okay, good. It's a short day today [for us], but I need to let you go because you really do have quite a bit to do today.

Will I get it all done??

Of course! And if you time it right, you may even get to bed at a decent time. It's all about priorities though. Don't procrastinate today.

Okay, thanks.

Yep. Now—go make it happen. Love you, girl!

Love you too, Dad!

January 23, 2014

Oh God, do you have a word for me for tonight? I know I'm late!

Yes, you are!

Sorry.

It's okay. What do you think about yourself?

Huh?

Earlier you asked what you should talk about and I said, "You."

Yeah, but I didn't get it. I thought maybe I'd figure out what you were talking about…but I didn't.

Right. So what do you think about yourself?

I don't know. I think I'm a mom. A wife. A teacher. [A slave!] But that's not what you mean, is it? Or rather, those aren't the right answers are they??

Ahh….you know they're not.

So how do YOU see me?

I see you as my child, my chosen, my called, my anointed, my gift, my treasure. my joy, my peace, my love, my creation, my fellowship, my time, my love. Everything that I LOVE—you are.

Wow…

Yeah, wow. Dear, I created you. I love you. I have a plan and purpose for you. You don't have to worry or wonder

about how I'm going to take care of you, because I always will. You're mine. I'm going to take care of you. And it doesn't matter where you go or who you talk to, I'm always going to be right there. Just waiting for you to invite me in, invite me to your circle, your conversation, your fellowship, your ministry. I AM the reason you minister, so ALWAYS invite me to what you're doing. Even if it's just a fun get-together, please invite me. I want to be welcome everywhere you are and in everything you do.

Invoke the Holy Spirit everywhere you are. Everywhere you go. Ask him to reveal himself ALL the time. Not just when YOU think the time is right or you happen to come upon a person who's in obvious need of prayer. Stay in my presence because I'm going to show you people who need prayer that's NOT obvious to the natural eye.

When you invite the Holy Spirit, this is when I give you revelations and knowledge and words that they are too afraid and ashamed to speak. But I've called you out TO speak those words to them. To show them that I AM the holy God. The maker of the universe, the beginning and the end, the alpha and omega, the one who sees and knows all.

I'm going to reveal to you the secrets of their hearts and their lives so they will know I am alive and real…and then you're going to bring them into my presence so they can know me for themselves. These ARE the things I have spoken to you. THESE are my words. Now go and speak.

Okay. So is THIS what you want me to say tonight?? In class? For my word?!

You can. But I really just want you to speak from your heart. Be you. Again…INVITE the Holy Spirit and just

wait and watch how he leads you…..and then just follow him!

Okay, Daddy. I will do this. I STILL feel unprepared though!

Yes, well, you waited until the last minute, so that's why you feel that way. Remember, time management, priorities, procrastination...things have to change…

Yes sir.

Okay, go get ready to go!

January 28, 2014

Good morning.

Good morning.

I sure do wonder what I'm doing sometimes. Thinking about Kay and all the stuff I need and should be doing. I know you've been getting on me about my priorities and time management, but I think I'm still missing it. I'm not truly getting what I'm supposed to be doing. Is it ALL good, but within certain and defined parameters? Or do I actually need to cut some things out?

Good questions. Jo, you do need to cut out some ideas and thoughts more than you do—actual THINGS that you are doing. Does that make sense? Your mind is telling you that you need to do certain things—not me. I'm not leading you that way. Your mind is. Those are the thoughts that need to become subject to your true priorities in a given day. You line up with me, and I'll make your paths straight. I'll show you what to do each day. You can simply ask me and I'll tell you; I've done it before for you. And when I do that, haven't you seen that

I don't fill up every single minute of your day? I give you a list of things to do and that's it.

With you, it's going to be more about priorities than it is "at this minute we do this and next, this, and lastly, this." That's not how you HAVE to be. If you want to go there, you can. But you don't have to be that rigid. Yes, your children will learn how to live by a schedule because you will teach them how to make and follow their own. But you don't have to live by a to do list and a thirty minute blocked time schedule. Just live following ME.

Okay, Lord. I will try to do that better than what I have been.

Good. You'll see change. It may not come immediately, but you'll see the difference it makes.

So you want to start today?? Do you want to tell me what to do? Because I sure do wonder about soccer practice.

Hahaha, I bet. And you want ME to let you know by telling you your schedule for today, huh? HA! That is funny. I'm not going to give you that. I want you to pray about your schedule and the effect it will have on your lives. YOU pray about it and let the Holy Spirit guide you.

Okay…

So you want to know about today? It's going to sound simple. Stay calm during school. Put your focus and attention on your children because it's SCHOOL time. Don't stress them; don't stress yourself. Don't follow the schedule with a buzzer, but give everyone the time they really need to get their school done. Talk to them about their own schedules and making a short one for today. But NO STRESS!

Got it!

Then, Jo, just get your work done around the house. Your service to the house, get it done. Cheerfully. Work on your bible study, your journals, your joy paper, read over all that and start thinking about it so you can write. Praise your children for the good jobs they ARE doing. Don't focus so much on the negative stuff. It will come; it will change; be patient. Fruit doesn't come off the tree in one day, season, or year. Give your changes time to mature and grow. Then you will see the fruit of your labor.

Okay dear, it's time for your focus to shift. You just continue to think on these things and bless your children with the peace you carry today.

Yes sir. Thank you.

Thank YOU for listening! Now let's see you obey. Love you, girl.

Love you too, Daddy. Bye.

HEY! We didn't talk about the house!

No, we didn't. We will. Just wait on and follow me. You know the drill. Wait on me.

Aww…okay…bye.

January 29, 2014

I know. I'm late today and behind on regular house life. I got distracted. I'm sorry.

It's okay. I still heard from you. I love your praise of me!

[Smiling.] Thanks. So what's on your mind today? All the stuff I need to get done?!?

Uh…no.

I know. I think I'm going to get it all done though.

I think you are, too. You're going to make it happen and that's good.

Thanks.

Yeah. You're getting better. The key is to do it without stress—on yourself AND your kids.

Right. Sometimes it seems that it doesn't matter what time I start prepping for the next day, it still ends up being stressful. I'm not sure how to get around that.

It's all in your tone and delivery. Try to keep it down today. Mellow. Cool. Collected. Yes, touch base with that friend today.

Okay. I will and I'll try harder on my delivery to the kids. I do need to get to the grocery store first.

But please plan the rest of your meals first!

Okay, okay. I wish you could just plan that for me each week, too. That'd be cool. But I know you have helped me with the food this week, too. And I thank you for that.

No problem.

Hey, what's going on with my mind? I feel like I'm having a hard time speaking to people lately. I keep hearing myself say that "I'm going blank." What's the deal? It's one thing to forget stuff someone was talking to me about a few days or week ago…but now I'm not articulating my thoughts well? That's

CRAZY for me! And I'm totally noticing it. It's not cool. I'm a speaker! I speak and communicate my thoughts clearly! I can't be going blank!! Tell me something!

Relax. Pray about it. Pray the mind of Christ, but also pray about your mind and whatever you think your condition may be. There are many factors to your memory and what aids or blocks the clear function of it. Come to me in prayer about it.

Okay. Well, I guess because I was late today and it's time to start life, I have to leave early today. Don't feel like you got to say much or impart anything.

Oh, but I did. You can get your priorities done today, and you're going to come to me in prayer about your mind and memory. Those are good things. Hold on to them. Stay focused on what I tell you every day, and keep coming to me. Continue to come to me in prayer.

Okay. That's cool.

Good. Now get going. You have papers to grade! Stay on top of your game. Finish what you start so you're not in the weeds next time you sit down. Don't let stuff carry over from one day to the next. Not with bible study lesson stuff, but school stuff, okay? Finish grading the same day.

Okay. I will work harder on that.

Good. Love you, dear.

Love you, too.

February 3, 2014

Good morning. Everyone really liked that word you gave me for class. Thank you.

You're welcome. I delight in talking to you and giving you words.

That makes me wonder, or rather, I've been wondering if all the things I've been telling Miracle about being responsible with her gift and being a good steward of what you give her, does that apply to me here with this?

Somewhat. You do ask me for words for people that you are to share. But most of the time it's just us talking to each other, and you don't always ask to share our talks.

Right. Well, I thought you've alluded to the fact that something was going to come out of these writings, it just wasn't right then. Or right now.

You're correct. It wasn't THEN, when you initially were asking those questions.

Ohh okay…so is it now?!?

It's closer to now than we when started, but it's still not yet time. You keep copying and pasting them into one, and I'll tell you when to move forward with the compilation.

Okay. And I've asked if you wanted me to share anything on FB too, right?

Yes, you have. Not everything, obviously, but why don't you just let me lead you and tell you when to post something on FB?

Well, yeah, I can do that. That's fine. I was just asking if I was being a good steward of this time?

Ahh…I think you could listen and obey more. Make sure that you're putting this time above the time required of others. I need to come first with you. Rarely do you skip these times together, and spend the time in prayer, worship, or reading instead. If you miss this, you usually do nothing else. And when you DO do this, you still skip the others. I told you that this is NOT a substitute for your worship and adoration and praise of me—or your time in the word to study and learn more, or your prayer time and intercession for others. You are still working on getting it together.

Yeah. I'm sorry for not being a good listener and obeying you. Will you forgive me?

Of course.

Hey. And where do you throw those?

Into the Sea.

Okay.

So. What do you think about our pastor asking us to pray about children's and/or youth ministry??? Let's talk about that!

You're going to pray about it though, right?

Yes, I am.

Okay, good. What do I think? Mmm…I think it's time. You've known for a long time what was in your future, and if you have hesitation now, it's because you didn't plan accordingly. If you didn't start taking steps to "prepare" yourself, then you may feel like you're not ready. But

being that I prepare and equip and call and train and fill in gaps when I pull people out of their comfortable place or their desert—**DON'T RUN FROM YOUR CALLING! I WILL EQUIP YOU. YOU** just have to abide in me. That means—**FULL TIME ABIDE.** Not the one percent that I've been given lately. I need **BOTH** of your attentions.

But don't get fidgety and run away from this. Don't worry about the job. The job will lie down; I will come first. I'll become your priority. You'll see me in EVERYTHING you do. Your eyes will begin to change, and you'll see my glory in things you didn't see before. Your mouth will open and become—not the mouthpiece it was—but an even louder roar will come out of you that YOU haven't even heard before. I will anoint you to teach and train, and it won't be without experience and knowledge.

You DO walk in my fullness. You DO walk in my love. I have anointed you from the beginning for this. In THIS time, in THIS season. It's time. Things will change, accelerate quickly. I'm moving you to new grounds and new territories because things are changing quickly, and I need things to grow and mature quickly. Dead things will fall off of you. Habits that are not of me will not satisfy and will be distasteful to you. Your desires will all change because I'm filling you with my spirit and my presence so much that it's going to seem like you're going to burst open you'll be so full [I see a big guy blown up like a balloon with light in him that's shining out, like he was about to pop].

My wind is going to carry you to places you haven't seen in your world travels—because now you're on my radar, my assignments, my missions. Your thoughts will be totally different as I start moving you out of this place you're in now. This city, this town, this job. It IS time. Open your eyes and see through mine. Stop questioning; stop doubting, and just start hearing. I lead you. YOU DO HEAR ME. YOU ARE MY SHEEP. Stop questioning so much, and just step out. It IS time. Pack your things, because it's time to go. [This was Wendell standing at a desk, like office stuff into a box, not the house.]

These are my words. Don't doubt. Don't question. You know my voice, too. Don't question what you should share. You asked, and I'm telling you. IT IS TIME. You will go when I open the door. That job has to end, because I have new things for you. Your new, focused, Holy Spirit-led eyes will show you. Go where I am showing you. Follow the open doors.

When? When I say. When I show. You just need to be ready to go. Start prepping and cleaning and reshuffling things now so you don't carry any weight or burden when I close the door on that job. It's time to go to your new home. The one that I have for you. Where you will work and love. It will make sense. Just stay with me. Keep writing. My plans are perfect. For both of you. Just keep listening. New eyes for you both. New ears to listen with love and compassion, not just for the lost, but for your children. There's a new love brewing inside of you both. And not just for your children, but for all people everywhere. You will become LOVE.

But I've said this before and I'll say it again—when I pull you out—DON'T LOOK BACK. Do NOT carry weight from the past because you're moving forward in me. If there are loose ends that you don't want to leave undone, then NOW is your time to mend those things. Because there will not be time when I say go, and you cannot

afford to carry the weight of the past and look backwards while I'm taking you forward. DO NOT CROSS THAT LINE. And I don't mean relationships/friendships. I'm talking about anything that you would feel responsible for. On and off the job. Relationships with those you impart to are fine. Keep those. They're good. But dead weight must go. Don't question. Just press, prepare, and be ready to go. No more will this job stand between you and your called place. It's time to go. I've spoken.

Um. Wow. I thought I was just asking about ministry at church! It's almost like you went a little overboard or extreme, huh?

Nope. It all went together. Yes, you can copy and paste it just like that. You can send him the whole thing really so he can hear the authenticity of this conversation.

Yeah, but do you think I should do it today? I just brought it up to him yesterday, and he's working may feel blind-sided if he didn't get a chance to pray about it today?

Well, why wouldn't he have time to pray about it?

Well I don't know, he's on the work trip…I don't know his schedule and how tired he is.

Mm hmm. The job. Do you see it?

We'll yes, I've seen it, but he's done okay recently. He's getting better than he used to be.

Yes, he's better than he used to be. But I know what I've put in him and where he's going. It's hard to watch idleness in any of my children. You, too. There's so much to be done, and until you start seeing with my eyes and hearing with my ears, so much time is wasted. There needs to be a hunger in my children that they cannot wait

to come and spend time with me so they can be filled, strengthened, get their orders for the day...why would anyone choose to pass on that?

I don't know. We get too busy.

Doing...

Other stuff. Not your stuff...

NOT MY STUFF. You're busy doing things that are not for me or led by me or even anointed by me. Seek FIRST the Kingdom of God...

Okay. So...the answer to the question from pastor was?

Pray about it. You haven't really prayed yet. Open your mouth and pray about this separately and together. And yes, listen to all the words I've given others for you. You already had these things put before you. If you don't know what to do, then you either didn't believe the men and women of God who were speaking to you, or you didn't take them seriously enough to start preparing yourself to be ready for the call, or you just forgot because you didn't LISTEN TO THEM!

You heard that man of God say to read those words EVERY DAY. You heard me say to say these things out loud EVERYDAY. These are declarations. These are truths. If you stayed before me with the words I have ALREADY SPOKEN, then when you get someone in front of you and it lines up with what you've already been told and prepared for, then you'd recognize it as so, and your prayer would just have to be for confirmation from the Holy Spirit. Not an "I don't know what I should do" prayer. Do you see the difference?

Yes.

If I've already said it, then it's just a matter of waiting for it to come to pass. And while you wait, you work towards it—not doing it on your own—but you're in the training and preparation stage, so when the door opens you can walk through. You shouldn't be confused right now. At all. This calling is not a new thought or idea. It's been over a year that I've brought this call to your attention. And don't get caught up on what you think was a wasted year because you didn't behave as if it was coming. I will equip you. Both of you. All of you. But you have to follow my lead, because taking it into your own hands will bring disaster.

Okay. So…go pray.

Yes. Get in my presence and stay there. Play my words back to you.

And send this to Dell today? I'm still unsure. I just don't want to put pressure on him while he's working so hard.

So don't put pressure on him. You send it, he reads it when he has time and when he wants to talk about it, then he'll bring it up. Don't pressure him. Simple as that.

Okay.

You have a lot of editing to do today, though! It's been awhile since we've talked this long.

Yeah, I know. Typos are crazy.

It's all good. I love you, Jo.

I love you too, Daddy.

Feel my presence today, because I'm with you. Today is going to be fine, and you'll do well. Stay focused and you'll get things done.

Okay, thanks. I love you.

I love you too, dear. Bye.

February 4, 2014

Good morning, Daddy. I realized that it's hard for me to come here each day, because I don't think you could possibly have something to say to me every day. Or that if I come you're just going to tell me what I did wrong or failed at the previous day. So sometimes I avoid this because I know I failed the previous day. I know that I didn't get through my to do list or I got too angry at the kids yesterday or that my house is still a wreck, and I'm home all day, so why isn't it clean? Why do I have things in my house from over a week ago that need to go back to the garage?

So it's hard to come before you because...I already know that I've messed all that stuff up. I don't want to hear about it from you. Not in a mean way—I just don't want to always talk about what I've done wrong or haven't done right.

Okay. So you think that my love is conditional?

No, I know it's not conditional...

But you're behavior shows me that you believe—deep down in your heart—that my love and thoughts towards you are conditional. And that my words to you are only those of correction and rebuke? And I say "deep in your heart" because your immediate answer of "no my love

is unconditional" is a head answer. Your behavior and actions show what you truly believe.

[No comment.]

And don't take THIS as a rebuke! This IS a correction—but it's for your own good, your well being. You HAVE to have understanding of the fact that I'm going to love you no matter what. This relationship isn't about what you've done or haven't done. What list you finished, what job is complete, or who saw your clean house. I don't love you based on those things!

I love you because I CREATED YOU, JO. I created you. I love you. I have a plan for you that's not wrapped around the conditions of "If you master a clean kitchen every night before bed." Those things are great, but that's not what I look at. I look at your heart, JO. What's in your heart. The corrections and rebukes I give you are based on what's really in your heart that needs to be dealt with now so you can carry out the future plans that I have for you. This relationship has nothing to do with stuff or things, this has everything to do with what's in your heart

Let's clean up the bad, let's sharpen the good, let's get you prepared for your next assignment. I want you ready to take that next footstep I have before you. I don't want you stumbling and falling because you're looking at how your footsteps aren't as neat and perfectly shaped as mine! Really? That's never going to be. You won't see perfection on that side. Now I DON'T mean, don't do your best at what you can do. Don't live sloppy and talk about your clean, purged heart! Because as your heart changes, your character changes, and you'll see that you

can handle more, you can do more, AND you can do it more peacefully, because your heart has changed.

You'll make it through to do lists, you'll keep your house tidy—not perfect because, honestly, you're at home with the kids—you have to LIVE there. Don't push your NOW OLD perceptions onto them and stress them out about keeping a "perfect" house. If you do that, you're creating the thought in their mind that I AM conditional, and I AM NOT! You've got to learn to abide in this place of peace so your children not just see me through you, but they know me because of you. They'll know me as the daddy that loves no matter what, who'll always be there to listen, who always has time—for the "big" and "small" stuff, that I CARE. I care deeply, Jo.

And that's why I don't want you to get caught up in the stuff that doesn't really matter. I want you kingdom focused, mind stayed on me, and you will have that perfect peace. Ha. That's the perfect you need to strive for! Rest in me. I have you. There IS nothing to worry about. Because I have it all—all in my hands. I love you. I'm here for you. Just come to me. Everyday. Just like this. Even if your mind gets cloudy and you think you don't "deserve" to come in my presence and talk to me.

Erase that. That's the enemy telling you lies to deceive you. You've got to stop listening to him. Don't let him get in your way. Put him back in his place and keep coming towards me. I'm going to take you where you need go next…and it has nothing to do with the looks of your house!

Thanks, Daddy. I love you so much.

I know. And there's SO much more of it for you to experience. It's coming soon. You're going to get a new wave of my love and my presence. Just press in.

Thanks. I will. Can I share?

Yes! You can share! I know you have some other friends who need to hear these same words. Please share so that they can come to me and rest in my presence and my peace. I love you Jo. You're doing a good job. Continue with your stewardship of this. It DOES have a purpose!

Oh, I think I knew that. Just get a little too excited sometimes and want to know early!

In time dear…in time…have a great day.

Thanks, God, I will.

February 5, 2014

Good morning, Daddy. How are you this morning?

I'm well. You're here.

Awww, thanks. What are we talking about today? I've got nothing on my mind, so it's all you. And so I'm guessing the answer is going to be "me," hahaha.

Yes, but we'll see how you take it.

Okay…

I want to talk about stress.

Really?

Yes, really. Stress. How it's affecting your life and the lives of others around you.

Okay.

I want you to think about Joshua and how he reacts to things. You see it in your head right? How he spazzes out, how he punches his legs, head goes back, complete frustration, right?

Yes.

Okay. Now see how Brianna reacts. Feet stepping on each other, hands fidgety, yelling. You got that?

Yes.

So your children are getting stressed even though you would look back at your life and say that being a kid is easy. There's no need to get that worked up, why are you stressing, etc. Am I right?

Well, of course! [Laughing.] But yes, you are. I get it!

So what is causing them to stress? What causes adults to stress?

Pressure.

Pressure, good. And where is that pressure coming from?

Me. Us. Our expectations of them. Our amazement that "they don't get it" without actually being taught or having it explained to their level.

Oh, so you've thought about this before, have you?

A little bit.

Well good. Let's keep going. But it sounds as if you already understand that you and Dell are a big part of the problem, is that right?

Yes, we are the biggest part of the problem.

And it's not that you two don't mean well. You TELL them that this is the place to make mistakes and learn and grow and ask questions, etc., but YOUR BEHAVIOR is different from YOUR WORDS. What you're saying is NOT what you're meaning, and they've picked up on that. It actually wasn't hard for them to see at all. You've got to work on lining those two things up. Your words and your actions.

It kind of goes along with what we discussed the other day. That you're representing me to them. If you tell them that I'm always there and always listen, then you have to be modeling that both in your spiritual walk AND how you parent them—in your relationship with them. You are plugged-in to represent me here on earth. So you have to act the part.

Okay. I get it.

So, choose your words wisely. Don't say things you don't mean, and don't let your body and actions say something different than your mouth. Do you have that? I see you getting sleepy again…you want a snow day too, huh?!

Yeah, that'd be nice.

But are you getting the point, Jo?

Yes, I am. Their stress is because of us…really, just like most things boil down to us and it being our fault.

I didn't say that. Why are you? If that's what I meant, don't you think I would've said it?

Yes sir.

Okay then. Don't speak for me unless it's correct. I didn't call you a failure. You're not one. Dell is not one. You have made mistakes, and the result is now evident. But we're going to work on that.. So don't bring it up as if it is law. People make mistakes; it's what you do with it that defines who you are. I don't want you moping around today because I brought this to your attention. It's about what you're going to do with this information now.

With this mistake—how are you going to react? Because to successfully fix this you need: me, prayer, endurance, patience. With your words, you're going to have to match what your body, your reactions, your tone of voice is saying. They'll see right through something that doesn't line up, so you have to make it count. Smile more. In and out of school, in and out of playtime. Smile JUST BECAUSE! It will carry further than you think, further than you can imagine.

Now I know that you're tired again. And hungry! Why don't you go lay down for a while, then get back up so that you're ready to go by 8:00. You can still have a good and productive day. It's not over just because you're tired and you're going to have to push things back an hour or so. It's all good, see? I'm not yelling, over-reacting, or causing you to stress because you've upset me and my plans. Ahh see? That's what we didn't talk about today... maybe next time....your triggers. Your day not going as YOU planned, you not having CONTROL of everything. Yes, we'll be talking about your triggers, too!

Great[(sarcasm]. That sounds like a really fun discussion... though not really!

I know. But remember, it's all for your good.

Okay, I know. I'm falling asleep. I love you, Daddy.

I love you too, dear. Now hit save and get upstairs. You can edit later, too.

February 7, 2014

Good morning, Daddy! I'm excited today. I've been happy and excited a lot lately. Just so in awe of you every morning without anything "major" happening. Just in AWE of you and your goodness! I love it! So how are YOU today?

[Smiling.] In awe of you.

No way!

Yes, way. I'm just so pleased with how your heart is changing and shaping into what I've created it to be. I'm so happy for YOU! Getting closer to this point. Going further down your road. It's going to be great to see you walk these things out. I am happy for YOU!

Wow. That is cool. To know that our obedient journey makes you HAPPY. Just like we get excited and happy when OUR kids do the right things, huh?

Exactly. I'm proud of you when you follow me…at whatever cost.

Cool. Okay. I have some questions from yesterday that we need to get to before I have to rush out of here! The book. What's the word on that?

Keep copying and pasting until you finish it. I'll give you instructions after that.

Okay. Should I email her back?

You told her you would.

Okay. And I should tell her?

That you have work to complete before you can give her a definite answer. Keep reading through her materials, though. And the cost involved—though you'll need your page numbers to determine that—hence, the importance of copying and pasting!

Gotcha. Okay, thanks.

The floor last night.

Your memory served you well, and you were able to make the connection. And yes, Miracle confirmed it for you. The method I used to get your attention? That's up to me. Yes, I made you stand there. Yes, you heard from me. And, yes, you were noticeable. You'll get over all that! The point is you DID hear me, you did recall the first time I spoke to you/hit you like that, and you were able to get the word you desired from Miracle. Ha. You didn't catch that part in the car did you?

I thought I did?

Not to the degree in which I sent it.

Okay. So now what? My husband. I can get words and confirmations, but what about him? He hasn't brought it up, and I haven't said anything! Woohoo me! Yes, I'm super excited, and amazed, about that! [Just got sidetracked thinking about him needing a roomier car that will hold more people comfortably—for driving kids/youth on "field trips."]

Don't worry about him. Just like others—your job is to DELIVER THE MESSAGE not babysit, or stalk, while they figure out what to do with the message, or

judge them based on their response and behavior. Just DELIVER. But I've got him. Just like I have you. You let me continue to deal with him. This has been a good two weeks for you two. And it does remind you of that fast you took from each other while courting…those were good times, weren't they?

Yes.

So it's all good, Jo. It's all going to work out in the right time. This has definitely been a season of waiting for you. I think you're doing well, but you have to keep it up and hold out until the end. Kind of like last night.

Yeah. I get it. I get that now, I mean!

Sure. Okay, love. You're getting distracted, and it's almost time for you to go anyway. Have a good day. Work on your book! And start planning ahead for next week so you don't get in the weeds with the Olympics thrown into the mix!

[Laughing.] Thanks, Daddy. You're so good to me!

I know. You're my child and I love you. I love to bless you and comfort you and give you peace. Just stay with me.

February 10, 2014

Hey Daddy—

Hey, Jo. What's up? [Smiling like he knows. I know he knows!]

Oh you know what's up, Daddy. I want some answers. Clear ones. The kind you'd spell out in the bible with CLEAR instructions. The kind you were giving us when we were prepping the house to sell. I want STEP-BY-STEP! THAT'S what I want! Now what do YOU want? [Why did I ask that? UGH!]

I want you to be content with what I DO give you.

Man, I kind of feel like you made me ask that! Was that the Holy Spirit talking on my behalf? Cause I think I sure was handling that open line of communication just fine. I think he should speak when I DON'T know what to say. But I was rattling off just fine!

Yes you were.

I just want the answers to MY questions. I don't want you to give me a crumb and tell me to consider myself satisfied! I want MORE! But more of everything. More of you. More of your presence. More of your knowledge and power and authority. I want more of YOU….but with that increase in wisdom and knowledge also comes some of these answers I need in life too, right?

Jo! Your mind is so busy today! Do you remember what you told Joshua yesterday? You need to slow it down. Keep your mind focused on me. I'll give you peace; I'll calm you down. I'm the one you seek and need. Just let me do it. Now calm down.

Okay. I still want some clear answers and direction, though.

In time, dear, in time. Bring your mind back in. Don't worry about the rest of the week or the time or your kids or school or any of that. If you want answers from me, then you have to be ready to listen so you can hear all that I say. Are you ready?

Not yet.

I know. I'll wait. What I pour out to you is not just for you. It is for others. Men, women, and children. [And by children, I mean the ones who are not adults! I don't get into the categories that you all do.] So My giftings are for all people, not just adults, not just you, not just your pastor. I have plans for everyone to use their gifts and talents for my glory, for my kingdom, for my purpose. It's all for me. Now. You want your role in that, right?

Yes!

Okay. So what I've asked you to do was to spend time with me in my presence. Have you done that?

Yes. Well, not every day…but somewhat throughout the year.

Good. It's a start. You'll get where you're going and where you need to be. Keep up the work, and continue to work on those good habits of time management where I come first. Got that?

Yes.

Good. You are going to minister to the people. It's all people. You're going to empower and teach them how to walk in the spirit. How to commune with me. How to stay in my presence because they've invited him there now. How to walk in love, see as I see, hear as I hear, set captives free. Pray for the sick. You want to raise the dead?

I really don't' know.

That's fine. We'll work on that. But all these things that you think are "just a part of you?" They are. I put them there. You're going to walk these things out more. It will start to become your norm. You'll have the stories to go

along with and back up the teachings. It'll come. But it's going to come soon, because your heart is changing. Quickly, because it's going to be on my time, not yours.

You're going to have boldness to walk these things out. No fear will be in you. You'll see who I want you to talk to, and you'll just go. No hesitation, no thought of the cost involved. Police and jail are not a preliminary thought of yours, you're just going to GO in a beeline to the target. And you're not going to stop with one [person] and one story. You're going to do it all the time. Because you're going to LOVE IT. Your kids are going to love it. Yes, even the ones who you think are grumpy or loud will love it too.

This IS a family ministry, Jo. Those were the words then, those are still the words now. You are a FAMILY of MINISTERS. You will minister my love, my truths, my gospel, and my healings. You will draw them in and keep them in my presence. Your kids are the magnets; allow them to be that. And then speak through me once contact is made. IMMEDIATELY ask me what to say when someone speaks to you. Do not have meaningless conversation. Its all for my glory. All of it.

Now I know this children's ministry church thing is nagging on you.

I'm not sure I'm going to believe everything. It's so hard to get a word for myself or for Dell.

YOU JUST DID IT! And you didn't doubt any of what I just said to you! ANY OF IT! What's the difference now? You think that if you get a word that contradicts what you THINK is right, or it's what you know Dell doesn't want to hear, that it will cause you to doubt? It will strain

your relationship if you give him a word that he doesn't want...again?

Well how do you think it affects OUR relationship when you don't receive all of the word? Or you choose not to type something? Or you doubt so you don't share it? Hello? Isn't this what you're saying to Miracle all the time—to be a good steward? Come on, Jo. Get ready to type. If you're going to ask the questions, then you have to be willing to listen to the answers. Let's go.

Okay.

Church. Yes, you are called to this house. Yes, you're going to serve in this house. Yes, sometimes it may be a challenge, but you're going to LOVE serving at this church. This IS your home. This IS your family. Don't move until I say move, and don't go back unless I say go back. Your plans are in my hands. I have them. Just let me keep them with me, because if you take them, they're going to go away. So just stay with me, and follow where I take you.

Will your kids be okay with you working in ministry? Yes, they will. They may act silly, but they really are maturing. Give them more credit than what you have been.

Okay.

I want you to work. Side by side. No, not your kids, your husband. You will be in ministry together. Things are going to shake off of you. [I see like scales being brushed off of the shoulder and arm.] Seasons and priorities are going to change. Things will become more simple when you become more simple minded—like a child! It IS that simple. You just need to walk with an "OKAY!" attitude.

It's all going to work out. There is a time and place for business, but life doesn't have to be run that way.

Enjoy the simple. You can enjoy life now, not just ' someday' when the kids are gone or you don't have to work in church or everyone is asleep or when you're retired. You can enjoy life now, and that comes from enjoying MY presence. Enjoy spending time with me and everything changes. Put me first—and everything changes! Your outlook, your attitude, your behavior, you goals, your temperament, your ideas, the things that give you earthly pleasure—those things will all change if you put me first and enjoy your time spent with me. I'll make everything change and be new.

I'll make it so you enjoy life—but first you have to enjoy being with me. I'm the one who changes how you see, hear, and feel. That's me. So let me do my work in you. Let me do that for you. I want you to be happy and joyful now. It's okay. You, too, can love your life. But you have to stay with me. Yes, Jo. Even when you're at home with the kids you can be happy and joyful. It IS possible! And you'll see—it's coming. With me.

So all the things that you two want, that you desire, they have to come through me first, or they're not going to be all that they can be. They won't bring the satisfaction that you think they will unless they go through me first. A house, a gun, a car, electronics. Yes, I AM asking you to be <u>that</u> serious about seeking me first on all you buy. You guys keep missing it. And it shows. Look at your kids. Look at yourselves. It's never enough. You never have enough to bring you the happiness and joy that your heart is seeking.

And with my touch, my love is always enough. My grace IS sufficient. I AM ALL you need. And because these things have come before me, they are like a curse in your house. I'm not saying you can't have them, but they're not in their proper place. There needs to be order in your house that is not there right now. I need to come first, and it needs to be visible to all. Not just some. This family must unite to become what I've called it to do as a unit. This family is not all about individuals. There will be moments that individuals shine, but you are a team, a unit, you're one in me. Get things in order.

Yes sir.

Do you feel your children's ministry question was answered?

No.

Well, keep praying for your husband. Miracles do happen. You used to dislike kids, and then you fell in love with them. But you feel that he's called to youth, huh?

Yes.

He is. He will minister to them, too. I know his heart is there. But you'd be surprised what comes out of him from working with the kids, too. I change people! I change things! I make things new! You two are not trusting in me. That I won't bring you to a place and then equip you for it. You're both acting like things had to be perfect before you could possibly think about working in ministry or working with kids. Is that how you came to me? Perfect? Were you blameless in my sight, or did I let my son wash and cleanse you so you could come before me blameless? Why would this be different?

I've called you to this house and this time and to this generation. These are your kids. Sure you're hesitant because you don't know them. I get that. So get to know them! It IS that simple! Relationships will come, and it will get easier. Just follow where I'm taking you. Stop looking around as if I'm talking to someone else behind you; I'm talking to you both. I have been. For the past year… pay attention, go back and see the words that have been spoken to you and over you…JO…it's all been lining up!

So YES! Get on the wave and ride it, because I've sent it to pick you up. And I know that now you're thinking about the work and the lesson and all that. Not now. Just accept your called place, then we'll talk more about the how. It's all going to work. Just follow and stay with me. Remember---I MUST COME FIRST IN EVERYTHING! EVERYTHING!

February 18, 2014

Good morning, Daddy. It's been a long time. Too long! I've missed you—our times together.

I agree.

So what have I missed? What have you wanted to say but I wasn't here? I want to hear it all! Well, I don't know how much I missed and how long that will take. I probably don't have an hour before the kids get up and I'm starting to get hungry already.

I understand, Jo. I know you. Everything about you, your quirks AND how much time you really have! [Laughing and shaking his head.] You're funny.

Thanks, Daddy, for making me that way! [Laughing.]

Okay, you want to know what you've missed? Nothing. I wait for you to come to get your daily dose. I don't just speak when you're not here so you miss all I said. There's no recording or playback for you to listen to when you come, or you'd be behind all the time! When you're listening, I speak. That's why we don't have to be HERE in order to talk. You know that. I've spoken to you in the last week; we just haven't met here so you can type it out.

Well, that's good to know. Thank you for that.

No problem! So what do YOU want to talk about? I see you've been pondering that Randy Clark question.

Yes, I have.

Do you want to ask it of me?

Well, I've been trying to make sure that what I think I want is actually what I'd want. Do you want to *tell me* what I'd want?

No. I want you to first present it to me. Then you see how you feel about it.

Okay. So I've been thinking. Wait. Here's the question [so I can come back and read this later and remember]. Randy asks what it is that people want from God. Then he tells them to be very specific so when God answers and starts to do it, they'll recognize it as God. So what would I ask God for?

Okay, right now my answer is that I want to see. I want to be able to see through people so I can know what they're dealing with and what they need. [What I can pray for, what I can pull out of them, what needs to be broken off of them.] I'm thinking that's what I want. What do you think?

February 22, 2014

Oh, Daddy. I feel so rushed and like I'm here just because I need something. But I do. I don't like not talking to you like this. I don't like being so tired that I never want to get out of bed. What time do I need to go to bed? Lord, I need your help. I want so much to be in your presence, be about your business, do things that are fruitful. I feel this life just gets in the way. Sometimes I don't want to play wife and mom and games and activities. I just want to be daughter and princess and servant and student and slave. This life, this stuff, just seems SO MEANINGLESS! I know we're here for purpose, but we get caught up in the stupidest things. And my family is no different from anyone else's. We are no better than others. There's nothing separating "us" from "them." It's all the same.

I've totally deviated from what I came for, but that's my heart. My heart longs just to be with you in your presence, learning things of you, what pleases you, doing your will, making YOU happy. I don't want all this other STUFF. Take away desires that are not of you, and change my heart to be more like yours. And then really—change my family's, too! Because being out here on my own is hard when I'm responsible to five other people. Show me how to do it. How to pray. How to live. How to balance my heart's cry with my role's responsibilities.

My hands that want to be doing something and see the productivity…you put that there. Show me why. Show what I'm supposed to be doing in the natural with my hands so that I can fulfill that desire and bring you glory. God, I just need you SO BAD. I cannot do this without you. I need you to show me and to teach me. So I guess it's time to listen, huh?! I love you Daddy, more than words.

I know, daughter. I hear you; I know you. I made you the way you are and your heart's desire for me—that's how I wired it. Come to me. With all your thoughts, all your hurts, all your cries, all your desires, all your questions… come to me with everything. I AM all you need. I have all the answers you seek. And the ones that you or someone else would say are "inside of you," that's because I've already placed them there through my words and my teachings. You're not relying on self when it's said that the answer is in you. You're relying on what you've already been taught by me. So go with me. Follow me. Keep walking with and in me. I'm all you need.

So let's talk. You have a house issue. Rather, a realtor issue that you want to know about. I'm not going to give you the answer you want, because you want a direct answer. Haha. I'm not coming like that. I want you to do the research. Look at the benefit of staying with the bank or staying with Janell. What matters most to you? Dollars and cents or relationship?

What are you going to say? No direct answer of whether to stay or go? Just that we need to look at it, huh? I wish I knew that my husband was praying and seeking for an answer instead of just being so caught up with life. THIS LIFE! SO DISTRACTING! I hate it! God please help us. Please.

I have to go now. But I'm going to do what you said to do. Thanks, Daddy. Love and miss you. Sorry about all those days missed. I love you so much. Thanks for being so gracious and forgiving. If only everyone knew you.

February 24, 2014

Good morning, Daddy. It's beautiful today. The sky is so pretty, and the sun is going to shine. It's going to be wonderful. Thank you, Daddy. What's on your heart today?

You. You're on my heart. You're always on my heart. Always on my mind. I love you so. You are my princess, my angel, my gem, my star. The one I love. You are my daughter. Walk with me today. Let me guide you—in school, at home, with your husband, let me guide you in everything you do.

Well how do I really do that? Should I be quiet all day?

No, not necessarily, but let my peace rest upon you. Stay joyful because you're staying in my presence. Don't get caught up in regular daily life issues. Don't be distracted because your husband is home. Do school as normal. Run your full day. Put me first. Bring the kids to me in prayer. Seek my face. Let me direct you all.

Okay. I can do that. Or try my best to!

You can do it. Just keep trying. Your family IS going to come around; just keep following me. Put me first. Keep me first. I have all you need. I'm so glad to see and hear that your heart cry is for me. What you have to do now is get more time in prayer. It will build and strengthen you then, as well as in these times that we have together. We'll be able to do more here if you do more there. Does that make sense?

Yes, it does. Hey, what's the deal with Brianna? She is SO moody and cranky lately, what's going on?

Same as what I said before. Let me handle her. You stay true to who you are and who you are in me. Keep being joyful around her. She's going to come around. She's my daughter, too, and I speak to and through her. I'm working on her. So in my time, things are going to work out.

Okay. I trust you. It just sure is hard.

I know. But there is purpose in all I do.

Okay. I hope she enjoys this conference coming up. It'd be great if YOUR TIME was next weekend, and she snapped out of it then! Hint hint hint! [Laughing. Like you need hints.]

Yeah, that IS funny, huh? I don't need that hint, but I hear you. Bring it to me in prayer.

[Laughing.] Okay…I gotcha. I'm going to try and do better! Time to get ready for school. Love you, Daddy!

Love you, too, daughter!

February 27, 2014

Good morning, Daddy. It just seems so long in between conversations. I've got to figure out how to do this throughout the day. I just feel like if you say something important and I'm not typing this out, that I'll forget it. And I don't want to forget anything you say. So…I guess teach me what I need to learn. Either how to remember what you say or how to communicate during the day so we don't feel so far apart. I need so much more of you and from you. I have so much to learn. Please forgive me for the days that I sleep in and this leaves from my number one priority. Please help me to put you first. I want to please you with everything I do, and I know you must be first in order for that to happen. Help me Lord, I need you.

Ahhh daughter. I am here for you. I always will be. Even when you feel like your memory isn't good and you'll forget something—I'm here, come and talk to me. I'll give you what you need. I always have and always will… but you have to come to me. Don't try to do things in your own strength, and that's what you often do. That's where things fall apart and you get riddled with guilt because you know you have not sought me first. Stay before me. Come to me with any and everything. I am all you need; and I have all you need. Just keep coming to me. Everyday, throughout the day if that's what it takes, if that's what you want. It doesn't matter to me, because I'm always here.

Oooh hey, so what's up with that yucky dream?

You do have things from your past that are still within you. You do need to root those out and deal with them.

Aren't you going to tell me what?

No. I'm going to let you think and pray and ask the Holy Spirit about it. I want you to explore your mind and your past and see the residual effects of decisions made in your past. I want you to be aware of the cause and effect of certain things. You may not like it, but it'll be good for you. Please force yourself to sit down and THINK. Think back and remember things. It will be okay!

Ugh…okay…if you say so, but not right now.

No, not right now. I know you have to get ready to leave. Do you still want a fresh word for bible study?

Well, I don't know, I read that other one, and it still sounds good.

Well, it IS good! I said it! [Chuckling like—duh!]

[Smiling.] I know.

But really, I can say a few more things if you like.

Will it fit with the other? Would I just break them up into two parts?

You'll know what to do with them. Now get ready.

Okay.

Let my love overtake you. It wants to be free in you. From your belly will flow the living waters of my love. That's what I give. Freely. Without repentance. Without regret. I hold nothing back from you. All the love I have I give to you. I want your love in return, but I don't hold back while I wait on you. Yes. I'm waiting. I'm waiting for you to allow me to come in. I'm waiting for you to put your guard down.

Those hurts. Those offenses. Those questions you ask that keep us separated. Those things you blame on me. Those things done to you that you can't even understand how I would allow that. GIVE THOSE THINGS TO ME. They are not yours to carry. Lay those things down at my feet. Lay them there and don't pick them up. My son already paid for them. He's already carried and paid that weight for you. That cost. That price. Those things that rob you from the joy you could be having in me. He's already paid for that. Don't pick it back up. Don't carry it yourself again. It's done.

Now. With those things that consumed that place in your heart—let me in THERE. Let me in to that secret place that no one else even knows about. That's where I want to be. I want you to let my love and my peace wash that place. Cleanse you there and inhabit all of your being. Do you feel my love on you right now? It's here. I'm always here. Just waiting on you to allow me to overtake you. I want you to feel my peace. I want you to have freedom in me to be the person I've called you to be. Yes, there can be peace and joy while parenting. While shepherding. While working. But you have to come to me. I have to be first. CHOOSE ME.

March 3, 2014

Good morning, Daddy! It's a great day!

Yes, but it's ALWAYS a great day.

Yes, I know. But today is my super great awesome birthday that you picked for me, and I just LOVE IT!

Well I'm glad. I'm really happy that you delight in your birthday. The representation of it all and that you're not afraid to get older and share your age!

[Laughing.] Nope. Not ashamed...hopefully I'll still look good like Mrs. Jane, though, in twenty years! Golleee!

You'll be fine. So, what do YOU want to talk about today?

Oh geez. Um. All things related to the youth at church, right?!? Can't believe Dell finally, actually, said yes. I'm thinking I may volunteer in the kids part, though. What do you think about that? Is that okay, or what you want?

Yes, I'm fine with that. I think you'll be good for, and with, the kids.

Okay. I need to go back to working on that Generation for Christ (GFC) type of stuff, then.

Yes, you should. I've noticed that you've seen the reminders and hints that I've sent too, huh? Your friend asking for your story and what you do, your niece asking if you've done anything else with it.

Yeah, I've been looking backwards and seeing the clues. It's much easier to look back at Dell's clues though! Help me to see your clues in real time so I can be aware and ready for when you say GO. I just want to please you so badly that I don't want you to always be waiting on me to get my act together. Did you speak to me this morning? Tell me that I need to be praying in tongues every day?

Yes. That's a reminder, too. My servant told you that before.

I know. And I'm not doing it. Why is it so hard for me to do that at home on my own? It's so much easier when I'm at church and praying for other people?

Because you haven't learned how to reach me, go behind the veil in your personal prayer and worship time.

And like this, I just see it as—you're sitting behind the veil and I just come right up, pull aside the veil and just walk right back there! It's funny, because I can clearly see this, but I still don't see you! It's just as simple as pulling back a shower curtain to get in the shower. That's how easy it is to just come in and talk to you. I love you, Daddy. You're so amazing.

But agh! I'm so distracted thinking about today!! [Laughing.] Dinner, the mail coming with a card from bible study, opening the box from my mom…I'm so excited! So please don't get upset that I'm all over the place. In fact, is it okay if I know my assignment is to work on GFC stuff, and I just go work on my task list for today and clean up and do hair and hopefully get to read? I feel like a kid begging her daddy…please??

Yes, my child, you may go

YAY! SO EXCITED. Thanks, Dad. I heard everything you said. I'm going to try to do better. I am. Gonna try to pray more today—maybe while I shovel snow out of the driveway… ugh…when is winter going to be over, huh?!? Yuck. I am so glad you see the plan we don't, because I don't think anyone is happy about all the snow and cold. I'm just thinking that the ground will have all the water it needs to start the year.

Okay. Thanks for the time off. I'm not all the way gone though, I promise! And I don't promise, but I know how thankful I am about today, so I know I'll be praising you all day! I LOVE YOU! THANK YOU FOR THIS AWESOME BIRTHDAY!

[Smiling.] You're welcome dear. You are welcome. Enjoy it. I have a lot more for you.

TODAY?

[Laughing.] More birthdays! I do have more for you today, though. You will be blessed. You're doing a good job, and you will get to taste some reward of it today. Allow others to bless you. Accept gifts. Enjoy your day and the blessing of being my servant.

Wow. Just to hear you call me your servant brought tears to my eyes. Wow. You've taken all my giddiness and turned it into humble unworthiness. Ooh, God. You are so good. Good to me. Good to your children. I can't thank you enough, because there aren't enough words. I love you so much. [But I do need to go because kids are getting impatient with me and each other! Nothing like people striving for that "perfect" birthday plan…]

March 10, 2014

Oh Daddy. I missed you soo much!!! It's so good to be back. Back with you, in your presence! It was a good week, though, huh? Did you like it?!

Yes, I liked it. I liked my children, too. It was good for them to be reminded, or some told for the first time, who they are in me. What I think of them. Who I've created them to be. It was beautiful to see people healed from physical AND emotional scars there. Scars that I didn't put there!

Yeah…that was good, huh? It was deep. I'm going to have to go back and watch that DVD again about Job, though. I need to fully hear and grasp it. I think I was distracted by Gabi a little that night.

It's all good. Go back and watch it.

Okay. So what's up?! What's going on? What do you want to talk about? Or hey—do you want to talk about this prophet thing?

[Chuckling.] Hmmmm…no, I don't right now.

What? How can you say that? [Laughing.]

Because you asked me what I wanted to talk about!

Yeah, but you keep telling people to tell me stuff, and it sounds like you're calling me a prophet, but I don't know what that looks like. I don't know the difference of how to walk out being a prophet versus walking in the prophetic. What does that look like? Who's taught on that?

I'M your teacher. *(His interruption was almost as abrupt as when He corrected me about Joshua not being MY son—as in—we've dedicated him and given him back to the Lord. So we are stewarding God's son.)*

Okay…so don't look for or at other people's stuff?

You can. But the answers you seek and need and what will take you where you're going…those things, those teachings, those directions will come from ME.

Okay. So…you still don't want to talk about it right now? Because what are we going to talk about? We could talk about VOA, Dell and his job mess, Miracle and the concert and fundraising.

[While typing, right after I said VOA, he said,] **"Go to VOA"**.

It will be okay [to go to VOA—like, financially?]

Yes, you'll be fine. I've always blessed you. I'm not going to stop. You will be financially able to go to VOA. It really is ALL about priorities. You're not getting it wrong, Jo. I hear you saying these things at home, and you're correct. Priorities, availability, time management…you're right. It does ALL have to get in order. And YOU need to work on getting a schedule you'll stick to.

Okay. Sorry I'm getting tired again…this snot and pressure in my head!

It's okay. But don't keep ignoring yourself when people are willing to pray. My healing is for everyone.

Okay. So we didn't talk much, and now my kids are all up and at it. I've got to get back into the swing of school. Hey, thanks for showing me something yesterday at church!

I'm always showing you things. You just doubt.

I really want to get better. Not at doubting, at trusting.

Good. That's where you need to be. You're in my will, just stay with me. Do your life, and doors will open— for you AND your family. I've got plans for you all, and you'll see how they unfold. But you have to stay with me and stay on course. You cannot afford to veer right now.

So then what about my kids? And all this fighting they do? We on course with them?

They will be okay! It's all going to work out. Keep on track, set a good example, and I'll do the rest. It's coming, you'll see.

So staying on course—his job. What's the deal there? And for real—why does he keep getting words from other people when you and I know he wants to hear directly from you! What is the deal?? Everyone keeps saying that he knows your voice... then why isn't he hearing it? Why isn't he getting it?

Are you asking so you can go back and tell him what I say?

Well probably. Mostly for me to get it, but yeah, I guess I would go back and tell him how he's getting the messages.

Yeah. Well, that's not what he wants. So we don't even need to talk about it. You can just pray for your husband... and I've told you to do that before. That's what you should be doing. Not coming to me to get the answer to report back to him.

Okay, I get it. I will.

You were asking the wrong question, though. Good job catching that. Now we'll see how his prayers and questions change.

Okay. Well, I have to be a sleepy parent/teacher now. I still want to talk about the prophet stuff.

I know. We will.

Okay. I won't ask when!

Okay! [Laughing.]

Love you, Daddy.

Love you too, Jo.

March 11, 2014

Oh, Daddy. You are good. I love you. You're awesome. You're the greatest. You're the best!! [Laughing.] You amaze me. And I just love you soo much. Show me how to love you more. Show me how to serve and honor you more. What can I do for you today? What can I do with my life? I just want to live a life that pleases you. I want you to say, "well done." What can I do for you?

Love. Love me, love others, love the one in front of you, love your children, and love does cover a multitude of sins! You can parent and look like me.

I don't know what that looks like. I don't know how to walk both sides of the line of discipline and love...while not spoiling the child by sparing the rod.

You do it, though. You are getting better with your anger, you're not disciplining out of it—not physically, anyway. You still get angry and yell, and that's unnecessary. But we're working on your heart, so that will change, too. You may not see it, they may not see it, but you really are getting better. The fact that you're even thinking about becoming a better parent, and you can remember the times you've held back your hand or your words, means you are getting better. It's a process. Just keep at it. It'll become easier as it becomes who you truly are. You're doing good, though. Just keep it up.

Okay. Thanks. I'll keep working at it.

So, dear. There are some things on your mind. Youth and prophet stuff. What do you want to deal with?

I don't know. Wendell wanted to know about this job, too.

Yeah. Asking me yesterday would've been fun, huh?! That IS good practice! Do more of it. So what were you going to ask me?

I don't know, he didn't really give a direct question. He just said, "Ask God about this job."

Okay. I think he should go for it. Send in his resume. Find out about the job, what it entails, what the hours will be, will it satisfy him to work from home, or will he find that he does like being out with people?

I think I'd like it. Though I can see that at times, I wouldn't!

Yeah, there are pros and cons to it. But you can weigh those once you find out more information.

God, he feels so lost and confused. PLEASE help him.

Pray. That's what I told you to do. That's your job right now. Pray for your husband.

Yes sir. Well, maybe I don't know how I should be praying. Just the mind of Christ? Is there something blocking him? Should this be warfare?

JUST PRAY. The Spirit will lead you once you get there.

Okay…and I'm back to feeling tired again…

You're not taking care of your body. You need to eat better and get back to working out.

Argh…

You'll be fine. It's for your own good.

Yeah…I'm just too tired to do it!

It'll come. Just get back to it.

Okay. So anything else we need to talk about?

Not right now. I'm going to let you go so you can start to get your work done for school and bible study. I know you have a lot to catch up on. You can do it. I'd love if you'd revisit your own music again.

Really? It's all unfinished.

Maybe we can finish it together, then. Meet me there this week. Let's write together.

Okay! Cool! I will try harder to get life done, or under control, so I can pull away with you.

I love you, dear.

I love you too, Daddy.

March 12, 2014

Remembering that Daddy died nine years ago today. So thankful I have you as a heavenly father who will always be here for me. I miss my dad being there to answer the phone and say, "It's going to be okay," but wow…how much more you do that for me. I know I shouldn't be comparing you two to sound like you're better, because that's just plain unfair for him! But JUST SO THANKFUL to have you in my life, to have you here to comfort and guide and protect me. So grateful, God. I love our relationship. Thank you so much for taking me to this deeper place in you. Thanks for inviting me in and letting me come back each day…and somehow, you always have something to say to me! You never get tired of doing this! Amazing! [Laughing.] You're just so good to me. Thank you.

Ahh, daughter, you are most welcome. It is my pleasure to spend time with you. I love you. You are precious to me. You always have been. I've always been here watching and waiting for you to come to me. I love you, but I will not push. I wait. I wait for you to feel my presence and draw near to me. I cannot force you; it always has to be your choice. I'm so glad that you come every day that you do. I do wish it were more often, but again, I cannot force! [Smiling.]

I want to talk to you even more, throughout the day, but you'll have to listen for me. I want to give instruction, guidance, peace, provision, unfailing and unconditional love to, and through, you. I want those same things you want. And now I want you to start turning these feelings we have for each other and the things that I show you into things that you show others.

I want others to know the thoughts I have towards them. I want you to tell them. I want you to be my mouthpiece. I want you to teach other believers how to hear my voice, walk with me, talk with me. Let me guide them so I can use them too. I want you to empower, not just the next generation, but your generation.

I have gifts to share and give and teach, but I need people who are willing to be taught. Will you teach them? Will you help them see I want to use them, too? I want to use them to build my kingdom, to walk unafraid, to be bold, to be led by my spirit. Will you teach them? Will you be my mouthpiece?

Yes. Of course I will. I kind of think I was doing that…a little!

You were and you are, but I want you to do more. It's time to do more. It's time to teach. YES. I want you to teach others.

Are you wanting me to contact churches to try to teach their kids? I thought I had yesterday.

I want you to prepare and follow me. First I needed your "yes." Now I need your time.

Hmmm?

I need your time. This preparation will take time. Time to work on things, time to listen to me. Whether you plan to give me morning, night, or both, we need more time so I can give you direction. Don't worry about that manual and book as your guide. Remember, I'm teaching you. You're following me. I will give you words to say and things to teach. Do you understand that?

Yes.

Just like we sit here now, this is how I need you to dedicate your time to me. Can you commit to doing this with me in order to teach my people?

Yes, I believe so.

Okay. Then we will start. You will have to go back and do your edits, because you're going to be typing fast, and I want you to keep your eyes closed for focusing purposes. Do you understand?

Yes.

Okay. I want you to teach my love.

Okay.

That it's unconditional, that it's for now, that it alone can heal…those broken hearts, those wounds, those scars left behind by others. My love can heal. It touches people where they don't allow others to come in because they've been hurt so much.

Okay.

I want you to teach that I heal. I heal today. Not just in bible times, not just those lined up at an altar. I heal today. Anywhere. Anytime. Through anyone. I don't care about what vessel is being used. If my love is flowing out of someone, I will heal. I know what you're thinking. That I don't care about the vessel? I'm not talking about those working for the other side. I'm talking about those who are operating in love, from our side.

[I have NOTHING in my head, completely blank almost like a trance. But nothing is going on. I completely forgot what else I was questioning when He spoke.]

I heal.

Okay. What is this?

It's a deeper place. It's less distracting for you.

Okay. It's weird. I feel weird. I'm about to cry, and I don't know why. God. Should I be typing or just sitting? If I sit, will I be stopping your talking. My head is so heavy. God?

Just wait.

[This was like weight, but not heavy. Not hard to breathe. JUST DIFFERENT. I could feel the presence on me, but it's hard to explain. There was nothing in my head. No care, no worry, just peace in his presence. This whole first bout lasted about 7-10 minutes (it seemed like).]

God I want to go back. Back there again. Take me back.

You will. Peace I give to you.

I don't want to go back out. [This was me behind a curtain and seeing the curtain pulled open at the top so I could see people outside, and I didn't want to leave where I was.]

You have to write.

Okay…Can I give this away?

Yes. Through your hands and your words.

Ohh, I just want to stay here.

You can. Just rest in me through your day. This peace will stay with you. Just walk with it on you.

That was amazing. Thank you for that gift.

Always my pleasure.

I feel like we've lost our moment, though. Were you done talking/teaching?

I can still teach.

Dude, I literally FEEL lower. Like I feel like my whole body was just let down back onto my bed. That was incredible. Man, I want to go back there. I want to do that again, to stay there. Aww, man. That was incredible! I want more!

It's on you. It's in you. You can have it anytime.

[He takes me back "there," to this place of extreme peace.] This is incredible.

You want me to teach from here?

Yes…

I give peace! That passes all understanding and all knowledge and all explanation. I give this. And this is what I have for the people. I'm giving it to you to give to pass on to the people. Carry it. Use it on my children who are lacking. Give it away freely; I'll always have more to give. I'll fill you up. You'll never run out. Just keep resting in me. You'll try to figure out how to explain this, but remember, it's beyond words. Beyond your understanding. You can try, but you just won't get it. My peace is amazing, unforgettable.

I give hope. Many are without it. They've lost it because they put it in false things. Wrong things and people. But I give it. There is hope in me. Hope for a future, hope of the second coming, hope for healing and restoration, I give that. And I'm real. I do not lie. There IS hope in me. And for some, hope will be restored by witnessing my miracles and feeling my presence like this right here. Some will

believe right away, and some will need proof to believe, but I GIVE HOPE.

I treasure My children. All of you! But I really love My kids. The ones who are so often dismissed. I've chosen them to do a good work. A special work. You know it. Those doors that are cut small for only them to enter through. I've chosen them to carry out my will and my purpose. They can carry it. Let them. Let them come unto me and seek me and follow me. Let them learn of me so they can go and do. I hold nothing back from them just like I don't hold anything back from you as adults. Let me use them. Especially if you've given them back to me [baby dedications], they're mine. Let me use them.

Don't worry about a repentant heart. Those things will come from my service. Trust in me. Follow me. I'll take them and use them because they are willing and have no fears or reservations. Let me use our children for our kingdom. Let them see how exciting the Christian walk can be. Let their eyes twinkle because they love me and they love being used by me. Let them get excited and carry that fire within them that you used to have. Or maybe you never had it, and you wished you did. That fire is contagious. It's not hidden away and covered up. It's out and exposed for all to see, all to touch, all to get lit by. Come and touch the fire.

Come and experience the fire that I have for you, too. I want your hearts on fire for me. I want you as excited about my kingdom work as your kids are. Don't just sit back and look and wonder and be left out. Jump in the fire and let me use you, too. I want to use you all. I have plans for all of you...if you'll just let me use you. I want to sing. I want to hear you sing. Sing my songs

to heaven. Sing my praise. Worship me with your song. I want you to love to worship me. Again, unforced... but uninhibited. Unashamed. Unabashed. Unafraid. Just come and worship me. Please.

I want to open your heart and come in and fix it. But you have to let me. I can't come in on my own or that would be forced, and I don't do that. You have to invite me in. Tell them that. I need to be let in for the real and true healing to start. But I'm waiting because I want to do it. I want to heal them. I want things to be right with them so they can operate and live the way they were created to.

So how are you going to write this up?

Huh? I thought you just laid it out? Like that was the order, right?

Yeah, but you'll need to fill in some stuff. You can't just read this to a bunch of kids and their parents.

Okay...I don't know how I'm going to write it. It sounded long, and I know there are tons of mistakes, so I have to start with an edit first! And I've got to get my kids up for school...

This is why I am going to need you both morning and night.

Yeah, okay. I get that. Wow. Now that my eyes are open I see I have a lot of work to do with this—editing. I'll need to do it now so I remember what you said! Okay, Daddy. My kids are late, and I'll be behind too. I love you!

I love you, too, daughter!

March 13, 2014

Good morning. I'm feeling quite good this morning. Like, a little tired, but just mellow. How are you?

I am well.

That's great. You're amazing, actually. I love you. You're super, the best, excellent, beyond all of my silly words that I could come up with! I love you.

I love you, too!

So what do you want to talk about today? Sorry about not getting back last night. At least I didn't skip for TV purposes, and it was so I could type out the *Power and Love* testimonies. Hey, I'm pretty excited about doing the blog, what do you think?

I think it can be good. Just make sure you're always writing with the right heart and motives.

Okay. My goal is just to encourage while sharing examples to help someone do the same thing or teach their kids.

Yes, it's going to be good. It's going to open you up to write more things. More trainings that you may not have even thought about. You will end up with all of your material right in front of you. It's going to be good. We won't go into what you see right now [invitations to churches] because we have to focus on what is right now. And right now is pure motives and sticking to your goal—to teach, train, empower, release.

Is there more? Should there be more to that?

No. It's good.

Okay. I'm already thinking about my first speaking engagement! [Laughing.] I'm sorry. It's just hard when I KNOW that I've always felt and seen that I was going to be talking in front of people…well, I guess I don't need to apologize because really you put that there, huh? I was never talking about bad stuff for Satan, so it's all for you. But yes, I hear your reminders to keep my heart pure and focused on you and not self.

And those thoughts will come, Jo. You're not exempt. The enemy will tempt you to get off track and look at yourself or how it benefits your children. But stay with me; stay on the path and course that I have for you. Do not veer.

Yes, God. I got off track today and didn't get on here early enough. May I be excused to get us ready for the day?

Yes, of course. I love you, Jo. Speak my words today. I am with you always. Just open your mouth and speak my words.

Okay. Yes, God.

March 14, 2014

Hey, Dad. Let's do this. Are we talking plans today? I don't know what we're talking about! But let's do business.

You're rushing.

I am. Full weekend, full day if I get it all in and done. And I really want the house to get cleaned up, too. Just ready to hit the floor running, you know?

I do. But I also need you to work on your listening, okay?

Yes sir.

I don't mind getting to the point with you, but that means throughout the day I need you to be CONSCIOUSLY LISTENING MORE.

Okay. Yes sir. Got it. I'm going to listen more while out today.

Oh, not just while you're out. I mean during the day at home, too.

Ewww...that's harder. I'm usually barking orders and not very quiet.

My point.

Rrrr...okay. I will try harder to listen more. Pray for me! Can you pray for me? Jesus can!

He is.

Okay great, because I'm going to need it! [Laughing.]

So, dear, you want to talk business stuff. What type?

Well the other day you were giving me a bunch of stuff that I think I was supposed to look over again, then I think I was supposed to start meeting with you in the evening, too. And that's going to be super difficult! So I haven't done that yet. Just didn't know if there was a part two to what you were saying to me or if I was supposed to process that all first?

Yes, there's more. I can give it to you now; we don't have to wait until you get it all digested. This is information for you to study and write something out of. You follow?

Yes. Well, I think so. I did until you asked me if I did! [Laughing.]

Sure, you get it. I am your textbook, and from this time spent together you are going to write a paper, a series, a sermon, an instruction manual, etc. Do you see that? No,

I'm not saying all of those things MUST come out of this, but all of those things COULD come out of this. It's up to you what you write and who you write to. Hopefully you'll seek our guidance when you get ready to write, and we can guide you in what to pull out for what audience. But you will have to decide what you write when you sit down to study this text again.

Okay. You keep saying text, and I keep thinking about how I was supposed to be printing these out.

Yes, you WERE. And ARE supposed to be. Keep working. Don't get caught up in what you should've done. You messed up, okay, now just pick it back up and let's move on. You'll find the time in your day once you commit and give the day over to me. You've got to make your plans and stick to them. Timelines, budgets of time for each task. It is possible to be successful in your day. First give it to me, then I'll give it back.

Okay. I get it.

Good. Now let's begin.

Whoo. I thought that WAS instructional! We haven't started yet, huh?

Give it to me, and I'll give it back to you.

Okay, yes sir.

Close your eyes to focus on me only. My voice.

[TOTALLY got off track and started thinking about Miracle's missions trip and t-shirts.]

Start over!

Sorry! [Laughing.]

Okay. From the beginning. Just focus on me.

[I think I'm distracted again. It was like I saw my dad's head, but it was all the way bald on the airplane that I was on. No real seats, but he's sitting in front of me at an angle so I cannot see his face to confirm it was him. Weird.] Okay, Daddy. I'm sorry. Please forgive me. Maybe I'm not ready for business or textbook talk today.

I forgive you. And you are ready, so let's keep trying.

[Rode up into the sky like on waves that looked dry but fluid. Reminded me of thin layers like magic shell. Rode up into the sky on these blue/green waves and at the center was an eagle just staring. Like I floated right into it, but I didn't. But now there's nothing around and I can feel my arms literally right now as if I've been carrying something heavy for a long time with my arms at ninety degrees. The muscles feel tired and weak.] God, what are you saying?

Come to me all who are weary and heavy laden, and I will give you rest.

But I don't feel heavy laden. I don't know that I'm carrying a lot. What am I carrying that I shouldn't be?

My time. [I knew the answer was my/Jo's time.]

I don't understand. Show me. Explain it to me. I want to do right by you.

Follow me.

[I'm just floating along in space. I thought I made this up, but not sure since it won't leave…the French guy we just met was stirring a big pot, steam coming up, can't see inside the pot, though. It's just all white everywhere. And then a miniature version of a leader from church goes into the pot. (Goes in versus being thrown, she just went in without a fight).] Then pastor. I don't see a specific person next; it's just a knowing of the name of the person. And another guy we just met at the *Power & Love School.* I'm just knowing the names now, not seeing the people going into the pot, so I can't identify who they are.] God?

You're still here.

What are you showing me?

My prophets.

Why is the French guy on the outside?

Because he just stirred you up. Your calling and your purpose. I'm your teacher. You come to me. You can listen to their teachings, but I AM YOUR TEACHER. Do you understand?

Yes sir.

What you carry is not yours. So you need to give it all to me, every day if necessary. Your job is to carry my mantel. That's it.

Well, that's a lot!

You felt some of it lift, now give the rest to me.

But I don't even realize that I'm carrying or what I'm carrying? How can I be sure to give it to you every day?

It's your time.

Do you hear that sound that sounds like a sonar ping?

The deep calls to the deep. I'm calling to you. I want to take you to new depths in me. Follow me.

Carry my mantle. Go with me and take me with you. Everywhere you go. You are at a different level, and it's time to work harder. You will figure out your life to make it easier for us to work together.

[The last time I heard the ping I thought, "This has to be Dell doing something," and it was like I was pulled farther away, then it all lifted, and the moment ended, and I never heard the ping again. Turns out that it was Wendell's email notification! But I KNOW God used that to get a point across to me, and his presence lifted after that, and I was just right back on my bed where it all started—no longer in the heights of the sky or the depths of the ocean.]

March 15, 2014

Hey. It's the afternoon/early evening...what are you doing?

Watching you.

Yeah...[laughing]. I love you. I love this. It's good times.

It is.

I missed our time this morning, so thought I could get some time in since I was supposed to be up here taking a nap, but this is better than napping...plus I'd probably end up sleeping too long! So what's the word? Do you want to talk now?

Yes, we can. Do you have anything on your mind?

Nope. Not at all. Wondering where you would pick up. I do have this little bit of wondering...like...would I be able to go back there, wherever or whatever "THERE" is, again. It's some cool experience I just want to take part in every day. And pretty messed up that the anticipation of it reminds me of sinful habits that dwell in our pasts, huh? But we should long to be with you, in your presence, and anticipate our times together with you. Such a shame how the enemy tries to destroy us before we come to the realization of who you are and who we are to you—how much we mean to you and as much as we want to spend time with you, you want to spend even more time with us. I love you. I love this! Okay, so you were going to tell me whatever you want to tell me because I have no thoughts and agenda. Just want to hear you speak… as soon as I hush! [Laughing.]

That's fine. I love your voice, too. Especially when it's praising me or showing adoration of me. I do love to spend time with you. If only for a few minutes like we'll have this evening. I love it, too! You make me happy, Jo. I'm proud of you. You please me with the smile that you give people and children. You're catching my heart and my desires. I like that. Keep staying with me and keep at it. It's a blessing to those around you and who you come in contact with. Some people really need those smiles you give.

Okay.

I want you to sit and wait on me and my presence.

Okay. Yippee! Is this it? [Laughing.]

Just sit and wait.

Okay. I had to get comfortable!

Now hush and be still.

Okay. [Lightheadedness.] God, I want to know it's you.

You will know. I give peace. You're not focused on me. Come in and focus.

Okay. [After about 5-7 minutes…] I don't know if I can. My mind is everywhere. You want to just talk to me instead?

Let's just wait awhile longer.

Okay…[7 more minutes… I worshipped quietly, but nothing]…I don't think this is working. I think we should just talk.

Okay.

Can you just say what you wanted me to see or experience?

Would that be the same?

No, but I feel like I missed out on something. And my mind is all over the place, and I'm thinking about making the family dinner and what we're going to eat.

You heard them [family in the house], but did you try to listen to me?

No. Were you speaking?

You weren't listening for me. I told you to listen for me throughout the day.

Ugh…so that was a test, maybe?

Not necessarily. But I want you to listen for me everywhere, all the time.

Okay. [Eyes closed again. I see snow. Reminds me of how I say it's so quiet and still and peaceful after a good snow. You can just hear the stillness of the air. It's beautiful.]

Now listen there.

It's gone. It's like the spring rain has washed away the snow and the branch I see is brown and wet from the rain, but part of it still has snow. The part closest to the tree, so the end is brown and wet. A bird has landed on it. The bird leaves. It's summer now, not just hot, but dry. Really, really dry, like things are burned out it's so hot and dry. No water. No animals at all. It's deserted. God where are you in this land? Where is the help for this barren land?

You are the help. You are the fresh water for this desolate place. You are the life that brings new springs. Find the heart of the city and water it. Dig wells that go deep. Bring new life to the town. Spread your living water everywhere you go. New life. New creation. Newness because of who lives inside of you. It's time to spring up and let your own waters flow. You are a spring, and it's time to pour out. Spread what's in you to those around you. Be the well. Be the vessel that carries the living water for all to drink from.

Don't let any die or be parched. Living water is in you. Pour it out. You bring the hope to the dry and dreary lands. Spread it, share it. You won't run out. It's ever-flowing. You will be refilled every time you pour out. You will never run dry as long as you share the living water that you have. Never run out as long as you are giving out, sharing, pouring out. You give, I'll give. Abundantly. Way far above what you can think. I give increase. Look at the land now. [It's green with plant life everywhere. Lush. Grass like a golf course! Flowers in full bloom.]

That's life. Those are the seeds laid and watered by you and your family. And you're blessed because of it. Your service, your attention, your love, your time, your giving. I give back and I am taking care of you. There's much more to come. Take what I am giving you and share it with others around you. Do not keep any for yourself.

This is all to give. My words, my thoughts, my plans. Give it all away.

Huh? What are you saying?

My words. Give them away. You can look at the book; you can work on your blog. Don't be dismayed by those who hate. You will become hated. But it's for my cause, so it's good. I'm with you. Your husband supports you. Speak my words. I'm giving you words; I'm opening your mouth to speak; I'm giving you this mantle. I know you don't take it lightly, but you have to come for training.

Remember I am your teacher. I'll tell you when to speak publically. You'll know. You won't be able to contain it. Where you are not welcome, you will not speak. You will speak where the way is made for you in advance. You will know it. It comes with peace and honor.

God? Is there anything else?

Not for now. Stay in my presence. Keep in my word. Stay buried and rested in me. Come to me all the time. All the time.

Okay. This sounds like a lot.

It is. But you have me, so it's not too much. You can do all things through me.

Jesus?

Yes.

Oh wow. Okay. Should I be talking to you now?

You can, but I was just reminding you that I'm here.

Oh okay. Okay. I don't know if this is presence or if I'm getting too tired. I'm going to call this and start working on dinner.

Okay, Jo. We'll be here next time you come.

Okay…this is going to be weird you if you both talk [laughing].

You'll be okay.

Alright. Bye.

March 18, 2014

Hello. Oh, God…

I know. But you're here. That's what matters. So let's talk.

What do you want to talk about? Because I just want to listen.

That's what I like…

[Smiling.]. Okay, so you start.

I want to whisper in your ear how much I love you. My thoughts are of you. No one else is like you to me. You are special. You have a special place in my heart; you're mine. I love you dearly. Walk with me. Spend time with me. Embrace me like I always long to embrace you. Allow me to come in and take over your life. Allow me to rock your world with the love I have for you and for the world. Allow me to show you these things that I have for you. These plans I have for you. These thoughts I think of you. Allow me to do that. I want to do that. I want to show you what I think about you. You are so special to me.

I want us to have that kind of relationship. One that desires to be in each other's presence all the time.

Just like when you're courting and you long to be with your fiancé, and you get all giddy when you're together, and your heart feels saddened when you're apart…that's the relationship I want to be in with you. I want your heart to be so focused on me that I'm all you think about—because you're all I think about. And you may think that sounds crazy—how can you do your job on earth if you're always thinking of me—well, it works. Because having your mind and heart on me means that you're thinking of me, you're living for me, you're operating like me, and it's giving you peace and love and joy that no man can give.

These emotions in their fullness come from me. There are NO substitutions to the love and joy and peace I give. Nothing can compare to me. You can mark that. There is no one or no thing that will ever satisfy your longing for these things to be fulfilled. I AM the only one.

Yeah…you are all that.

And then I just have more to give! It's incredible all that I have for my children. They just have to want it and come to get it, too. Just have a desire for me. Oh how I love them and miss them and want to be with them more. I'm always with them, but I want them to know it, to experience it, to walk in the fullness of my presence. Ahh my children.

And just like you were thinking about those women in those ad relationships last night and the women who sell themselves because they don't understand their value and importance…ahh…that's my heart. I just want everyone to experience the joy and the hope I give. Those women are there because they've lost their hope and think that there's

no other way…but I am the way. I am their hope. I am the life that they seek. We must find them and tell them.

And yes, you CAN be apart of that even though you're called to kids! You're going to be alive and active and spreading my love and truth wherever you go, Jo. You're my vessel; I'm going to use you wherever you go. Keep looking for opportunities to share my love and just keep doing it. You're doing right.

Thank you, God.

Oh you're welcome. 'Cause it's in you and it's just time to start pouring it out.

You're going to show me what that looks like?

Of course. You'll know. You'll be ready to speak when it's time. Just learn to trust my voice when you're speaking out loud and when you're in public. I'm speaking, you're just not used to my voice…because you didn't follow my directions a long time ago and start talking them, you know??

Yes…I know. I do take responsibility for that.

No shame or guilt, just a reminder to get back at the consolidation and then print.

Okay. Got it.

I want you to do well today. Continue to keep your voice low with the kids and ask questions. This is a good start for you. Well done.

Thanks.

Okay, I want you to go now to prepare and get things in order. Let's try to talk again today.

Okay, I will try harder! Love you.

Love you, too.

March 19, 2014

Hey. Feeling quiet today…how are you?

I am well.

Yeah. So what's on your mind to talk about today? I'm feeling really behind in a lot of areas right now. It could get overwhelming if I let it.

So don't.

I don't plan to, but I'm just thinking about cleaning the house, packing, school, bible study, plans for the kids and youth at church…and I'm still supposed to be combining these and I haven't been. So what do YOU want me to do today?

I want you to think about me…that will give you peace. [Smiling.]

[Laughing.]

Then I want you to get your bible study things done, your school done, get to the store to pick up the items you need for bible study tomorrow. Plan your dinners for tonight and tomorrow early today so you're not waiting until the last minute. Wash those dishes that are still out. Contact someone about the garbage disposal. Do work on getting those grades in the computer, because your folder is large, and pick your curriculum. You can clean, but get these things done first, before you start to run around doing other chores.

Okay. Thanks, Dad.

No problem. Now what's really going on?

I don't know. Nothing, I think. I'm just replay things that happened and conversations from previous days. Like the little boy—she said they prayed for him, but I still felt like something needed to be dealt with. Is there something they missed? Or what should they be praying for or over or against for him?

They need to pray my spirit down on him. At an early age, they need to ask for the indwelling of the Holy Spirit to come and fill him with evidence. They need to include him in their family prayer. They need to incorporate family prayer time. The kids need to see and hear their parents praying for them and for others, both in tongues, and in English. Tell them to pray against bad habits. For all of them. Tell them to ask the Holy Spirit to reveal deep, deep roots that may go back a generation.

I don't want to tell it all to you because I want them to search back so they can see the areas that may still be affecting them from their own generation lines. I want them all to be free in me, so they have to let the Holy Spirit walk them down this journey so he can pull up things that may either be buried or unknown. It will be a process. But I, we, are with them. We will help and guide them along. There needn't be fear or doubt.

I know these are hard for you Jo, but these are my words. Just speak them and let them receive what I am saying through you. If there is doubt, I will confirm. For all of you.

Okay. Thank you, Daddy.

I want you to pray these things: life, the ability to love fully, trust, walls and guards down, loyalty, trust, peace,

patience, justice, fairness, humbleness, truth, kindness, virtue, honesty.

God I don't think I liked this. It just seems too close. I think I like asking and speaking to people I DON'T know.

Of course. You can hit or miss and it won't hurt your relationship too much. But here you're pushed outside of your comfort zone. You have to TRUST that I'm speaking to and through you. We'll see how you decide. I would just suggest that you're honest with her and tell her what you did, asked me, and what you think you got back from me. Sure, go look up those words that don't make sense to you. I don't mind you checking your source, I put that in you! Do check, so you can learn what they mean. You can leave them or take them out. But know that I speak through you.

Yes, this IS like a test of different things. We'll just see what happens. In fact, I'm going to let you go now so you can look these up and start on your full day! We'll talk later. Bye!

Uh, okay. Bye.

March 25, 2014

Good morning. I know it's been awhile…I'm sorry. There's always this feeling of wondering if you'll still talk to me when I sit down after it's been so long.

I will always speak.

Okay. So I saw that there are other people with conversations with you who wrote it down and have books out. That last one

I saw had real topics though—that were important to other people. We don't have those types of conversations.

Do you want to? We can.

No, I don't think I really want to. I don't want to help people figure out why the world is falling apart and wonder what you're doing about it. I think I like how Bill Johnson put it when he said, "I just talk about what I'm responsible for." I don't want to ever get caught up in those debates that are completely over my head and beyond my scope of knowledge anyway. So if I asked you big questions about the world and earth and origin and public leaders…I might open doors to get into that stuff. And I don't want to. I don't even watch the news!

You should.

I know…so I can know what to pray for?

And so you can know what's going on. What other prophets ARE talking about. You follow?

Yes, I do. So do YOU want to talk to me about those things??

Not really. That's not why I talk to you.

Why do we talk?

To show others that I speak.

Hmm…

If it appeared as though I only spoke to people about big news, political stuff or how the world began, then people would think that they'd have to be smart in order to hold a conversation with me.

Yeah. I'm not going to take offense to how that looks coming off the tail of my previous comments! [Laughing.]

And you shouldn't. That's basically a summary of what YOU said, NOT ME. I know how smart you really are, and you CAN comprehend those topics. They're not beyond you or "above your head." You are very capable, as are many others who read this. But I want people to know that I am here and willing and WANTING to speak to anyone who will listen. This doesn't have to be uncommon or an anomaly. This IS my norm. This IS what I want for my children, my people. I don't want us to be separated. I want us to be close, like friends, like family. I love you all so much, you just have to believe me.

Some don't believe without seeing, and so for them I have to appear in some form. Whether it be a sign, miracle, healing, or written down on paper or in a book. Jo, you ARE carrying out what I'm calling you to do. All those months and years of me telling you to write and you not knowing WHAT to write?! That was ME. Preparing you for THIS. THIS is what I'm asking, calling you to do right now. THIS is the writing that I want from you. THIS has a purpose, and there is a destiny in this.

IT IS OKAY to get your word for a person and write it down. Think how much you like having something written down so you don't lose it or forget it? Do not discredit what I am doing here. I'm training you. I'm preparing you. Yes, you will speak from a pulpit, but THIS is a part of that ministry. Those days will come, but THIS comes first.

Wow, okay.

My plans are greater; follow me. Stay with me. Stay on course. You know all this.

Yes, I've heard you say it many times. And when you say it, is it because I AM off track? Am I not inline with you??

No. I'm just reminding you of where to stay.

Okay. Alright. Where do we go from here? What's next?

I want you to talk to my people.

Huh???

I want you to talk to my people.

Is this a test?? I think I'm about to fail. I feel nervous in my stomach. You mean SOME DAY speak, right?

No, dear, I mean prepare to speak to my people.

I don't understand why this sounds so different and my stomach is getting nervous like we're about to go to church and you're asking me to speak right now.

But I am asking you to speak right now.

You don't operate in time…

Aha. You've got it. I give you a fresh word every day. I want you to know when to give it.

On Facebook?

Wherever. To whoever will listen.

Uh…okay. Are you giving me something today?

Perhaps. If you stop getting nervous and stop talking!

Haha!

[Laughing.] Are you ready?

I don't know. I don't know why you've got me nervous today.

I don't. That's my point. Stop it.

Okay, cool. I'm ready.

My grace is sufficient, but it's not to be abused. Stop abusing my grace. I give it in love, not to justify poor choices and wrong behavior. Do not try to take advantage of me. You can't out give me, so don't try to take more from me. I am all you need, and I have all you need. I will supply all of your needs according to my riches and glory. Ask me for what you need, and I will supply it according to what I know you need. If you're not getting what you're asking for, then our desires are not lined up.

Get in my will. Get yourself in tune with me. As we become more inline and are operating the same, when you're fully in my son's image, then our desires and heart cries will be the same. Then you will ask for things I want to give. Our hearts will beat in sync, and you won't have to wonder if you're in or out of my will for you. Your life, your desires, your choices, your words, your actions, your thoughts… they'll all be pleasing me and be for my glory to build my kingdom. When your thoughts are set on what pleases me, then I can use you and provide things for you and move mountains for you, because we're operating in the same spirit.

No, I am not saying that I do not answer the prayers of "baby" Christians. I am not saying I ignore the requests of those who don't know me. I am speaking to those who are seasoned in me. Know my face, know my voice, know my hand. LINE UP. Get in my will full time. Stop bending to the right and left. Stop getting off course. You know who you are. You know those things that you do that you think no one sees. I SEE. I KNOW. And I know

your heart when no one else is looking. I see what you are putting in front of you. I see what is poisoning you. I see the lies that are being told to you and spoken over you, and I see that you are believing them.

But I am here to say that I AM YOUR GOD. I AM YOUR FATHER. THE ONE WHO MADE AND CREATED YOU. I MADE IT ALL, AND IT WAS GOOD. AND YOU, MY CHILD, ARE GOOD TO ME. You are beautiful—because I made you that way. You are wonderful—because I made you that way. Stop believing the lies that you aren't good enough, you aren't pretty enough, you aren't thin enough, you aren't worth it. You ARE smart. Don't buy into the lies of the world.

They are here to bring you down, but I sent my son to lift you up. He is your righteousness. It is him that you stand behind, so that I see only purity through him. So stand behind your brother. Get in line. Get in order. Let me see who I created you to be, because you're standing behind my son. My grace is sufficient. But do not abuse it…

And what did you want me to do with this again?

Speak to my people.

Mmkay.

You are hesitant this time. It's not a sweet love song, is it?

Uh, no.

So let's see what you do. Because this is where being my mouthpiece carries weight. Coming and talking to me each morning doesn't step on toes—it may just cut into your sleep or personal time. But THIS, this is where the rubber meets the road. This is when that old stuff is

sloughed off. This is when you are truly picking up the mantle.

Yeah. This doesn't sound that pretty…I liked that love stuff better.

And that's fine. You'll get those, too. But when I give you a message, I need you to deliver it.

Oh, well, when is this for, anyway?? Like one day…

No. It's for today. Right now. Edit it and send it out.

You have a title for it?

For those off the path. Okay. Don't be hesitant. Just do it. It's not like I'm telling you who to go personally to and say it to their face, you know?!?! [Laughing.]

I know! Okay. I'm gone then. I've got to hurry before my son finishes his breakfast and is ready for school when I'm not!

Alright, daughter. Go get it done today!

Thanks, Dad. I will.

May 6, 2014

[It's been a REALLY LONG time since I've done this. Written and communed with God. Not all the way sure why. Got busy a little, NEVER want to wake up early in the morning to do this before the kids wake, and it never did seem the same when I tried this later in the day. So there's the guilt of not coming, even though I know I shouldn't feel guilt.

And I know that there were times that I'd just talk to him to see if he was still there and still listened even though I wasn't a "regular" anymore, and he'd answer. But I never said much, so he never had to answer much. It was almost like a sonar ping just to make sure I was still in proximity.

So here I am today, trying to get my life back in order. Convicted by comments of other people of words I've spoken of God's in the past and how it's still ministering to them and me just taking those times and words so lightly. My hesitation to actually get started and hear his voice again and at the same time hearing Larnell Harris in my head singing, "I Miss my Time With You." Now being pushed by the time on the clock…ugh…let's do this.]

Oh God, please forgive me.

Your Daddy forgives you. Nothing has changed. How I speak. That I speak. My love for you. Our relationship. My distance and lack there of…I'm still here. I still love you. I'm still not going anywhere! I'm just glad you're here. I'm glad you're back today. I've missed you so much. Our time together. I've missed this time to talk with one another. I'm glad you're here.

Mmm…thank you, Daddy. I feel like I've missed so much that I just want to ask—what did I miss?! What do you want to say to me?

Your house. It's under attack. You need to be persistent and fight for your house to sell. There are forces coming against you. You need to fight. Stand firm. I sent that confirmation so you would know that this is your called place. You are to move. You have heard from me. Don't get distracted by other's selfish desires and ambitions. You follow ME. So fight for your house. [Yes, clean your house!]

Argh! Okay, [laughing]—the cleaning part!

I know. [Smiling.]

So what else do you want to tell me?

That I love you.

I know. You always tell me that.

But I do. I always love you, Jo. Yes, I always tell you that and always tell you to tell others that…they need to know. Don't think of it as being a cheesy sticker. When someone is down and feeling alone and rejected and that no one cares—they need to know that I love them that I care, that I'm there for them. So tell my message—even if it's something you've heard before. Tell my message.

Okay. I'm sorry for that.

No worries. Just do better.

Okay. So what's my day look like?

Opportunities to show my love. To your children, to people you encounter. You don't even have to go out of your way. Love on the people you see today.

Okay. I can do that. With your help, of course. I need your words.

And I will give them.

My husband's job. What's the deal with that?

He should stay until I move him.

WHAT?! For real? He is really down, you know?

I know. But I'll be with him. Giving him wisdom for the replacement and giving him peace during this time. I'll

move him. The next move is mine. Just wait for it. It'll come. It'll be clear.

Like, he should take the next job that approaches him? [Smiling. I feel like it's a yes, but he's not coming out and saying it.]

You'll know when it's the right job, just wait for it.

Yay. I feel excited. Thanks so much. Is there anything else that you want to tell me this morning?

Are you ready for Pagan Picnic? Are you ready to trust what I say and give to you? Are you ready to listen and present it? I'm going to need you to start trusting me more, because it's time. My voice hasn't left you, so trust it and speak. Listen for my voice more. It's time to move forward in and with me. It's time to advance, but you have to listen and speak. Are you ready?

Yes.

Good. Then we're done here. Meet me again tomorrow, but listen for my voice throughout the day.

Okay, yes sir.

I love you.

I love you too, Daddy.

May 29, 2014

Okay. It's been too long, I know. I feel ashamed, but I know I shouldn't. I just need you to talk to me today. I know that I know you're still here and you listen and you SPEAK, but I still just need that today. I need your voice. I need some new, deep revelation. I know you love me. I know you want everyone to know that you love them. I know it seems like that's the only thing you say when I ask you what you want me to tell someone—and that I don't say it. Is it fear? Is it stuck behind the "Jesus loves you" pins and pencils and erasers and everything that used to have that plastered on it that has desensitized me from the meaning and magnitude of that?

I feel like everyone grew up with 'Jesus Loves You' on all of the kiddie toys from church, and me saying, "God loves you" won't mean anything to them. "Smile, God loves you." Those just seem like cheap band-aids to me that some woman with her hair curled and pinned up high and hair-sprayed down with her church suit on would say when you're upset or crying or walking in a room without a smile—"'God loves you!'" Like that was going to immediately take all the pain away and make everything better.

So when you tell me to "tell them that I love them" and I don't, that's why. Those are the back thoughts in my head. "They already know." "They've heard that before." "Give me more than that." You just want me to go up to them and tell them that you love them and that's it? "God loves you." And then walk off? I want to say that's not enough, but I know what that statement is actually saying and that saying it's not enough is untrue. I know that. I know it's enough. I know the reality of living and operating and accepting the fact that you DO love us IS enough to make pain go away, perception change, and frowns turn to smiles when we walk in a room. But it's the deep down, sinking in thing that has to happen. I just don't know if me saying, "God loves you" will do that to a person. Don't they need to be touched way down deep for that to really minister to them? Where's the more?

And even still, I know you're coming with the fact that you ARE the more. You'll bring the increase. You'll open the dialogue. You just want my obedience in that first step before you can give me more. They're drawn by your love and your kindness. I'm just a mouthpiece when you tell me to speak—or at least I should be.

Well, you said a lot. I heard your heart, and I thank you. I always want to hear your heart. I want to hear your thoughts. I don't want to just see everything; I want to hear from you, too. And I know you want direction. I know you want closeness and to know you can trust me because I have you in my hand. I know that. I get that. I want that, too.

I want you to trust me, and I want to be able to trust you with what I give to you. What I bless you with. Will you take care of it? Will you steward it? Will you watch over it? Keep it safe? Keep it right with me? Do your best at all times, not just when it's convenient or your kids are around? Will you do right by me when you are alone? And yes, I know you have, but in relation to what you spoke of here today—I want you to speak, because you asked what I wanted to say, and I've told you what to say. So go and say it. All boldness will come to you. Take the phrase "God loves you" out of the box. I have no box, so if I tell you to say it, it's for a reason. It's not going to leave your mouth and then go into a box. I am love. I encompass everything, I'm everywhere, I am love. So when you tell someone I love them, you are releasing into the atmosphere, THEIR atmosphere, the love I have for them. So do it.

Okay. I'm sorry.

It's fine. Just do better.

Is there anything else you want to say?

Mmm…I know that you want to talk about the house. Just wait on me. My timing is perfect. I know things are moving on all around you. Just wait; I have it all in order.

What about the carpet? Do we have to get it done?

No, you don't have to.

I mean first, do we have to do it right now?

No, you don't have to.

What about his job?

I told you about his job. He needs to put it out there. His job will approach him, and you will KNOW.

Okay. But I'm feeling pushy almost. Should I be? Should I keep telling him to get his resume out there now, or should I say, "When you're ready to leave, get your resume out there?"

He needs to do it now. It'd be best if he put it out there now. The timing is right. This is the season. Things will fall into place.

Okay. I'll try to be careful about how I do it. Will you help lay it on his heart then, too, please?

Yes, I will.

Okay. I probably need to pretend to do school stuff now. I want to be productive today and clean out some stuff, but I hurt.

You'll be okay. You will be able to do the things you need to do.

Okay. Thanks. I love you.

I love you, too.

June 4, 2014

Hey. How is it?

It is well. Are you doing well on your own?

Hmph. No, but you knew that.

Of course. So what are you going to do differently?

I don't know. I could sit here and say I'm going to do better, come every day, get back to a schedule…but in reality…I haven't done too well, and I'm not sure how much of that would be true. I don't want to lie.

I know.

So I'm not sure how I'm going to do better. I'm just going to try.

That's all I want. That's all I ask. Is that you try. Just give me your heart. Whether you're here and we're face to face, or if you're not and I'm just over your shoulder, I'm still here. I'm still present with you. I know that to you it's not the same, but to me it is. I'm always here. Just remember that. Make use of that. Stop making me seem like a far away person. You must learn to talk to me all the time, anytime, because I'm always right here. Always. Just ask, seek, knock, speak to me. You'll see that I'm here and I answer. Listen for me more throughout the day. If you do that, you'll rely less on this time and recognize you're not away from me even when you're not sitting down at the computer. You hear my voice, so use it. Use our relationship throughout the day wherever you are. You may enjoy writing and writing letters, but that's not always going to be how you receive it. And you must be able to give when you receive it.

Okay. I'm going to try to do better. Talk to you throughout the day.

Yes.

Okay. What else do you want to tell me? Because I know there's more!

That I love you. I do. You mean so much to me. I love you dearly, just want to pinch your cheeks you're so precious to me! [Smiling.] I want to hold your hand. I want to walk you down beside the water. I want to calm your soul. I want to refresh you.

This feels like it's supposed to be song lyrics.

It can be. You choose. But I want you to feel the way I feel for you. Not just how much I love you—how you feel on the receiving end, but how I feel on the GIVING end. I want you to know THAT. I want you to know how excited I get about you and spending time with you. I love watching you worship, love, give, play, pray, and share with people. Oh, it makes my heart sing! I LOVE IT! I LOVE YOU! You're amazing! I love the way I made you! You're incredible. And you're walking with me! You're mine! You've chosen me. You love me. You serve me. YOU'RE MINE! Hee hee. You're mine! I just love it so much. You make me SO HAPPY! It's unbelievable! You wouldn't believe it! YES YOU! Yeah, you have faults and make mistakes and sin and do wrong things, but I just love you so much because you chose to follow me! You're mine! [CHEESY SMILE. So giddy like I would be about something!]

[Laughing.] It's crazy!!

Aww man…but it's not. I mean I get how you say it is, but it isn't. I'm not crazy. My love isn't crazy. Not wrong. I'm head over heals for you. I LOVE YOU! It's not crazy to me, but there on earth to love someone this much and get SO EXCITED about them DOES equate to crazy. But that's because it's all twisted there. That's okay though—it doesn't stop how I feel about you, and it doesn't stop me from making sure I do all I can to make sure YOU know how much I love you. My love is unstoppable. There is nothing you can do to stop my love for you. YOU'RE MINE!

You're funny.

Good. I like funny, too! But did I take you down to the water? Could you see it?

Yes.

Did I give you peace and rest there? Does it satisfy your soul and your thirst?

Yes. But I want to be unquenchable, right?

Haha. Yes…but I want you to be fully satisfied with me, too. See, unlike food or drink where there are point of satisfaction that shut off the hunger or thirst, with me, the hunger and thirst continues—grows even. And yet, while your longing continues, you're being satisfied by my presence at the same time. Do you understand that?

Yes.

I am the only one who can fill those voids and appetites, no one or nothing else. In my presence is fullness of joy, of peace, of love…in MY presence. That's where I want to take you.

The still waters? Where my cup runs over?

YES. That is it.

Ahhh…I see. Thank you. For taking me there, for leading me by the hand to that place.

We can go to it anytime, you know? It doesn't have to be organized or set up. I can take you there anytime; you just have to let me. Come to me…<u>stay with me!</u>

[Smiling.] Yeah…you're so good to me.

I am.

I often wonder why, though.

Well, why wouldn't I be?

Well, I mean in comparison.

AH! We don't compare. Don't do that. That's from the enemy. They're lies straight from him. We don't entertain those thoughts here, so you shouldn't there. And if you can handle that without a teaching, then let's move on. Do you need a teaching?

No.

Great. Now if you do in the future, for you or for someone else, that's fine, you just come back and ask. But if not right now, then let's just leave that alone. I'm good to you. I take care of you and cover you and bless you. I even have others bless you! I do that. And I can. Do you need to ask anything else about it?

No.

Well alright then, just give thanks and keep giving to others. That's all I'm asking of you. Give and receive. Not a law for greed, Jo, or false motives—

I know. I know what you mean. Keep loving to give. Whether I get stuff or health or spiritual stuff from you, just keep giving, because I love to be a giver.

Yes, that's great. Great job. I love it. I love you! You're great! [Laughing.]

[Laughing.] Oh my goodness, you're nuts tonight!

[Laughing.] That's fine. Just fine. I like to have fun, Jo. I love to have fun with my children just like you like to have fun with your children. I know what you're thinking, but there's still time, you can still have fun, you can make things better. Just get on the floor. Get on the same level and HAVE FUN.

Okay.

I know there's more you want to ask about this weekend and that's fine, but we need to talk tomorrow, because you need to get ready for bed now. Just do it. I love you!

I love you, too, Daddy.

June 21, 2014

Good morning. I know it's been awhile, but I need daily instructions like you used to give me.

Well first I want you to love me and know that I love you more! You can't stop that or break that, so just live in the fullness of love that I bring. You are my chosen, and I love you very much. You ARE doing a good job, and you DO please me, so carry yourself as such!

Okay. God come into this place and send your peace. Let it wash over my children, my family. Let them get along because your peace is so heavy in this place. Take us to another place in you, another level, another depth, take us higher and take us deeper! Just have your way in us, Lord. So what else do you want to say or want me to do today?

Look for people to bless today. Look for my children. They're lost. Point them towards me today, Show them there IS good in the world, even if it's just by your smile.

Okay. I can do that!

Walk in my fullness. Walk in my peace and my presence, in my love. You carry it. You all do. You're all carriers of all that I am—so today, give it away. Intentionally—give what you have away.

So will we have to clean the house today for a showing?

No. Just be with your family today.

Uh. Okay. When's the next time we're going to have a showing?

Soon.

You know I want a REAL answer, right? The kind that we humans operate in…like WHAT DAY are we going to have another showing? [I think I got Thursday, but then it was like Tuesday, and then it was Thursday. So I don't know.]

God is there something we're NOT doing? Is there something we're doing WRONG? Why are we still here? Why are we having to wait so long and drive so much?

What do you want me to answer? My timing is perfect, Jo. Do you want to rush into something that isn't my choice for you?

No.

Okay, then. Just wait on me. I'll show you. You'll know.

Yes, but what about the price range? Is it wrong? Are you going to find him a house that fits in his budget?

You'll see how that works out. Keep looking for the house you want. I'm with you. It's okay to look.

But you know I hate seeing all these things I can't have, then we look at houses in the budget and they're so plain and small and there's no yard or they're far away...you know my desire is to live south of the church. I want to be CLOSE.

I know. I know your heart's desires and I know your motivation. And it's good. But you are going to have to just wait on me or things won't be right—the way I planned them for you.

Well can you give us some kind of clues? You didn't say if there's something we need to do here?

No, just keep doing what you're doing. Maintain there. No real investments right now. You can always declutter and repack things more. There's plenty to do in the garage and storage shed—if you're just trying to stay busy. Or you could just wait on me. It's your choice.

But is it going to be SOON? Like—REALLY SOON? What's coming first? Selling this house or buying the next? Those houses are going so fast, and if you're going to get us a nice house at his silly low price, I know it's going to go fast. UGH! I'm so tired and frustrated by this!

So don't be. Stop. The answer is that you have to wait on me anyway, so just be quiet and wait. Stop fretting over

this. If you can look at houses calmly, then go ahead. But if you can't, then just stop and wait on me.

Okay. Fine. I need to back away for a minute. I'll just focus on what I do TODAY.

That's a good choice.

Giving myself and what we have away. Got it. I think I'm done if you are.

I can be done. I love you, Jo. You know that, right?

Oh, absolutely. I know. You tell me and show me. Thanks for letting me sing! That was the best thing ever! I love it! Oh my gosh I love it so much. THANK YOU.

You're welcome. Keep up the good work.

Thanks God, I will.

July 5, 2014

When it takes me so long to come back here I always wonder if I've lost it. My ability to hear. That you'll come each time. Which is actually pretty silly since I'm always telling people that you're real and you hear and you answer! Of course you're going to be there, right? Because I'm here. And you want to be with me. You want to be with each of us. Today I'm just really feeling this desire to do more, be more, create more. I know you put the desire for more in us, but I also don't want to get ahead of myself and ultimately, YOU. I don't want to get ahead of your plan for me.

I feel like I want to start writing a message to go out somewhere and preach—but I don't feel like that's a complete prompting from you. Like it's not a bad thing to be prepared, but honestly, my heart is not in the right place with those thoughts. So it makes me feel like I shouldn't begin to try to write anything, because it won't be coming from your breath. It'll be coming from my own mind, and I don't want that. I want it God-inspired and God-breathed. So I'll wait on you.

Oh, my daughter…I love you so. We'll never be separated. I'm always with you, I always will be. Have no fear of that at all. I love to spend time with you. I loved being able to partner with you last night as you opened your mouth and let me fill it. Light was shone last night. Lives were changed, lives will continue to change because of the work you all did last night.

Thank you, Father. That's so good to hear. I loved it. I would love to just sit in one of those circles all the time! But I know I can't…mainly because I just said that! Like, if that's comfortable to me, then it's time to work on another area that's NOT so comfortable. Let you use me in a different area that I know is not something I can just figure out on my own.

That is good. I do want to use you in other areas. And I know that you're thinking about the kids coming up, too. Yes. Let's do that. Do you have a day you'd like to do?

No, I was going to ask you all of this and let you be in control.

I see what you're hearing in your head. Don't worry about that. If you know that your motives and your heart is pure for wanting to teach and work with the kids, then you just ignore those thoughts and kick them out. Just remind them whom you work for and that those tactics won't work on you.

Okay.

Okay. Now—you're thinking about this week. Monday or Thursday. I'm going to go with Thursday, because I know that Monday you'll be tired. Plus, you're not giving people too much notice right now!

Yeah, I guess you're right.

But those who need to be there will be there, so it's all good. Do you need help with what to say or are you going to pull up the stuff from last year?

Well, I wasn't sure if I was going to just call it a one day event on hearing the voice of God, how to apply it in your life, and give some homework stuff? Are we going to talk about this, or do you want to just give me what I should do and say?

Ha…I could. But I want you to think, too.

Ugh.

It's good for you. So we have Thursday, and you're trying to nail down a topic—for a one-day class, huh?

Yes.

Okay. Welcome the Holy Spirit.

Huh? No. That doesn't sound right.

No, I mean YOU. RIGHT NOW. Welcome the Holy Spirit into this meeting time, remember?

Oh yes, I do. Sorry. I always forget.

That's because you don't read what you've written. I need you to read it all more. I've shared some very important things with you that you need to re-read.

Okay. I'll try to keep working on the consolidation of it all.

We'll that's not my whole point, Jo. I'm talking about going back and reading what you need to read.

Alright. So where are we now, because I just go super tired! Crazy. Okay, I'm awake. Let's do this. Talk to me. Can I do a session in one day and give the kids enough tools? Would it be too much? Do I need smaller sessions over a period of days? Forget it. I really just want you to talk and to lead me. I don't want to think; I just want you to speak.

I want you to hear my voice and write what you hear. You're not thinking; this is me speaking. Just follow me. I have your purpose and your destiny. Even the things you spoke about today, I have all that. Those are in my plans. You're thinking them because you're sensing them. It's coming, you're right, but it's coming by my doing, not yours. You just keep following the unction and silencing the negative voices. Do the work, put the time in. I'm going to show you what to write. I'm going to show you ways of doing things that will make sense to whoever your audience is. You'll have to listen and pay attention to me, though, or you'll miss it. Remember, don't over think. Don't make it deep and complex. We're going to keep things simple so everyone can understand.

They need to bring their own notebooks and writing utensils. They need to take notes. You'll need to use the white board. Yes 1pm to 3pm is fine. I want you to talk about the different ways I speak and give examples. I want you to let them share about how they've heard or seen me speak to them before. I want the new kids to feel at ease. I want older kids to feel that they're being a part of the training of the new kids. I want an atmosphere that encourages everyone to get something.

You're really going to need some one-on-one time, if the parents allow it. Some will, some won't. That's fine. You take whoever will come. Don't push, don't argue, don't defend me—because you shouldn't have to. No one is being forced to come, this should all be free will.

Start looking at the calendar now. Have a date set up that you'll be able to take kids out and use what they've learned. You'll need to read this week. Pick up the children's book, your bible, and just stay consumed by me, the word, the ways people operate with kids this week. Get online and look things up. Be consumed with me this week. CONSUMED!

Okay!

And I DO want you to work on your art. Once again, it's time to get your days in order. You need to budget your time wisely. Get important things done, and don't stress over things that don't matter. Clean house is nice, but it does nothing for your heart and your soul at the end of the day or your life. It doesn't matter. Focus on what needs to be focused on. Let ME train you. Let ME teach you. Let ME empower you. And let ME release you. I will. Just watch me. Stay with me. Those other things you desire will come. They're down the road—and they're NOT far. You're not far off on what you feel, but let ME guide you. You're right to not do it on your own. Stay in tune with me, and when I call you, I need you to come to me then. Stay in prayer, stay in worship, stay in my presence, stay in the teachings. BE CONSUMED THIS WEEK! Now GO. NOW!

Yes sir![After editing, just having this feeling of peace and empowerment already! LOVE IT!GENERATION FOR CHRIST!]

July 8, 2014

Good morning, Daddy. I know that I didn't do too good yesterday. I think you wanted me to do more than I did. I don't feel I was in my Bible enough. For some reason I feel like I actually NEED to be reading my physical bible, is that the case? Instead of listening to or reading on my tablet?

Either is fine, but if you feel you get more by reading your physical bible, as opposed to reading on your iPad, then you do what feels most beneficial. I just want you in my word…it doesn't matter how you get it. So don't beat yourself up because you feel that you're not living up to my expectations.

Okay.

Okay. Now I do have plans for you today. You need to pull out your old papers and read over them. Do spend time in the bible today, do listen those videos [Curry Blake].

Anything else?

Just stay in my presence, Jo. Work on RESPONDING more than you're REACTING. You're fine until one of the kids does something you don't have control over. You've got to let go of that feeling of having control of everything. You don't have it. You never will. Just roll with it. Go with me. Lean on me for understanding and what to say and do. You need to consult me more during the day.

Again, it's not just about this quiet time. You have to work up to the point where it's you and me together all day. Where you're constantly listening for my voice or the prompting of the Holy Spirit. This time is good, but this is not all there is.

Okay.

Just listen for me, Jo. Follow my lead. I'll lead you.

Okay. Hey I'm struggling with trying to make something of myself.

Yes, I've seen all that going on. You're handling it well. Keep reminding yourself of who you are, who you stand for, that it's my timing. Keep shutting those thoughts down. I'm glad you recognize them for what they are and who they're from. Just keep resisting and keep yourself humble. You're following my steps, and I know the more you hear those wrong thoughts and see those around you who are self-promoting, it is easy to get distracted. But keep following me.

Follow my leading. Promote ME, lift up my name, my Son, my plan, my purpose, my destiny to the ones around you. Lift ME up, and I will draw them in. You just keep following me and following my lead. I'll take you where you need to go when it's time to be there.

Okay. Is there anything else you want to share with me today?

No, just don't forget to spend time with me in prayer. That's what you're lacking. That full on, intentional, crying out to me prayer. You need to get back to that. Start building that time back up. And when you wake up in the middle of the night, it's not just to think about all that you did or didn't finish. ASK ME what I want you to do with that time!

Okay. Yes sir! Sorry about that.

It's all good. But I just want you to start thinking like me more, and that comes from time spent with me.

Okay, I will. Thank you.

Yeah. Sure. Now go and have a good day with me!

[Smiling.] Okay. Love you, Daddy!

Love you, too, babe.

July 9, 2014

My wandering thoughts…God where are we going? (in regards to the house and moving)

I almost feel like we should take our house off the market, should we?

No.

Okay…so what's going on with it?

Are you following me? That's what I told you to do. Follow me. Let me lead you.

Yeah, I think we are. Aren't we?

You are. There's more, but you are following.

What do you mean there's more?

I mean there's more that you can do. There are more lives to touch and activate while you're where you are. You could be doing more…as a family.

Ah, okay. Yeah, I kind of figured that. Trying to figure out how to keep my kids engaged and excited about you and working for you—WITH you really.

Yes, with me. But don't push them towards me. Lead them, but they have to make their own choices. By leading them you've taught and shown them all they need to do to

get to me, follow me, love me. You've trained them. But that final step is theirs to take. And if you've done what I've commanded you to do, then at that point you have to let them make that choice for themselves. The Spirit will draw them in. You just keep praying and covering them. Keep being a REAL example for them. You've got to have a transparent life, because they can see right through you.

I need to calm down and stop reacting. I think when I lose my temper is when I look most like an unchanged, unsaved person that I'm asking them to look like. I have to control my emotions and anger and losing control. I think that if I can show Brianna and Gabi how to lose control without reacting that that would help them.

Yes, it would. You just keep renewing your mind each day. You keep doing quiet time. You keep reading in front of them. YOU have to change your lifestyle for them to see it, respect it, desire it. They have to see it in YOU if it's something they're going to want to duplicate.

Okay.

Look at that…

What?

You actually left the conversation about the house…ha haaa…you're growing up, Jo! [Laughing.]

There was a little shift in focus there, huh? That's funny. That is good, though. That makes me feel good. I have been feeling like I need to pay attention to the house less lately. Like we all do. Wendell is totally asking for a miracle for what he wants AND what he wants to pay for it. And if you're going to do it, and if this is the time that we're going to get what people have talked about, then we're going to have to follow you. Because it seems like you're going to have to lead us to the right people, in the right place, at the right time, and hook it all together.

Sure…follow me.

So…what about the house?

What about it?

Uhh…are we ever going to move?

Yes.

[Laughing.] I mean, soon?

Yes, soon.

No…your "soons" are long! Are we supposed to be at this new church?

Yes.

Are we supposed to move over to Missouri?

Yes.

Is Wendell supposed to get a new job?

Yes.

Hmmm. Is HE supposed to find it?

It will come to him.

Are we going to have to settle for a house that we don't really like?

No. You will like your house.

Do you want to tell me the price of the house? Or the range of it?

No. You just follow me on that. I will take you to/show you your house.

Okay…so it will have a three car garage?!

[Chuckling.] It will have what you want in it. You don't have to worry about that. You will not be settling like the feeling you've had with some other houses you've looked at.

Well, when are we going to sell THIS house?

Soon! [Smiling.]

[Starting to feel like this cat and mouse game is not funny anymore.] Well, can you continue to let me know in advance when we need to start cleaning? I appreciate the heads up even if my kids don't.

Yes, I can do that.

[So now I'm feeling like one [a showing] is soon.] Is there one coming up?

Soon.

Well how soon? [We'll be out tomorrow morning, GFC here in the afternoon, and Let Them Eat Art Friday night. And we have to go out today!]

Just keep maintaining the house and clean things when you're able. Don't wait, just do it when it pops in your mind.

Okay.

It'll be okay, Jo. The buyer is going to like your house regardless of its slight imperfections. You just need to do your part.

Okay.

Do you have anything to say about anyone?

I always have something to say about people! [Chuckling.]

Well, I mean do you have a word I need to deliver for you? Or someone I need to be praying for?

Tell Vee that everything is going to be okay. I see her tears and her struggles that she holds inside. I hear her silent prayers. I've got her covered. Her children, her husband, the house, it's all in my hands. I hold their future; I hold their plans. Their lives are in my hands. I've got them covered. Don't look to the right or the left; just keep your eyes stayed on me. I'll keep you in perfect peace. There's nothing too big for me and nothing too hard for me. I know all, I see all, and I hear all. Do not be afraid.

Nice. Anything else you want to say today? To me or anyone else?

My love is perfect. It casts out all fear and doubt. To walk with me is to know me. I want you to know me more. I want you to be aware of my presence with, and in, you all the time. I want you to walk in the fullness I bring. I've come to set people free, and that is what I want you to do. Set people free by the messages you've been given and the things you've been taught. My grace is sufficient, and my word brings rest. Rest in me. I have all you need. Follow me.

July 11, 2014

Good morning. Where do we start today? I've got nothing on my mind!

That's a good place to be.

Yeah… But I do know that if I don't lead with a question, you're going to start in on me. Hmm…I wonder what needs my attention to fix today, do tell?

Well, I hope that's not how you look at this time. Like all I do is tell you what you need to change or fix, as if I'm complaining.

I don't.

Because it's all for your betterment, which is what I thought you've said you've come to do. Your goal is to become a better follower, right?

Yes.

Okay then. Please don't make it sound like I sit up and list all the things wrong with you that you have to fix in order to do whatever it is you think you need to do to accomplish something. That's not how I operate, Jo. When you cry out to me in prayer or worship or tears and say, "Change my heart God," then I take that literally. And changing someone's heart is a process—which I thought we were both in on. Are we not?

Yes, we are. I didn't mean it the way it sounded. I'm sorry.

Which is simply a reminder of what your husband reminds you—that you need to think about what you're saying before you speak. How does it sound? What's your tone? How's it going to be taken—not just how do YOU mean it?

Yeah, I gotcha. So….anything today? This is going to really test my hearing, because I really have NOTHING in my head!

So just trust in me today, okay? When you go out, listen for me. Even when talking your husband, listen for me. I want you to hear my voice today. I want your smile to be on, your joy to overflow, and my spirit to lead and flow out of you with the words you speak. I want you to speak life to dry and dead situations. I want you to experience my love in a new way. The love of the father who has good gifts for his children. The love of a father who shares things with His children. The love of the Father who teaches his children how to do work and fix things.

I want you to fix things today. Fix those things that are broken, those lives that are broken. I want you to work for me, using me. I'm your guide, so let me show you and lead the way. Don't be like the child who hears and tries to take over because they think they know what the teacher is going to say or do next. FOLLOW ME! LET ME LEAD!

Stay in my presence today. Get before me in my presence. Come to me in prayer. Let me surround you with my angels. Call on them for help and protection. Call on the Holy Spirit to be present and active, and listen for Him the whole time. The whole day—not just when you think you need something. Be present today…in my presence. STAY in my presence. Yes, you can. Even in your home with the noise and interruptions.

Stop getting mad at them when they "interrupt" you. Learn how to stay peaceful. They're not breaking the flow; you are with your anger. Stay in my peace. Yes—that WILL be an indicator for you that you've changed—how you respond to your children! The loss of your control over everyone and every situation. How you will learn to respond and not react. They'll notice it, too. It'll be a

great testimony for them, as well. So you MUST stay in my presence. Learn how to abide in me at all times.

I'm really wondering how you want me to parent in this peace that makes you feel "out of it"—like a high—though I've never been high to compare it! How do you want me to handle their disobedience when I'm in a state of peace?

Calmly.

Mmm. And consequences for their actions?

Deliver it calmly. Your peace doesn't change the outcome from their disobedience; it changes the delivery of their consequence. In my peace you can easily respond. There is no reaction going on. If you don't react, they won't react. Over time! It won't be immediate just like YOU'RE process of change is not immediate.

Right. Gotcha. Okay. I'll try my best.

That's all I ask. But remember you've already got all that you need to do it. It's just a matter of walking it out.

Yeah, okay. So is this what you want me to do today? I'm guessing you've given me direction for today knowing that I'll be at the doctor and the ministry thing tonight?

Yes, I have.

I didn't talk to you about teaching on Sunday. I need to do that. Figure something out for them. Wondering if I SHOULD wait until tomorrow after Let Them Eat Art in case something spawns out of that time tonight?

You could. Or you could just talk about something that's on your heart already.

I don't know what's on my heart already.

You do. What gets you all excited? When you're smiling because you're bubbling over and you just want everyone to...what? What is that? THAT'S what's on your heart. That's what is your heart's desire to teach.

Wow. So did I just 'get it' by titling it? Fix Broken Things. That's what we should be doing, right? That's what these kids can do. Either recognizing it in themselves or recognizing the brokenness in someone else and giving them hope. We need to Fix Broken Things. I think I like it!

I think I like it, too!

Yay, God!

Yay, Jo. I told you it was already on your heart. That's what you keep having a desire to teach people. How to pray for those who need healing, and that's the physical part, but it's just as powerful to heal those emotional breaks. Yes, dear. Let your mind go with that today. It's okay to stop and sit and write! Yes, you have time. You will get the housework done! Spend time with your pen & paper today and write. And keep your mind stayed on me. I love you, girl. It's time to go!

Yes sir. I'm ready now. Thank you, Daddy.

Thank YOU, baby. Thanks for coming to me today. Just stay with us now.

I will. If I get off, please one of you just bring me back in, okay?

Okay.

Alright, I'm excited. Maybe so excited it's bringing on a slight headache...or I need to go eat...but please heal my head. I don't want any physical [or any other] distractions today before going out tonight! Thanks.

Done. You're welcome.

[Yes, the pain is gone!]

July 16, 2014

God what are you saying to me? [After reading the email I got back from the salesperson—after watching John Bevere on Sid Roth right after asking God what he wanted me to do about the communions/book.

Stopped to pull up a prophecy that I thought spoke of me writing, couldn't find it, fixed a cup of coffee, now I'm ready for this heart-to-heart conversation I'm about to have with my daddy!]

Okay, Daddy. What's the word? What are you trying to say to me? What is it that you want me to do?

I want you to live. I want you to live as if no one is watching, and I want you to live free in me. Sing, praise, paint, write [music], write our talks—LIVE FREE! It's the freedom that I bring, that I give to my children… that's how I want you to live!!!! [He's really excited. Like how I get when I'm talking about spiritual stuff and kids! But I'm not quite at His level.]

So….what about this book thing though?

[Taken aback.] I just told you to live free and you want to know about a book? You want to be under someone's rules and deadlines instead of listening to my voice when I speak to you? Is that what you want?

No.

Well then. Rest in MY words, and stay there until I tell you otherwise.

Like right now, huh?

Yes, right now. Just sit. Don't type unless I speak to you. Just sit in my presence and wait.

Now write. Write as the Spirit leads you in this drunken state.

I give utterance. I speak in the utterance. I understand in the utterance. My words come from the father and the son, and I speak them. I speak on their behalf and yours. The heaviness you feel is the weight of the glory of God that rests upon you. With the mantle he's given you, you will go and change many. Many lives will be changed by the words given unto you. You have a greater purpose not yet tapped into. You are at the brink, the beginning of a new thing, a new career, a new beginning. You are at the start. Don't despise small beginnings, and understand them for what they are. You're going to show many children how God wants to use them and how what they sense is not just okay but should be celebrated. You're going to snatch kids from the hold of the devil simply by them understanding whose giftings they carry. Some relationships will fall, but you're planting truth in the lives of the next generation. Go and set them free—where you are. They are not always going to come to you. You will have to go and find some in order to set them free. That is okay. The father just wants his children free. Speak truth always. No lies. No omissions. Speak truth only. Study. Read. Pray. Listen to others' teachings. Stay in his presence ALL DAY. Don't be so distracted by life that you react instead of respond. Stay in his presence, and you'll be able to respond more and

more accurately and more like your father. I am here to comfort, to teach, and to train you. I need you to remember to call on me. Call on my presence, ask me for help, ask me for guidance. I will help you; that's what I'm here for.

Okay.

I will open your ears to hear more, your eyes to see more, if that is what you desire.

It is.

Okay, then. With that comes more weight, more responsibility. Are you ready for that?

I think so.

Okay. Then I will reveal more. But be aware—you have to be ready to respond immediately. You're going to see things before they happen, and you have to be willing to respond accordingly. Some things will require quick action. You must be proactive. You must take the things you see and immediately begin to pray for and about and often against them. Are you ready for that increased responsibility?

Yes.

Because you will see how this is going to come out in your children. Now I'm letting you know this in advance that you're going to be able to identify the spirit involved with your child's behavior, and you're going to have to deal with it right then. Do you understand that?

Yes.

Okay. Then eyes and ears be opened to see and hear more. Now!

Should I open my eyes? There's a weight and a peace here at the same time. What do you want me to do?

Live your life as you normally do and as God said, but now you'll be aware of more. Be on guard, be vigilant, aware and fight the good fight when you're aware of the presence of darkness around you. Ultimately, this should have you in constant communication with the father, because this should keep you in prayer! [Laughing.]

Oh. [It's funny?]

No, it's not. But this will create the necessity of the traits you're all supposed to have already...praying without ceasing.

Hmmm. Okay. So this was OUR first time talking like this.

Yes, it was. And not the last. You remember God said Jesus and I were always there in your communions; it's just a matter of who you're talking to. You will still need to have conversations with Jesus, as well.

Yeah. Well, unless there's anything else, I just got REALLY tired.

Enemy, Jo...enemy...be aware, be awake, be vigilant, be on guard. You have to stop letting your guard down. And just so you know, your lack of rest at night let's your spiritual guard down, too. It's not just about your physical being that's being affected; it's your spiritual man, as well. You've got to work on your military mindset, and hopefully you do that quickly since I've already asked that your eyes and ears be opened more.

Mmm, okay. So we'll be talking later then, I'm sure. I'm going to get off of the computer now.

Okay.

July 21, 2014

Good morning, Daddy. I had a good weekend. Productive craft-wise! Thank you.

You're welcome. I heard you ask me to bless your hands; I have. They are anointed for greatness. So much more than just yarn and paint, though. You know that, right?

Yes. I know.

I've called you to do a great many things. Still creative. Both in the arts and in the supernatural.

Ah cool! Like creative miracles?

You'll see!

Sweet!

But your voice is anointed, too. You will speak into the lives of many, and they will be healed and restored to their right standing with me. That is as beautiful as art, too. The beauty of life in alignment. That's beautiful. That's the art and masterpiece I created! That's what I want to use you for. You can draw them in with your hands and your talents, but it's your voice that will put them in alignment with me. Use your talents to draw them close, then use your voice to point them to me. See how it all goes together?

Yes. I love it.

Sure you do. You get to see how I give gifts and talents, but they're still all for my glory when used correctly. Just stay in alignment with me, Jo. Stay with me. Let me guide you. Even with that book you've been toying with. I know

I told you there was a book inside of you. I know that. But let ME guide you. You go back and do what I told you to do a LONG time ago—put it together, print it out, and read back through it. YES, you can see that benefit now. It's not just for spiritual purposes. Yes, that is your editing, too. Just do it! Just be obedient!

Ahh, Daddy, I will try harder to be obedient. I just need to get over the fact of that I need to sit at my computer and WORK. It's something about the way it looks to be sitting at the computer. But I DO need to do work on here. For you, for school, for church.

Yes, dear, you just need to sit down and work. Do it today when you get home. Do it tomorrow after you meet with the kids. You have time. Just do it. Block off the time so you can still work on your yarn, still meet with me, still read the books you have to read, still do the work on the computer you need to do. You can do it. So what are your plans for today?

Huh? Aren't I supposed to ask YOU that?

Yes, but I asked you first today. I want to hear what you have planned for today, then I'll tell you what I think about it.

Weird, but okay! When I finish with you I'm going to get ready for the day, go downstairs, get some coffee going, get the notebooks and pencils ready, hook up the computer to the TV so the littles can copy from the screen maybe. Hmmm, I'll need to copy and paste the bible for them to be able to see it on screen. Or I can just look for other NKJV Bibles. Oh duh, I'll let them copy from their iPads. Yuck, though. Anyway. Then my son has an eye appointment this morning, and I'll read *Keep Your Love On* (Silk 2013) there.

When I get home, I have no plans. Probably fold clothes; maybe dig up the DVDs for the Randy & Bill book and start watching those while I knit?? No real plans to work when the house is clean. I love it! Though somehow I still end the day feeling super unproductive. OH! You told me to do some work on the computer! Okay, I'll block my time as you said and work on the communions, then school stuff, then I don't know what.

Okay. You're turn! What do you think?

[Chuckling.] Well, I can see how you can go a whole day and feel unproductive. Why don't you look for ways to minister today? Be it while you're out or online—with all the social media. Speak life into someone's life today. Ask the Holy Spirit to guide you as to what to say.

Okay.

'Cause really, Jo, isn't that when you feel productive and fulfilled? When you've done something for the kingdom?

Yes. I love that.

So do that. Work for the kingdom today. Everyday. Speak life into those around you. Use that voice that is anointed and speak on behalf of Daddy!

Okay. I will, Daddy.

That's it. Unless you want to talk more.

There's more I could talk about, but I feel a peace about stopping here. Thanks for allowing us to touch my sweet friend at visitation yesterday. PLEASE bring in income for me so I can bless people. You know I just want the money to bless people. I don't want it for myself; I just want to give it away.

Please open doors for me to bring in money. Okay, I'm done. We can talk later. I love you, Daddy.

I love you too, princess.

July 22, 2014

Good morning. I think yesterday went kind of well. I worked on everything on my list at least! That's a good day to me! How about you? Was it good for you?

You mean did you please me? Yes, you pleased me. Remember, I delight in you. Everything about you. You're my daughter, how I could I not be pleased with you? DON'T START QUESTIONING WHETHER OR NOT EVERYTHING YOU HEAR IS BIBLICALLY SOUND!!! Just LISTEN to me. You know me. So stop doubting and thinking about the lies being spoken to you. Listen to my voice. Hmph. It's the same thing you tell your kids really, "When you hear my voice, stop and listen. It doesn't matter who else is talking around you. Listen to MY VOICE!"

Ha. If only we, your children, did that, huh? I know that would make you happy!

Yes, it would. There are so many who I want to speak to like this. You need to help them. Jo, you've been right, this isn't just for you. Haha. Again, just like you say to other people—though normally when they're going through hard times—"It's not just about or for you, it's for the one coming behind you." THIS is for the one coming behind you. Yes, put this out. Yes, people will read it. And it doesn't matter how many and it's not for a profit—it's to help the one behind you.

I'm telling you stuff you know. This is your heart. I know it's not about money. At first it is because of the investment on your end, but I'll take care of that. Watch me. Whether it be your husband, whether it be a gift, whether your crafts sell, don't worry or think about the HOW. Just wait on me and watch. You'll see how I do it when I do it. Just get the book edited. Start combing back through it now.

What YOU think is personal and useless, to a book reader, might be exactly where they are. So don't go through it and start cutting stuff out. You don't know what the audience needs. If it's something that needs to come out, I'll let you know. And be sure to ask me while you proof, but don't just go crazy and start changing everything around. And even leave the punctuation. Again—this is how I speak to YOU. I don't talk the same to everyone. You know that, but someone else may not. Someone else may talk like you and need to know that I, God, their Father, wants to talk to them AND I don't speak in the "Thou's" and "Thy's" so they can understand me in their speech—that's going to be a big deal for someone. Put the book out there close to how it was written. I say close, because I know you have to change some names. But I really want you to put this out there the way it is. My voice to yours.

Is this going to be as hard as I'm starting to think it is?

Well, you're looking at the editing and someone else's opinion of the book as being hard. So that's your choice to allow that to seem hard to you. What I know is going to be hard for you is to put it out there the way it is. To bare all that we've talked about with the one to one hundred people who may read it. Comparing this journey to the copied journeys of others. So it's not deep, and you didn't

ask me about the affairs of the world and parts of the Bible…that's not what **EVERYONE** is interested in.

You came to me like a daughter asking for guidance in your marriage, your parenting, your house, your ministry, your hobbies. How many other people do you think are out there who wonder about the same things? How many do you think know they can come to me and talk just like this?

Jo, this is the point I'm trying to make to you. This is what I want you to get across. This is your assignment right now. Work on the book; I'll show you when it's time and who to go with. Just do your work; do your part. Now go, the kids are calling you.

AFTERWARD

August 29, 2014

I would love to tell you that I did everything God told me to do. I would love to say that when He told me to combine and edit the communions that I did it right away, but I didn't. I worked on a few, but not like I knew He wanted me to. I wish I could share that my husband got a new job in Missouri and we moved into our new home. It would even be great to share that my kids are always loving and kind, because of all the prayers over them and all of the spiritual battles we fought for them. It'd be great to say that my husband and I never disagree and have the best communication because we let Holy Spirit give us every word to speak.

But oh my goodness, this is real life! Real life is hard. Real life has ups and downs, and we go through times that make us question what we're doing, where we're going, who we're going with, and if our faith will stand through the test. Can we still love and follow Daddy God when our kids are disrespectful? Can we still love and follow God when we watch friends become widows? Can we still love and follow God when He keeps telling or showing us what's coming, but it takes years to come to pass?

The answer should be an easy "YES." Why should it be easy when we're in hard times? Because we have RELATIONSHIP with our DADDY GOD. It's relationship that keeps us close even when we're mad or upset and at our lowest point. It's relationship that reminds us we can always come to Daddy—no matter how far we feel or how long it's been since we've talked to Him. It's relationship that makes it easy for us to smile at a stranger, minister a prophetic word, or tell someone "God loves you" out of obedience.

DADDY JUST WANTS RELATIONSHIP!! With ALL of us, with EVERYONE! We are ALL God's children, some of us just may not know it yet. Accept God as your Father. Let Him be the Daddy you never had. Let him introduce you to his son, the BEST BIG BROTHER EVER, Jesus!!!! He's AMAZING! The Holy Spirit is AMAZING. Relationship with them is AMAZING!!!! There is no place I'd rather be than in their presence.

Nothing compares to the love of our Father; he just wants relationship. Come to him. Follow him. Serve him. Love him. Listen to him. He's always speaking, He's just waiting for us to listen to and obey his voice.

WHAT COMES NEXT?

If you read this book from beginning to end, you saw how our communions evolved. I want to encourage you to do communion. Just get before him and sit at his feet. Talk to him or ask him a question, then just wait and listen for his answer.

I tell the kids that God speaks to us in different ways. You may hear Him audibly or just in your head, see something with your eyes open or closed, awake or asleep (visions/dreams), feel something, smell something, or taste something. He's God. He's limitless. Don't put him in a box and think he can only speak in one way. Yes, he speaks in his Word, but we also hear God minister to us in the psalms, hymns, and songs sung today.

Are these all of the ways God speaks? No! There's so much more to God than we can ever imagine. These are just *some* of the ways he speaks and communicates with us. I just offer these as suggestions so when you ask him to speak to you, you're open to some of the ways he may come to you.

I know you've heard before, "Don't despise small beginnings." Look at the beginning of my communions compared to the end! If you get one word (that may or may not make sense), don't quit! Just keep at it. The more time you spend with him, the more you will begin to recognize the difference between your voice, his voice, and the voice of the enemy. You saw how much I struggled with trusting which voice I was hearing, but when I get into a rut where I question everything, I can think back to all of those conversations that I did NOT want to have! There's no way I would've made up those conversations that called out the areas that I would have rather kept hidden. I wouldn't do that. Only my daddy would call those out to make me a better servant; that's why spending time with Daddy is so important.

Take the time to start talking and listening to Daddy God more. He's always right there with you, just waiting for you to remember you are his son or daughter and you can come to him anytime. I'm excited as I think about you on your journey in this relationship—maybe it's a new thing for you, or maybe you're just remembering how you used to talk to him, and you're going to pick up where you left off (like I did so many times). Whatever the case, walk with him. We have the BEST daddy ever, and what he wants most with us is… RELATIONSHIP.

WORKS CITED

Batterson, Mark. *Praying Circles around your Children.* Grand Rapids, MI: Zondervan, 2012.

Clark, Randy. *Thrill of Victory/Agony of Defeat.* Apostolic Network of Global Awakening, 2014.

Dawson, Joy. *Forever Ruined for the Ordinary.* Seattle, WA: YWAM, 2001.

Kim, Yong Doo. *Baptized by Blazing Fire.* Lake Mary, FL: Creation House, 2009.

Schambach, R. W. *The Price of God's Miracle Working Power.* Tyler, TX: Schambach Revivals, Inc, 1991.

Silk, Danny. *Keep Your Love On.* Redding, CA: Red Arrow Media, 2013.

Toledo, Jennifer. *Children and the Supernatural.* Lake Mary, FL: Charisma House, 2012.

Printed in the United States
By Bookmasters